Paul Auster

CITY
OF GLASS

ADAPTATION BY
Paul Karasik and
David Mazzucchelli

NEW INTRODUCTION BY
Art Spiegelman

PICADOR

HENRY HOLT AND COMPANY
NEW YORK

Printed in the United States of America. For information, address Picador, 175 Fifth Avenue, New York, N.Y. 10010.

www.picadorusa.com

Picador ® is a U.S. registered trademark and is used by Henry Holt and Company under license from Pan Books Limited.

For information on Picador Reading Group Guides, as well as ordering, please contact the Trade Marketing department at St. Martin's Press.
Phone: 1-800-221-7945 extension 763
Fax: 212-677-7456
E-mail: trademarketing@stmartins.com

 First printed by Sun and Moon Press.

Library of Congress Catalog Card Number 93-91005
ISBN 0-312-42360-8
EAN 978-0312-42360-5

This book is a revised version of *Neon Lit: Paul Auster's City of Glass,* which was first published in the United States in 1994 by Avon Books, A division of The Hearst Corporation.

20 19 18 17 16 15 14 13 12

PICTURING A GLASSY-EYED PRIVATE I

It was a misnomer that started it...

A "Graphic Novel!" Bah!

What would Peter Stillman, Paul Auster's cracked seeker of Ur-language in *City of Glass* call the visual adaptation of the novel he figures in? A *Crumblechaw?* A *Nincompictopoop??* An *Ikonologosplatt???* Comics may no longer be the "real name" for a narrative medium that intimately intertwines words and pictures but isn't necessarily comic in tone.

In the mid '80s some well-intended journalists and booksellers tried to distinguish a handful of book-format comics from other, less ambitious, works by dubbing them "graphic novels." But even though my own book, *Maus,* was partially responsible for making bookstores safe for comics, the new label stuck in my craw as a mere cosmetic bid for respectability. Since "graphics" were respectable and "novels" were respectable (though that hadn't always been the case), surely "graphic novels" must be doubly respectable!

It was a wrong-headed notion that started it...

It would take another decade before enough long, ambitious comics gave the concept critical mass—until enough work *worthy* of critical attention made a bookstore section of some sort inevitable—but, tired of seeing my *Maus* volumes surrounded by fantasy and role-playing game manuals, I tried to jump-start the process. In the early '90s I groused to one of my editors that if my work was fated to be ghettoized in a graphic novel section, perhaps the neighborhood could be improved by hiring some serious novelists to provide scenarios for skilled graphic artists. I got permission to approach several well-known novelists, including William Kennedy, John Updike, and Paul Auster.

It was a number of friendships that started it...

I was fortunate enough to become friends with Paul Auster in the late 1980s, and my repeated cajoling got him to toy with the possibility of collaborating with a cartoonist. He had the glimmering of an idea: a vision of a boy floating above water. Next thing I knew, that glimmer became his next novel, *Mr. Vertigo,* and he kindly invited me to provide a jacket drawing. *All* the novelists I contacted were intrigued by my proposal, then fled.

(Updike, who early in his career wanted to become a cartoonist, said it had taken him fifty years to finally become reconciled to making his cartoons with words.) Even I was a bit dubious of my own idea, secretly convinced that the "purest" expression of the comics form demanded text and pictures made by one person.

And so the project languished, only to be replaced with what I believed was an even worse idea. At some point Paul had suggested that I simply adapt one of his already published works. I shrugged that off until another friend, Bob Callahan, in turn cajoled me into coediting a series of books with him: comics adaptations of urban noir-inflected literature. I couldn't figure out why on Earth anyone should bother to adapt a book into...another book! To make the task more difficult, the goal here was not to create some dumbed-down "Classics Illustrated" versions, but visual "translations" actually worthy of adult attention. *City of Glass* was exactly the sort of novel Callahan was reaching for to define what we eventually called "Neon Lit," but rereading Auster's slim volume made the choice seem downright daunting—and therefore actually worth a shot! For all its playful references to pulp fiction, *City of Glass* is a surprisingly nonvisual work at its core, a complex web of words and abstract ideas in playfully shifting narrative styles. (Paul warned me that several attempts to turn his book into a film script had failed miserably.)

I enlisted David Mazzucchelli, whose art on Frank Miller's *Batman: Year One* had shown a grace, economy, and understanding of the form that made the superhero genre almost interesting. The astonishing avant-garde comics and graphics he then went on to self-publish after abandoning the "mainstream" at the height of his acclaim made him seem ideally suited to the challenge of grappling with our proposed adaptation. But after a number of attempts, David began to look disheartened: he was more than able to tell the "story" in Paul's novel but couldn't quite locate the inner rhythms and *real* mysteries that made the story worth telling. Maybe it was impossible.

Grasping at straws, I called Paul Karasik, who had been a student of mine at New York's School of Visual Arts back in 1981 and 1982 (the very years, it turns out, that Paul Auster was writing *City of Glass*). As a teacher I had come up with some resolutely implausible assignments—like asking students to turn a rather nonnarrative passage of Faulkner's *The Sound and the Fury* into comics—and Karasik had consistently demonstrated a gift for intelligent, plausible solutions.

After explaining our impasse, I remember him cockily telling me he was born for this assignment, but I didn't hear his Auster-like back-story till much later. It seems that back in 1987 (the year, it turns out, that Paul Auster and I first met) Paul Karasik was teaching art at Packer Collegiate in Brooklyn Heights. Learning that one of his most talented eleven-year-old students, Daniel, was the son of the novelist, Paul Auster, Karasik read several of his books, and for a lark...broke down a few pages of *City of Glass* in one of his sketchbooks!

The new breakdown sketches he did six or seven years after that first experiment were inspired. When I got to the pages that captured Peter Stillman's memorable speech to Quinn, my jaw dropped. It was an uncanny visual equivalent to Auster's description of Stillman's voice and movements: "Machine-like, fitful, alternating between slow and rapid gestures, rigid and yet expressive, as if the operation were out of control, not quite corresponding to the will that lay behind it." By insisting on a strict, regular grid of panels, Karasik located the Ur-language of Comics: the grid as window, as prison door, as city block, as tic-tac-toe board; the grid as a metronome giving measure to the narrative's shifts and fits.

There was one problem with the sketches: Neon Lit's small final page format couldn't accommodate all those relentless rows of tiny panels without looking uncomfortably cramped. The scrupulous compressions (Paul K had shaped the adaptation so that each cluster of panels took up proportionally about as much space as the corresponding paragraphs did in Paul A's prose original) needed to be rethought so the pages could "breathe" a bit more. Occasional larger images were needed to beckon the reader's eyeballs into the congested grid. Fortuitously, this allowed David back in as a full participant in the further condensing and reshaping whereby he could engage the work with all his formidable skills.

As for Auster, I'm convinced he behaved generously throughout...

Paul Auster, appreciative of the wiggle-room translations and adaptations demand, spent a long, fruitful day with Mazzucchelli, Karasik, and I, studying the draft and offering suggestions. Generous as always, he was pleased and supportive, but I don't think he fully realized just how overwhelming the odds against success had been or that his novel had occasioned a breakthrough work. By poking at the heart of comics' structure, Karasik and Mazzucchelli created a strange doppelganger of the original book. It's as if Quinn, confronted with two nearly identical Peter Stillmans at Grand Central Station, chose to follow one drawn with brush and ink rather than one set in type. The volume that resulted, first published in 1994, overcame all my purist notions about collaboration. It offers one of the richest demonstrations to date of the modern *Ikonologosplatt* at its most subtle and supple.

—ART SPIEGELMAN 12/31/03

It was a
wrong number that
started it...

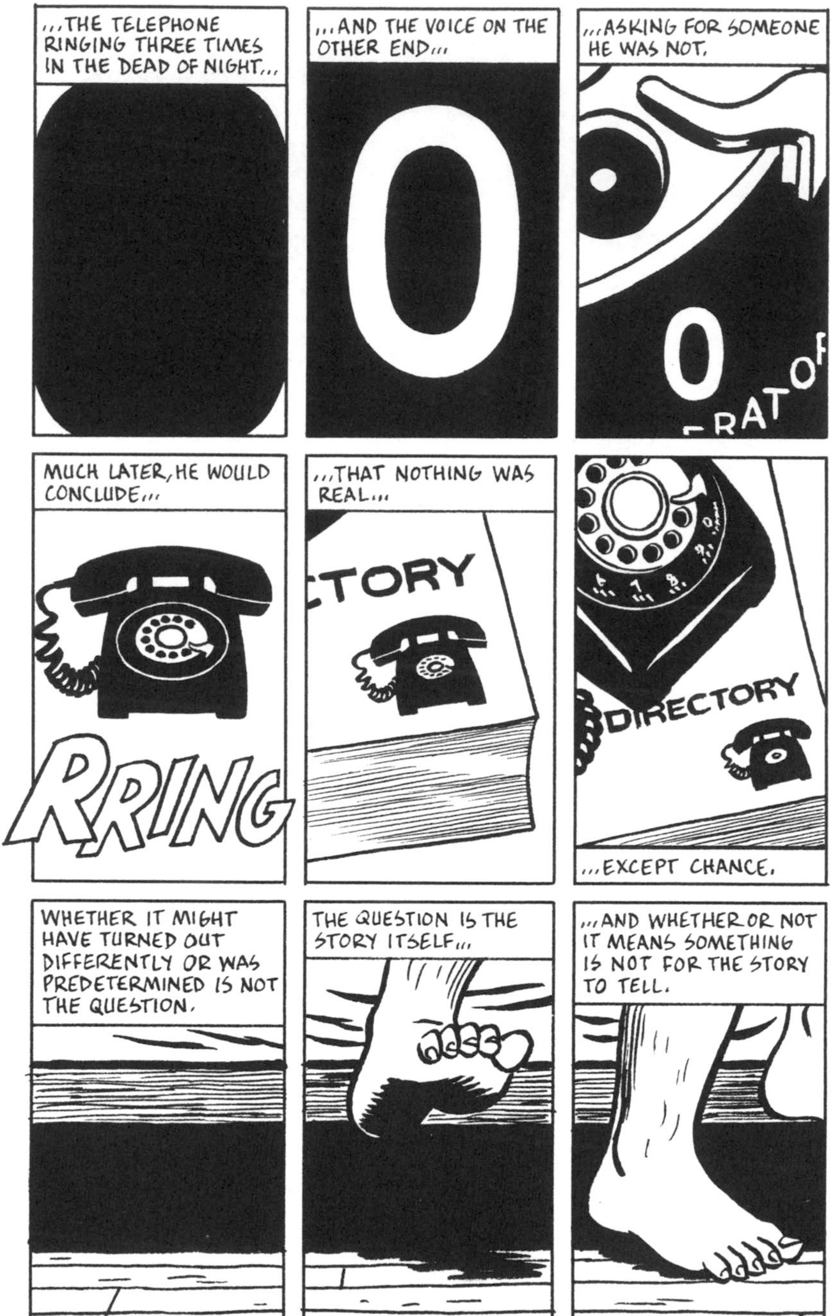
...THE TELEPHONE RINGING THREE TIMES IN THE DEAD OF NIGHT...
...AND THE VOICE ON THE OTHER END...
...ASKING FOR SOMEONE HE WAS NOT.
0
MUCH LATER, HE WOULD CONCLUDE...
RRING
...THAT NOTHING WAS REAL...
CTORY
DIRECTORY
...EXCEPT CHANCE.
WHETHER IT MIGHT HAVE TURNED OUT DIFFERENTLY OR WAS PREDETERMINED IS NOT THE QUESTION.
THE QUESTION IS THE STORY ITSELF...
...AND WHETHER OR NOT IT MEANS SOMETHING IS NOT FOR THE STORY TO TELL.

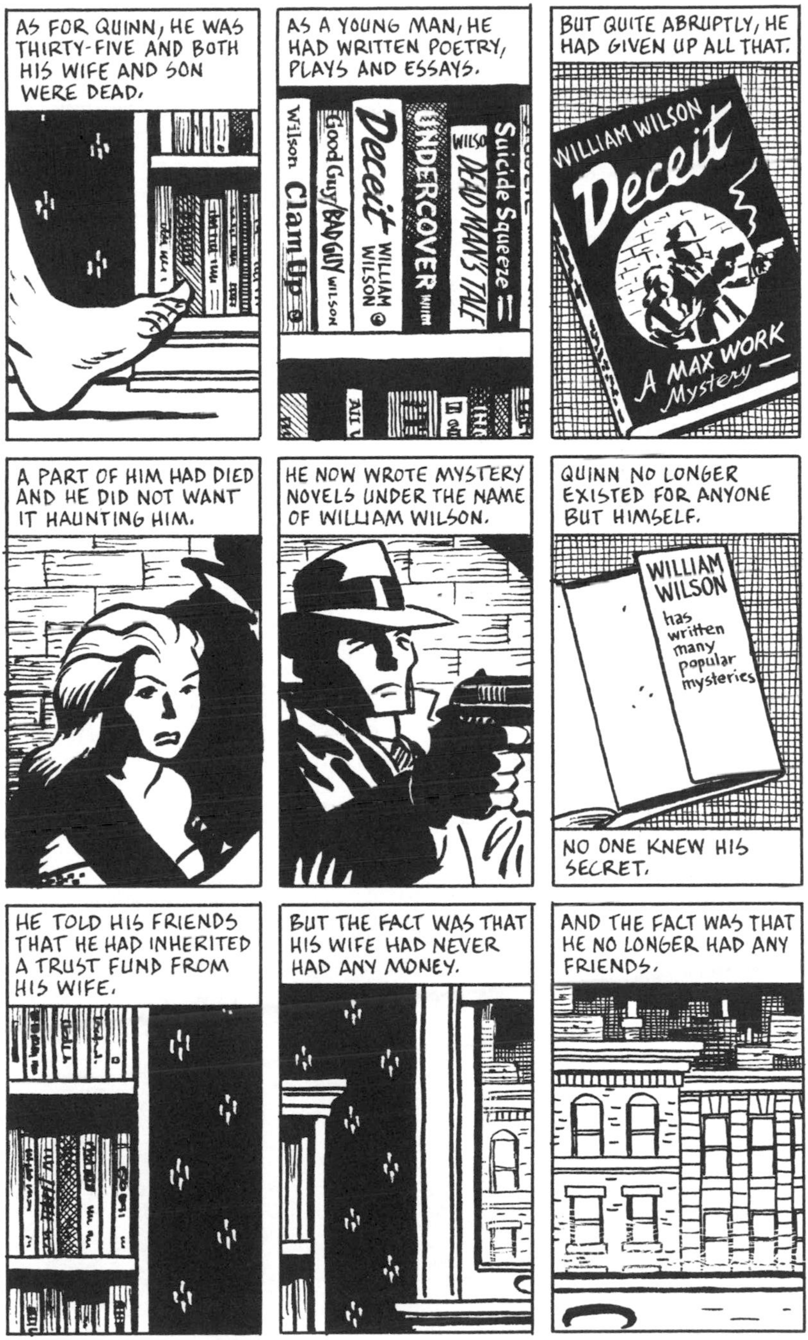
AS FOR QUINN, HE WAS THIRTY-FIVE AND BOTH HIS WIFE AND SON WERE DEAD.
AS A YOUNG MAN, HE HAD WRITTEN POETRY, PLAYS AND ESSAYS.
Wilson
Clam Up
Good Guy/BAD GUY
WILSON
Deceit
WILLIAM WILSON
UNDERCOVER
WILSON
DEAD MAN'S TALE
Suicide Squeeze
BUT QUITE ABRUPTLY, HE HAD GIVEN UP ALL THAT.
WILLIAM WILSON
Deceit
A MAX WORK Mystery
A PART OF HIM HAD DIED AND HE DID NOT WANT IT HAUNTING HIM.
HE NOW WROTE MYSTERY NOVELS UNDER THE NAME OF WILLIAM WILSON.
QUINN NO LONGER EXISTED FOR ANYONE BUT HIMSELF.
WILLIAM WILSON
has written many popular mysteries
NO ONE KNEW HIS SECRET.
HE TOLD HIS FRIENDS THAT HE HAD INHERITED A TRUST FUND FROM HIS WIFE.
BUT THE FACT WAS THAT HIS WIFE HAD NEVER HAD ANY MONEY.
AND THE FACT WAS THAT HE NO LONGER HAD ANY FRIENDS.

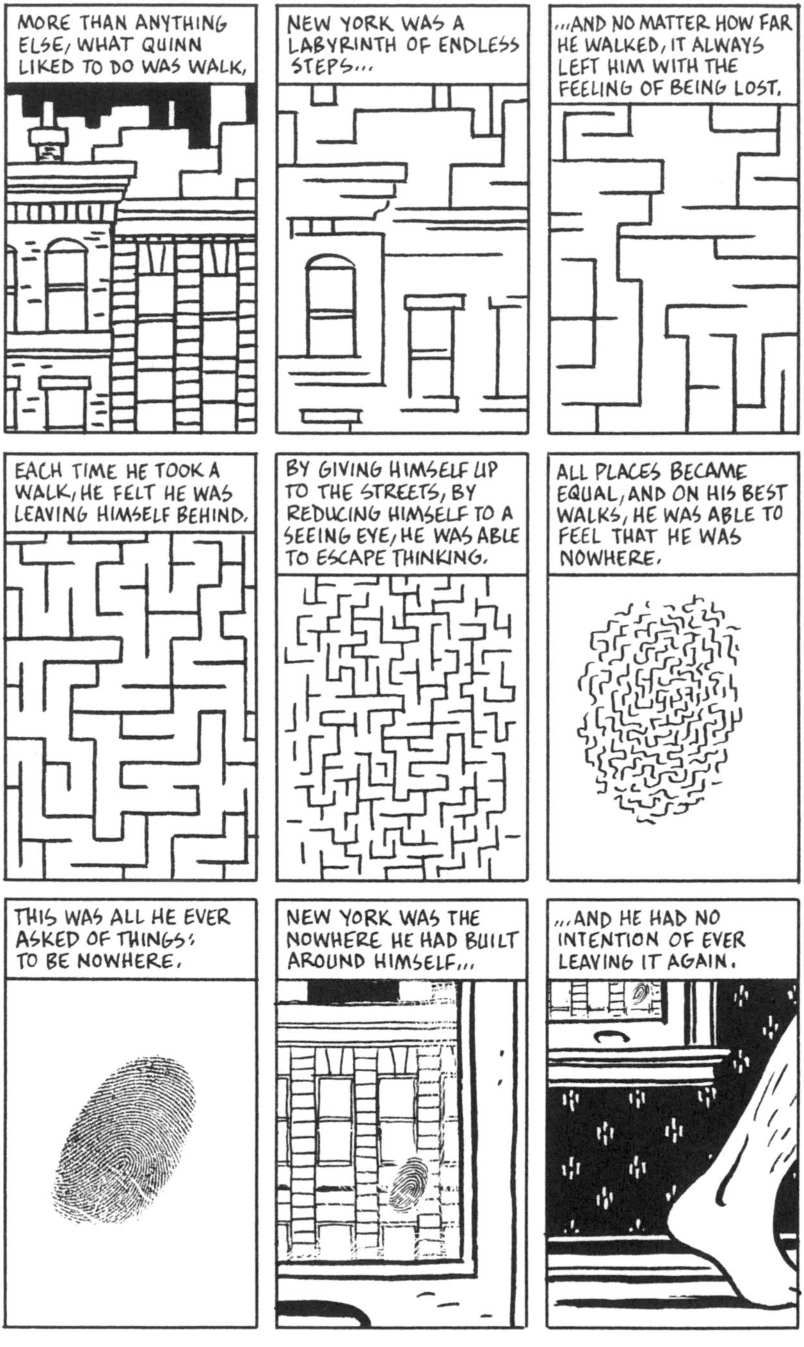
MORE THAN ANYTHING ELSE, WHAT QUINN LIKED TO DO WAS WALK,
NEW YORK WAS A LABYRINTH OF ENDLESS STEPS...
...AND NO MATTER HOW FAR HE WALKED, IT ALWAYS LEFT HIM WITH THE FEELING OF BEING LOST.
EACH TIME HE TOOK A WALK, HE FELT HE WAS LEAVING HIMSELF BEHIND.
BY GIVING HIMSELF UP TO THE STREETS, BY REDUCING HIMSELF TO A SEEING EYE, HE WAS ABLE TO ESCAPE THINKING.
ALL PLACES BECAME EQUAL, AND ON HIS BEST WALKS, HE WAS ABLE TO FEEL THAT HE WAS NOWHERE.
THIS WAS ALL HE EVER ASKED OF THINGS: TO BE NOWHERE.
NEW YORK WAS THE NOWHERE HE HAD BUILT AROUND HIMSELF...
...AND HE HAD NO INTENTION OF EVER LEAVING IT AGAIN.

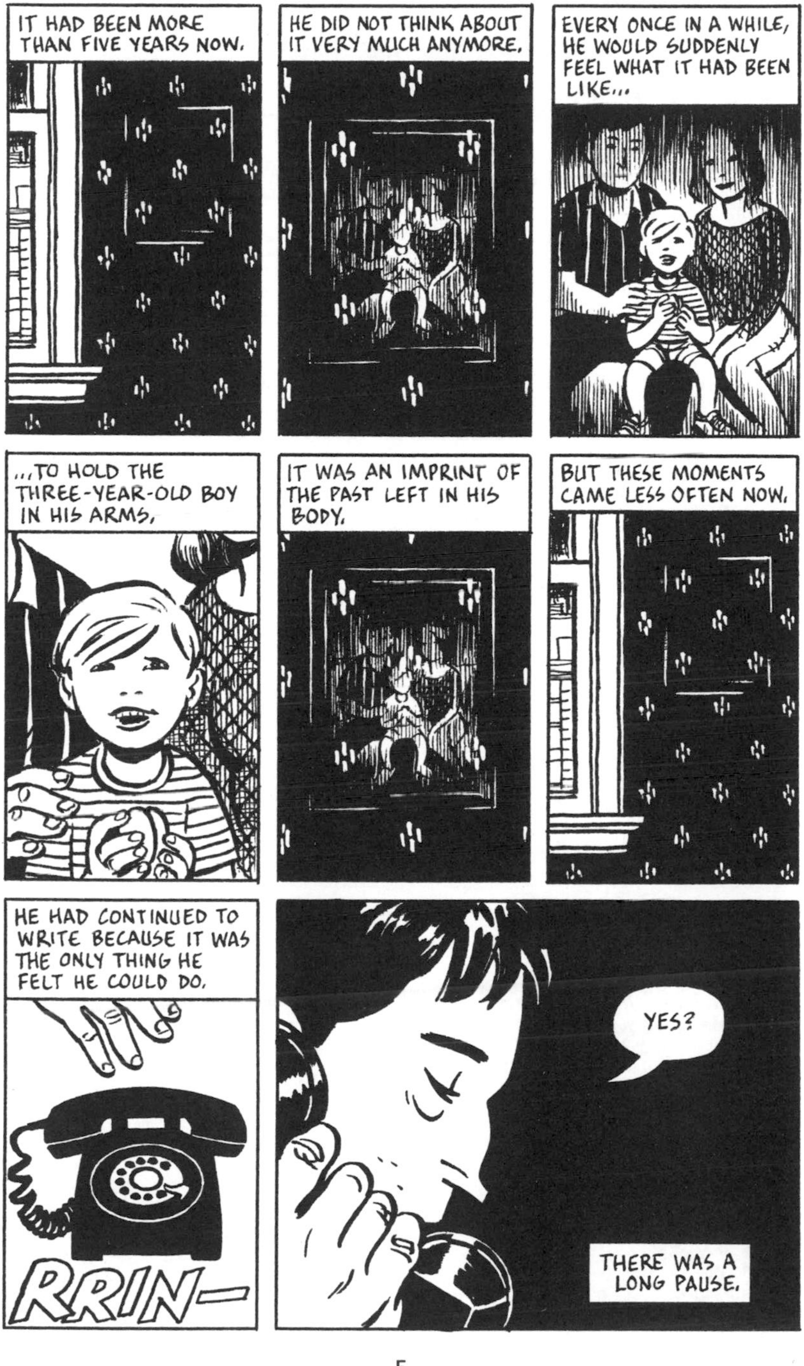
IT HAD BEEN MORE THAN FIVE YEARS NOW.
HE DID NOT THINK ABOUT IT VERY MUCH ANYMORE.
EVERY ONCE IN A WHILE, HE WOULD SUDDENLY FEEL WHAT IT HAD BEEN LIKE...
...TO HOLD THE THREE-YEAR-OLD BOY IN HIS ARMS.
IT WAS AN IMPRINT OF THE PAST LEFT IN HIS BODY.
BUT THESE MOMENTS CAME LESS OFTEN NOW.
HE HAD CONTINUED TO WRITE BECAUSE IT WAS THE ONLY THING HE FELT HE COULD DO.
RRIN—
YES?
THERE WAS A LONG PAUSE.

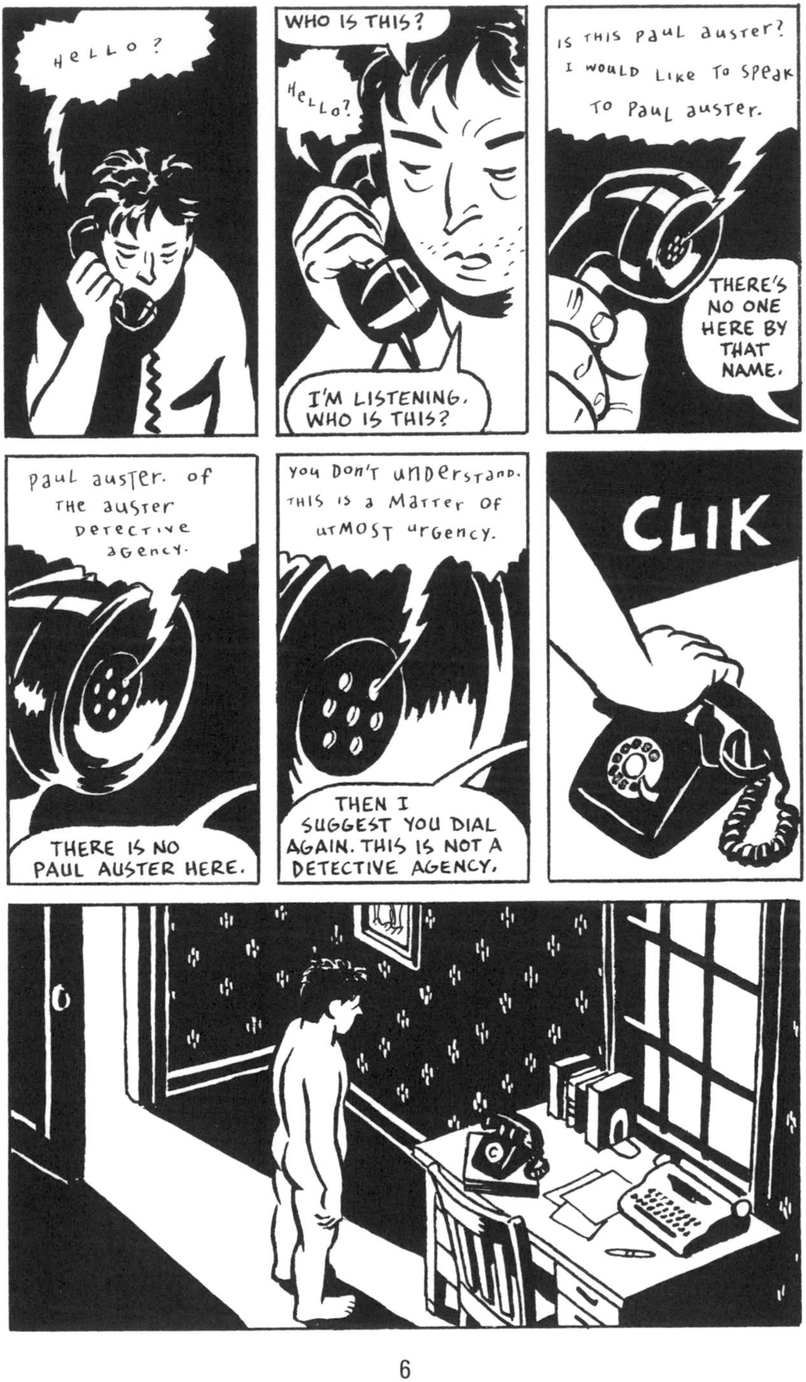
HELLO?
WHO IS THIS?
HELLO?
I'M LISTENING. WHO IS THIS?
IS THIS PAUL AUSTER? I WOULD LIKE TO SPEAK TO PAUL AUSTER.
THERE'S NO ONE HERE BY THAT NAME.
PAUL AUSTER. OF THE AUSTER DETECTIVE AGENCY.
THERE IS NO PAUL AUSTER HERE.
YOU DON'T UNDERSTAND. THIS IS A MATTER OF UTMOST URGENCY.
THEN I SUGGEST YOU DIAL AGAIN. THIS IS NOT A DETECTIVE AGENCY.
CLIK

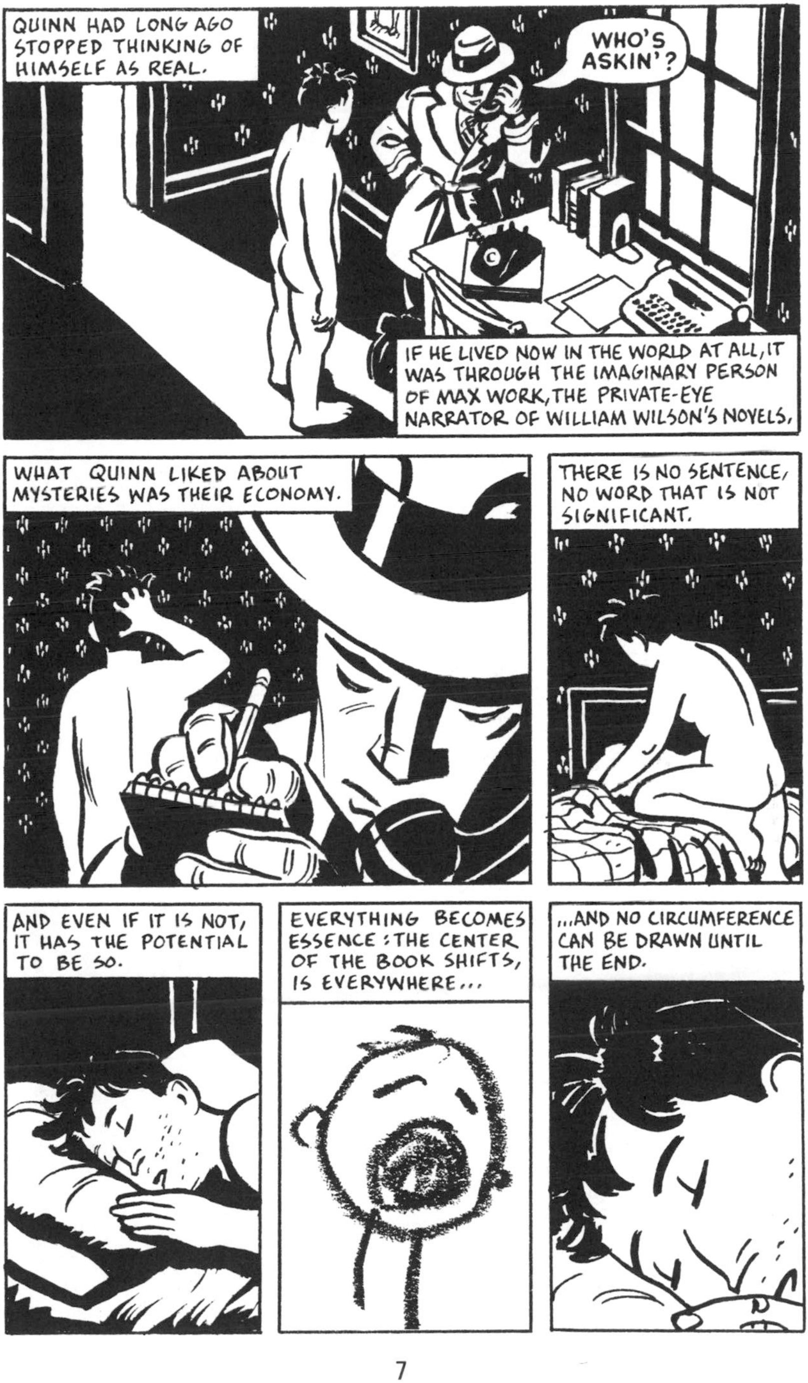
QUINN HAD LONG AGO STOPPED THINKING OF HIMSELF AS REAL.
WHO'S ASKIN'?
IF HE LIVED NOW IN THE WORLD AT ALL, IT WAS THROUGH THE IMAGINARY PERSON OF MAX WORK, THE PRIVATE-EYE NARRATOR OF WILLIAM WILSON'S NOVELS.
WHAT QUINN LIKED ABOUT MYSTERIES WAS THEIR ECONOMY.
THERE IS NO SENTENCE, NO WORD THAT IS NOT SIGNIFICANT.
AND EVEN IF IT IS NOT, IT HAS THE POTENTIAL TO BE SO.
EVERYTHING BECOMES ESSENCE: THE CENTER OF THE BOOK SHIFTS, IS EVERYWHERE...
...AND NO CIRCUMFERENCE CAN BE DRAWN UNTIL THE END.

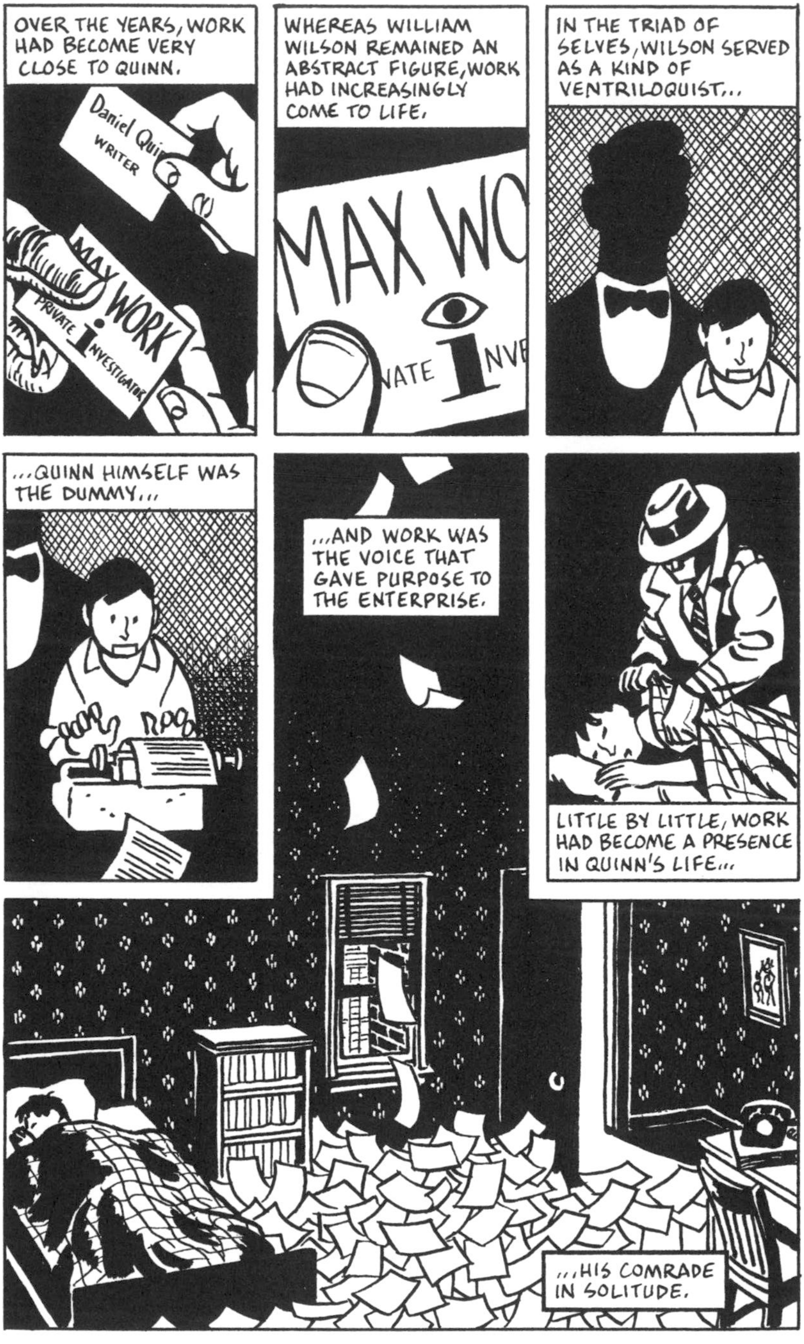
OVER THE YEARS, WORK HAD BECOME VERY CLOSE TO QUINN.
Daniel Quin
WRITER
MAX WORK
PRIVATE INVESTIGATOR
WHEREAS WILLIAM WILSON REMAINED AN ABSTRACT FIGURE, WORK HAD INCREASINGLY COME TO LIFE.
MAX WO
VATE INVE
IN THE TRIAD OF SELVES, WILSON SERVED AS A KIND OF VENTRILOQUIST...
...QUINN HIMSELF WAS THE DUMMY...
...AND WORK WAS THE VOICE THAT GAVE PURPOSE TO THE ENTERPRISE.
LITTLE BY LITTLE, WORK HAD BECOME A PRESENCE IN QUINN'S LIFE...
...HIS COMRADE IN SOLITUDE.

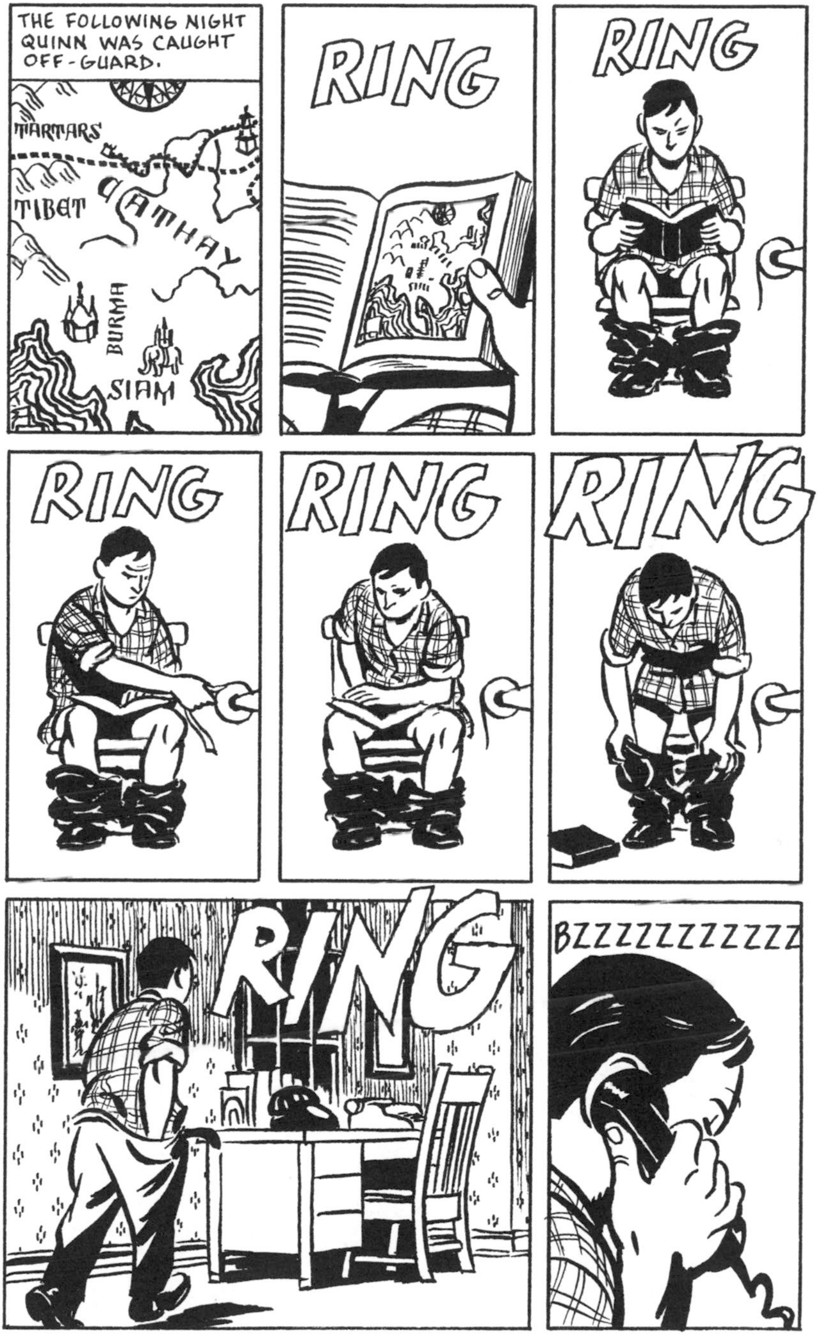
THE FOLLOWING NIGHT QUINN WAS CAUGHT OFF-GUARD.
TARTARS'
TIBET
CATHAY
BURMA
SIAM
RING
RING
RING
RING
RING
RING
BZZZZZZZZZZZ

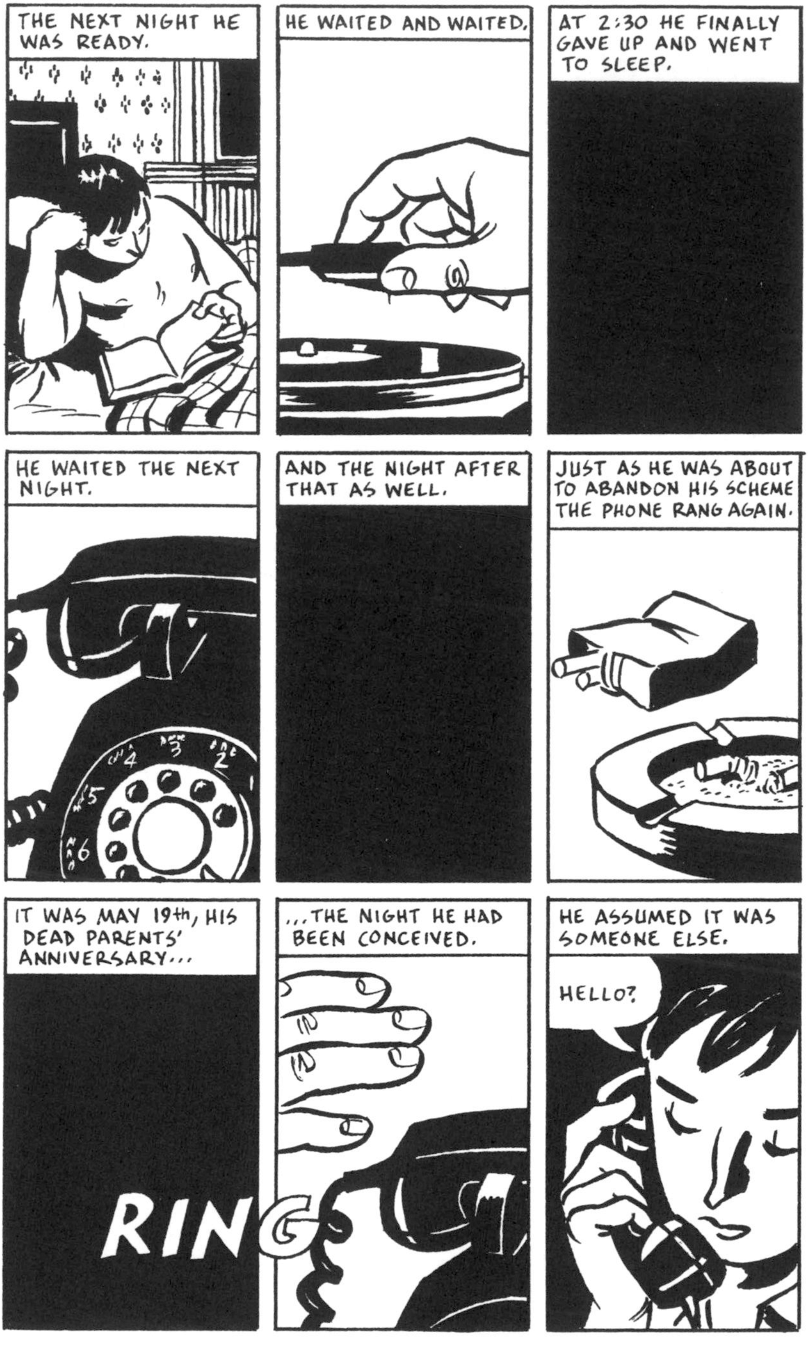
THE NEXT NIGHT HE WAS READY.
HE WAITED AND WAITED.
AT 2:30 HE FINALLY GAVE UP AND WENT TO SLEEP.
HE WAITED THE NEXT NIGHT.
AND THE NIGHT AFTER THAT AS WELL.
JUST AS HE WAS ABOUT TO ABANDON HIS SCHEME THE PHONE RANG AGAIN.
IT WAS MAY 19th, HIS DEAD PARENTS' ANNIVERSARY...
...THE NIGHT HE HAD BEEN CONCEIVED.
RING
HE ASSUMED IT WAS SOMEONE ELSE.
HELLO?

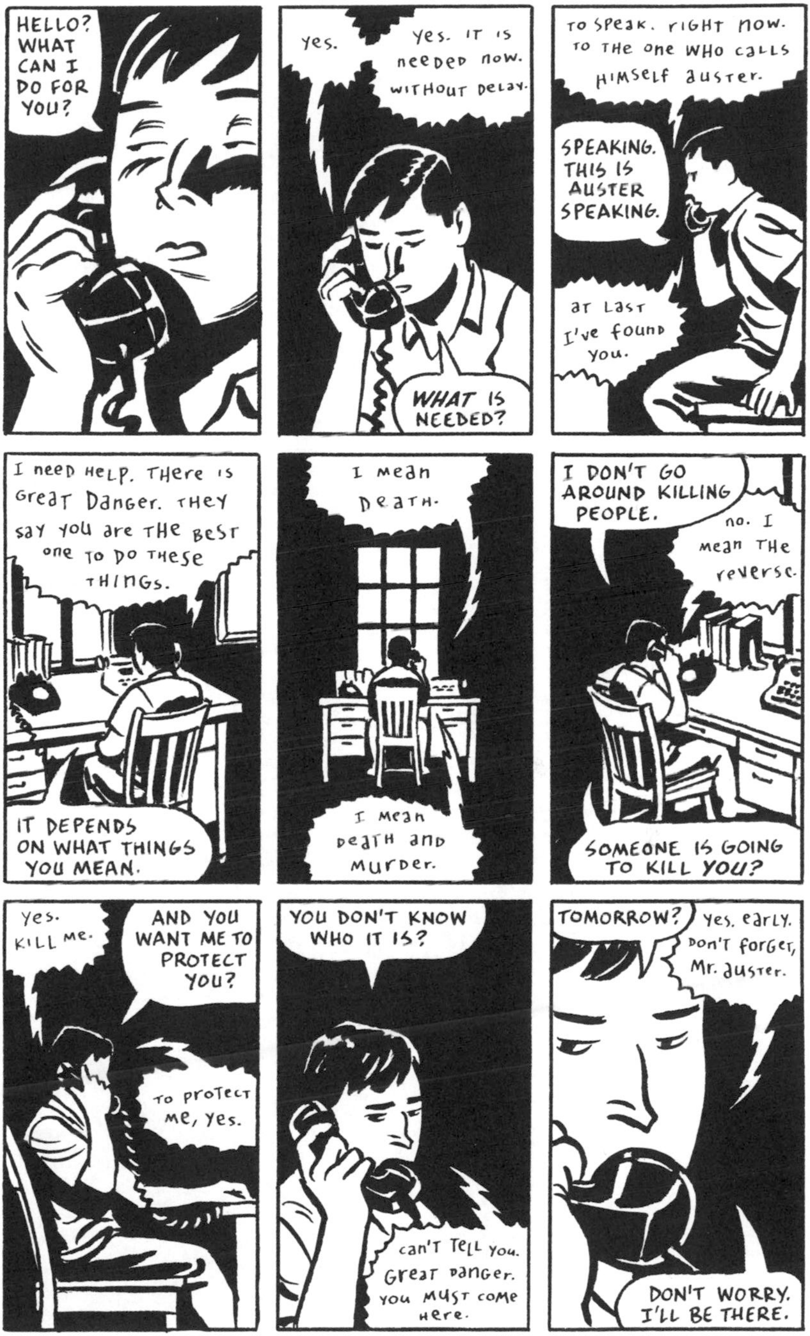
HELLO? WHAT CAN I DO FOR YOU?
yes.
yes. IT is needed now. WITHOUT Delay.
WHAT IS NEEDED?
To speak. right now. To THe one WHO calls Himself auster.
SPEAKING. THIS IS AUSTER SPEAKING.
at Last I've found you.
I need Help. There is Great Danger. They say you are THE best one to do these THINGS.
IT DEPENDS ON WHAT THINGS YOU MEAN.
I mean Death.
I mean Death and Murder.
I DON'T GO AROUND KILLING PEOPLE.
no. I mean THe reverse.
SOMEONE IS GOING TO KILL YOU?
Yes. Kill me.
AND YOU WANT ME TO PROTECT YOU?
To protect me, yes.
YOU DON'T KNOW WHO IT IS?
can't TeLL you. Great Danger. You MUST come Here.
TOMORROW?
Yes. early. Don't forget, Mr. auster.
DON'T WORRY. I'LL BE THERE.

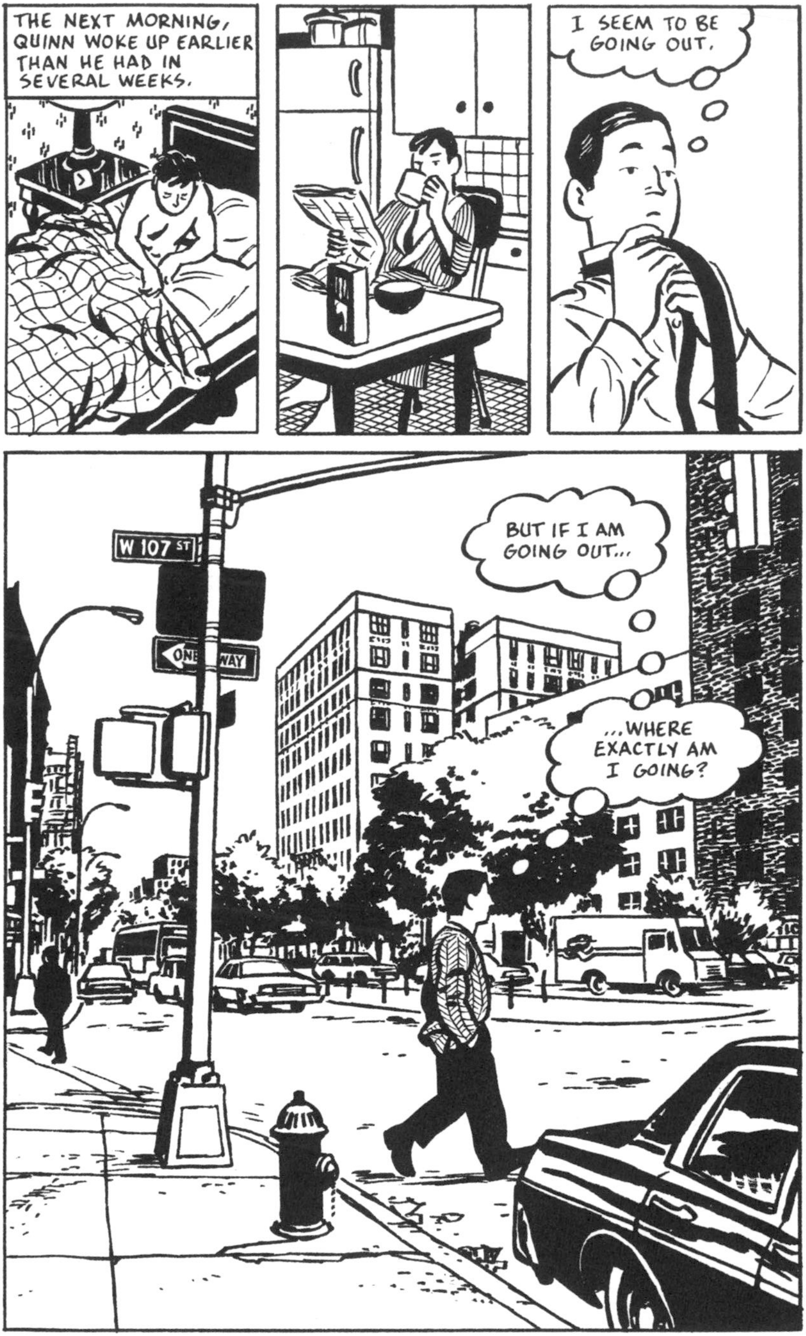
THE NEXT MORNING, QUINN WOKE UP EARLIER THAN HE HAD IN SEVERAL WEEKS.
I SEEM TO BE GOING OUT.
W 107 ST
BUT IF I AM GOING OUT...
...WHERE EXACTLY AM I GOING?

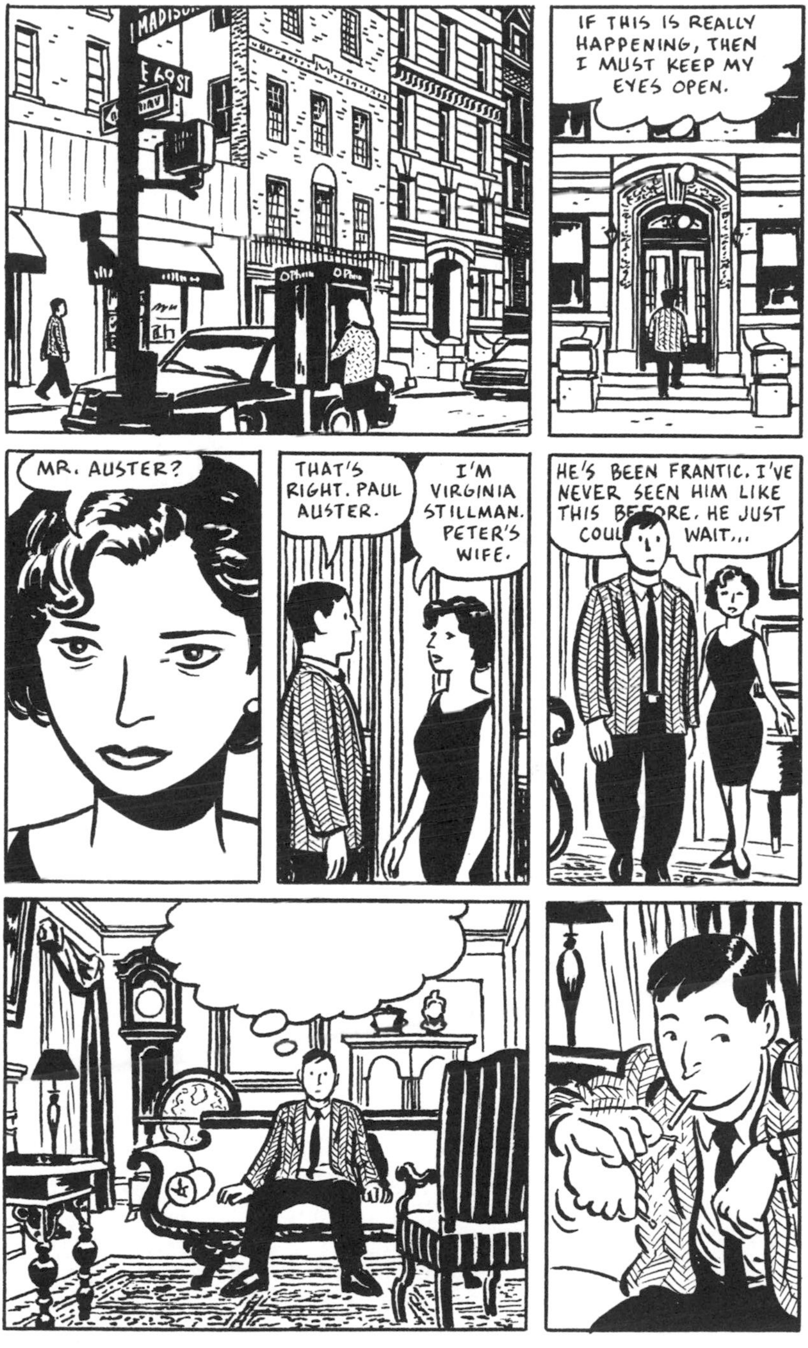
E 69 ST
IF THIS IS REALLY HAPPENING, THEN I MUST KEEP MY EYES OPEN.
MR. AUSTER?
THAT'S RIGHT. PAUL AUSTER.
I'M VIRGINIA STILLMAN. PETER'S WIFE.
HE'S BEEN FRANTIC. I'VE NEVER SEEN HIM LIKE THIS BE ORE. HE JUST COUL WAIT...

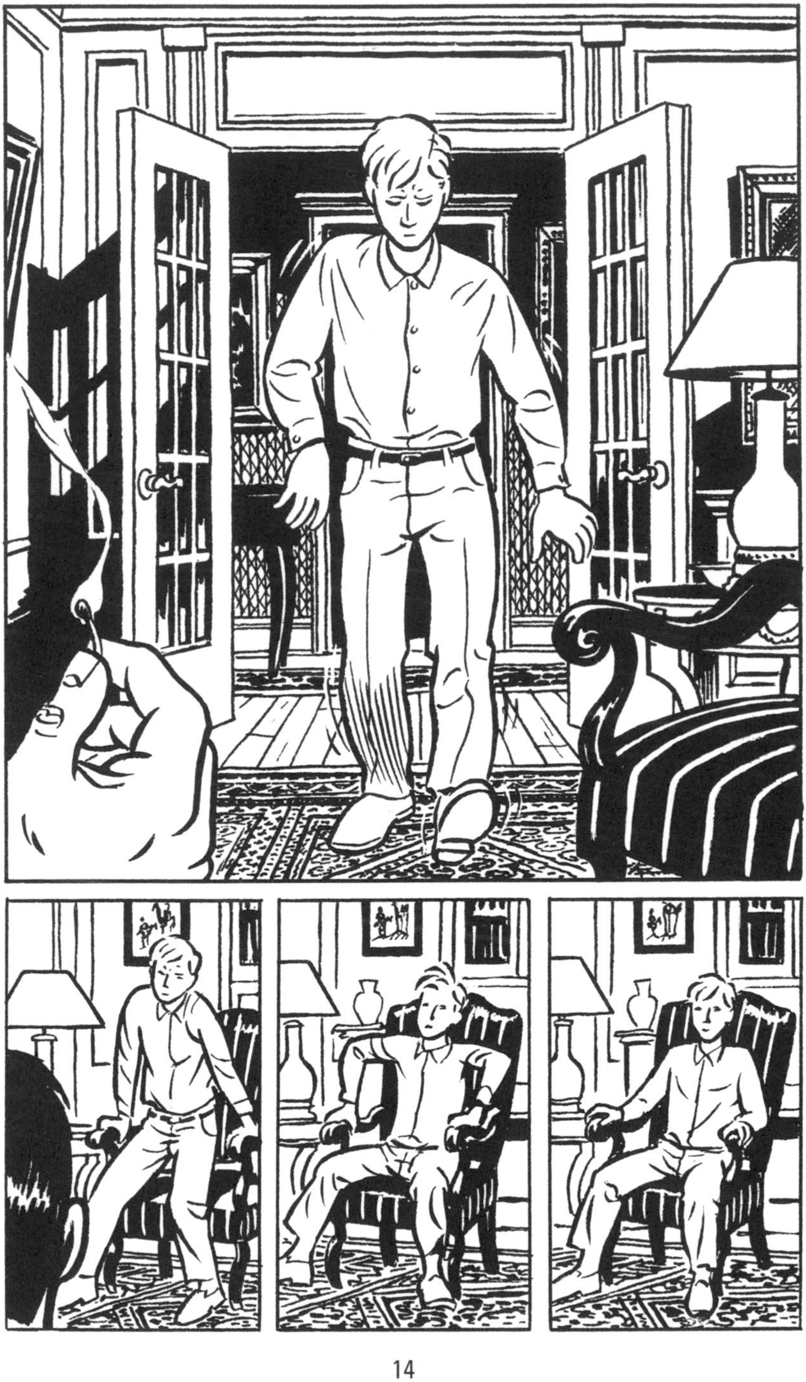

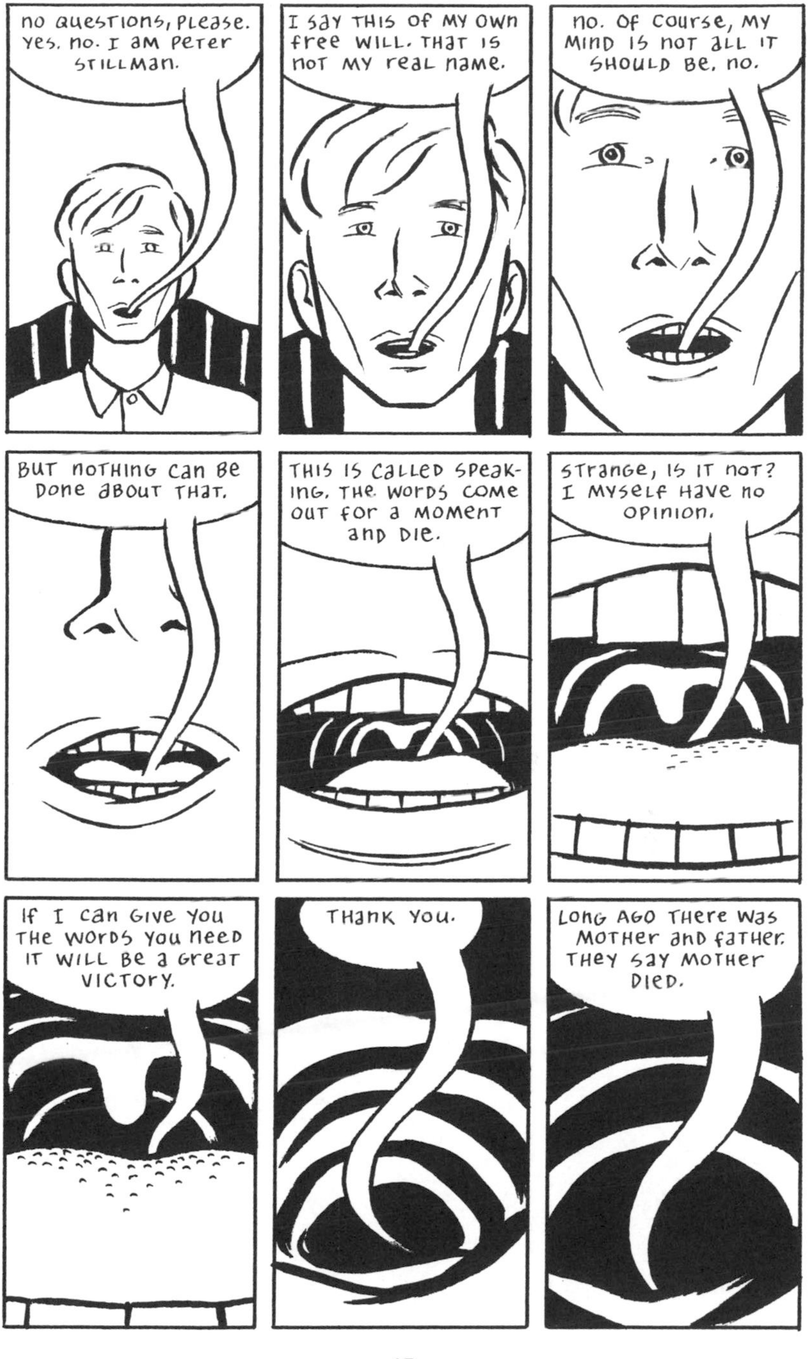
NO QUESTIONS, PLEASE. YES. NO. I AM PETER STILLMAN.
I SAY THIS OF MY OWN FREE WILL. THAT IS NOT MY REAL NAME.
NO. OF COURSE, MY MIND IS NOT ALL IT SHOULD BE, NO.
BUT NOTHING CAN BE DONE ABOUT THAT.
THIS IS CALLED SPEAK-ING. THE WORDS COME OUT FOR A MOMENT AND DIE.
STRANGE, IS IT NOT? I MYSELF HAVE NO OPINION.
IF I CAN GIVE YOU THE WORDS YOU NEED IT WILL BE A GREAT VICTORY.
THANK YOU.
LONG AGO THERE WAS MOTHER AND FATHER. THEY SAY MOTHER DIED.

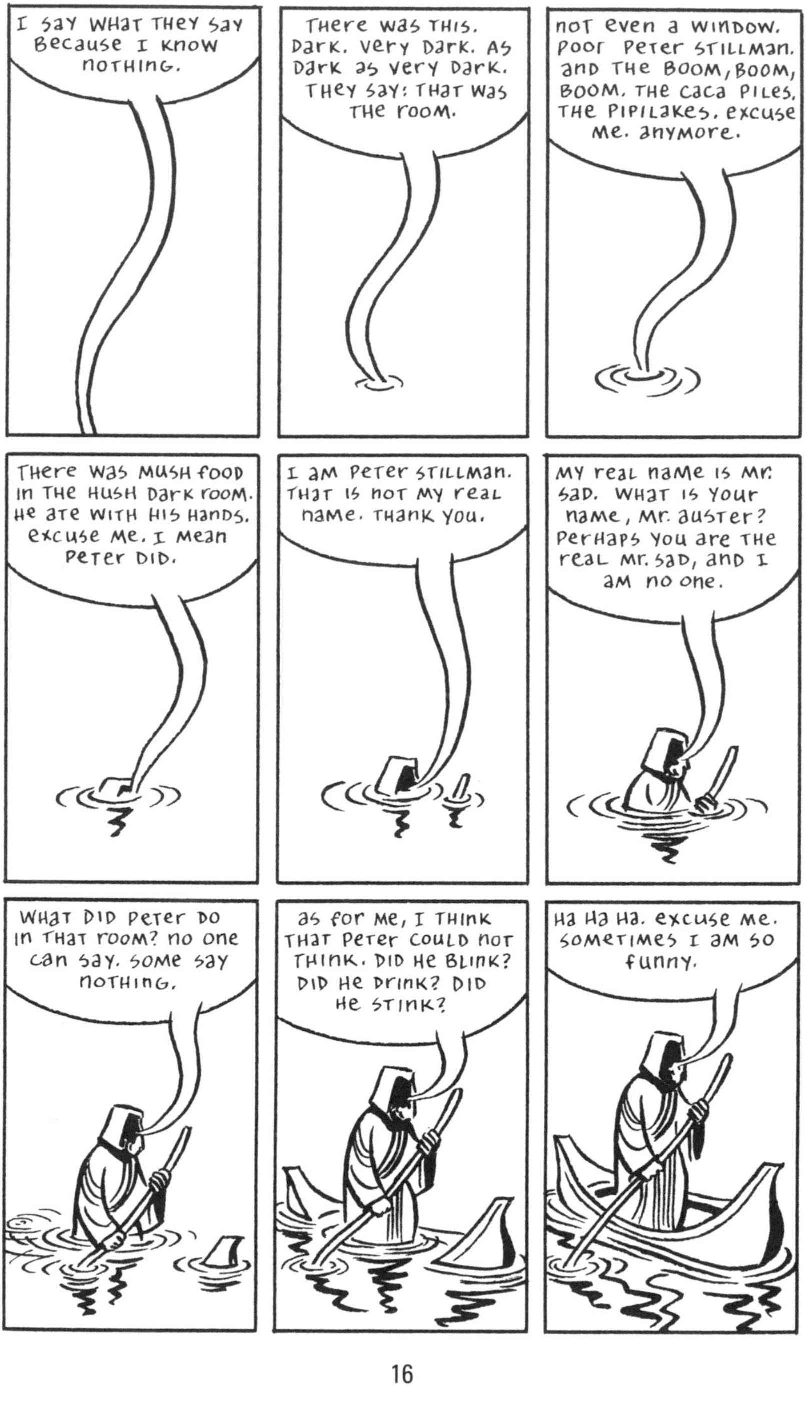
I SAY WHAT THEY SAY BECAUSE I KNOW NOTHING.
THERE WAS THIS. DARK. VERY DARK. AS DARK AS VERY DARK. THEY SAY: THAT WAS THE ROOM.
NOT EVEN A WINDOW. POOR PETER STILLMAN. AND THE BOOM, BOOM, BOOM. THE CACA PILES. THE PIPILAKES. EXCUSE ME. ANYMORE.
THERE WAS MUSH FOOD IN THE HUSH DARK ROOM. HE ATE WITH HIS HANDS. EXCUSE ME. I MEAN PETER DID.
I AM PETER STILLMAN. THAT IS NOT MY REAL NAME. THANK YOU.
MY REAL NAME IS MR. SAD. WHAT IS YOUR NAME, MR. AUSTER? PERHAPS YOU ARE THE REAL MR. SAD, AND I AM NO ONE.
WHAT DID PETER DO IN THAT ROOM? NO ONE CAN SAY. SOME SAY NOTHING.
AS FOR ME, I THINK THAT PETER COULD NOT THINK. DID HE BLINK? DID HE DRINK? DID HE STINK?
HA HA HA. EXCUSE ME. SOMETIMES I AM SO FUNNY.

WIMBLE CLICK CRUMBLE-CHAW BELOO. CLACK CLACK BEDRACK. NUMB NOISE, FLACKLEMUCH, CHEWMANNA. YA YA YA.

EXCUSE ME. I AM THE ONLY ONE WHO UNDERSTANDS THESE WORDS.

THEY SAY SOMEONE FOUND ME. I DO NOT REMEMBER WHEN THE LIGHT CAME IN.

I WORE DARK GLASSES. I WAS TWELVE. I LIVED IN A HOSPITAL.

PETER WAS A BABY. THEY HAD TO TEACH HIM EVERYTHING. HOW TO WALK. HOW TO EAT. HOW TO MAKE CACA AND PIPI IN THE TOILET.

EVEN WHEN I BIT THEM, THEY DIDN'T DO THE BOOM, BOOM, BOOM.

BUT IT WAS HARD TO TEACH PETER WORDS. HIS MOUTH DID NOT WORK RIGHT.

AND OF COURSE, HE WAS NOT ALL THERE IN THE HEAD. BA BA BA, HE SAID. AND DA DA DA.

IT TOOK MORE YEARS. NOW THEY SAY TO PETER: GO NOW, THERE'S NOTHING MORE WE CAN DO. PETER STILLMAN, YOU ARE A HUMAN BEING. THANK YOU SO VERY MUCH.

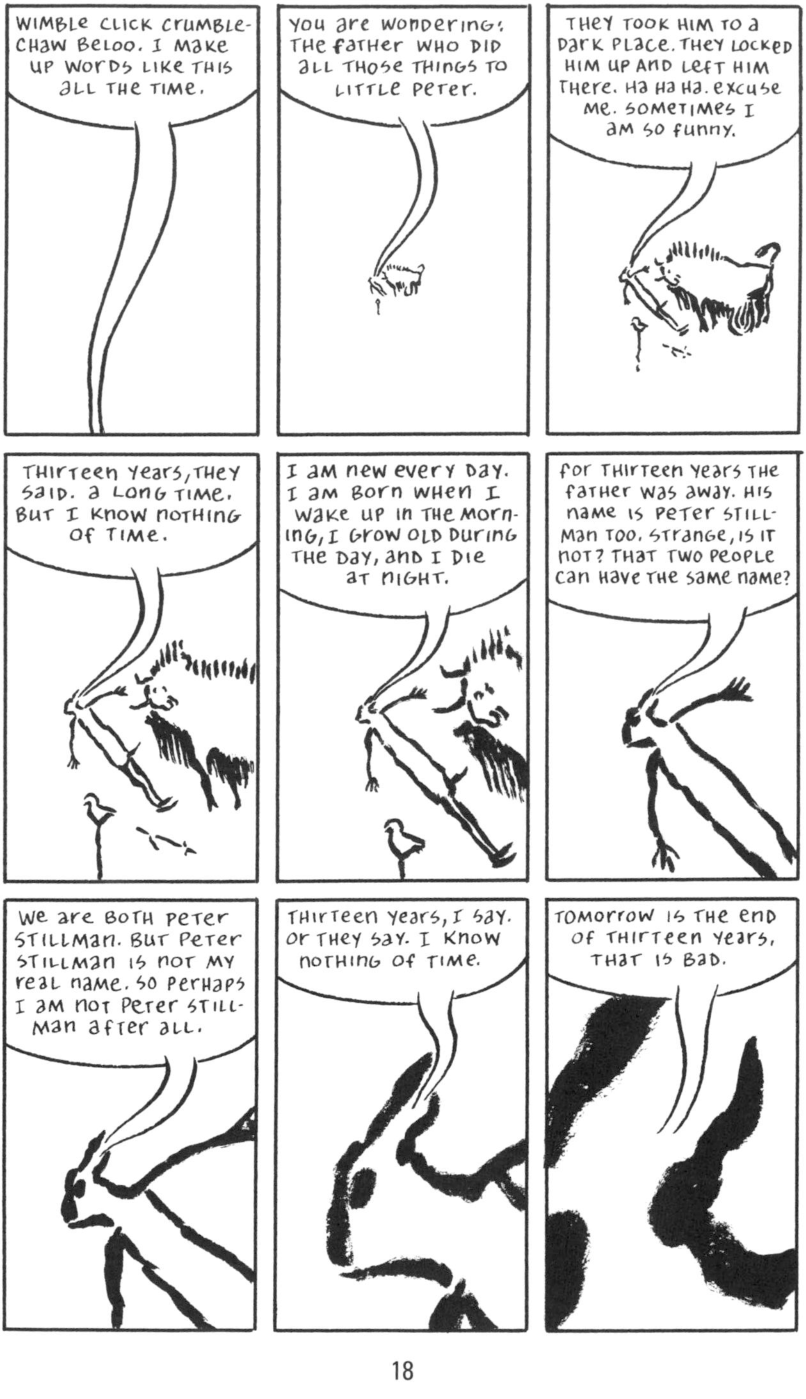
WIMBLE CLICK CRUMBLE-CHAW BELOO. I MAKE UP WORDS LIKE THIS ALL THE TIME.
YOU ARE WONDERING: THE FATHER WHO DID ALL THOSE THINGS TO LITTLE PETER.
THEY TOOK HIM TO A DARK PLACE. THEY LOCKED HIM UP AND LEFT HIM THERE. HA HA HA. EXCUSE ME. SOMETIMES I AM SO FUNNY.
THIRTEEN YEARS, THEY SAID. A LONG TIME. BUT I KNOW NOTHING OF TIME.
I AM NEW EVERY DAY. I AM BORN WHEN I WAKE UP IN THE MORNING, I GROW OLD DURING THE DAY, AND I DIE AT NIGHT.
FOR THIRTEEN YEARS THE FATHER WAS AWAY. HIS NAME IS PETER STILLMAN TOO. STRANGE, IS IT NOT? THAT TWO PEOPLE CAN HAVE THE SAME NAME?
WE ARE BOTH PETER STILLMAN. BUT PETER STILLMAN IS NOT MY REAL NAME. SO PERHAPS I AM NOT PETER STILLMAN AFTER ALL.
THIRTEEN YEARS, I SAY. OR THEY SAY. I KNOW NOTHING OF TIME.
TOMORROW IS THE END OF THIRTEEN YEARS. THAT IS BAD.

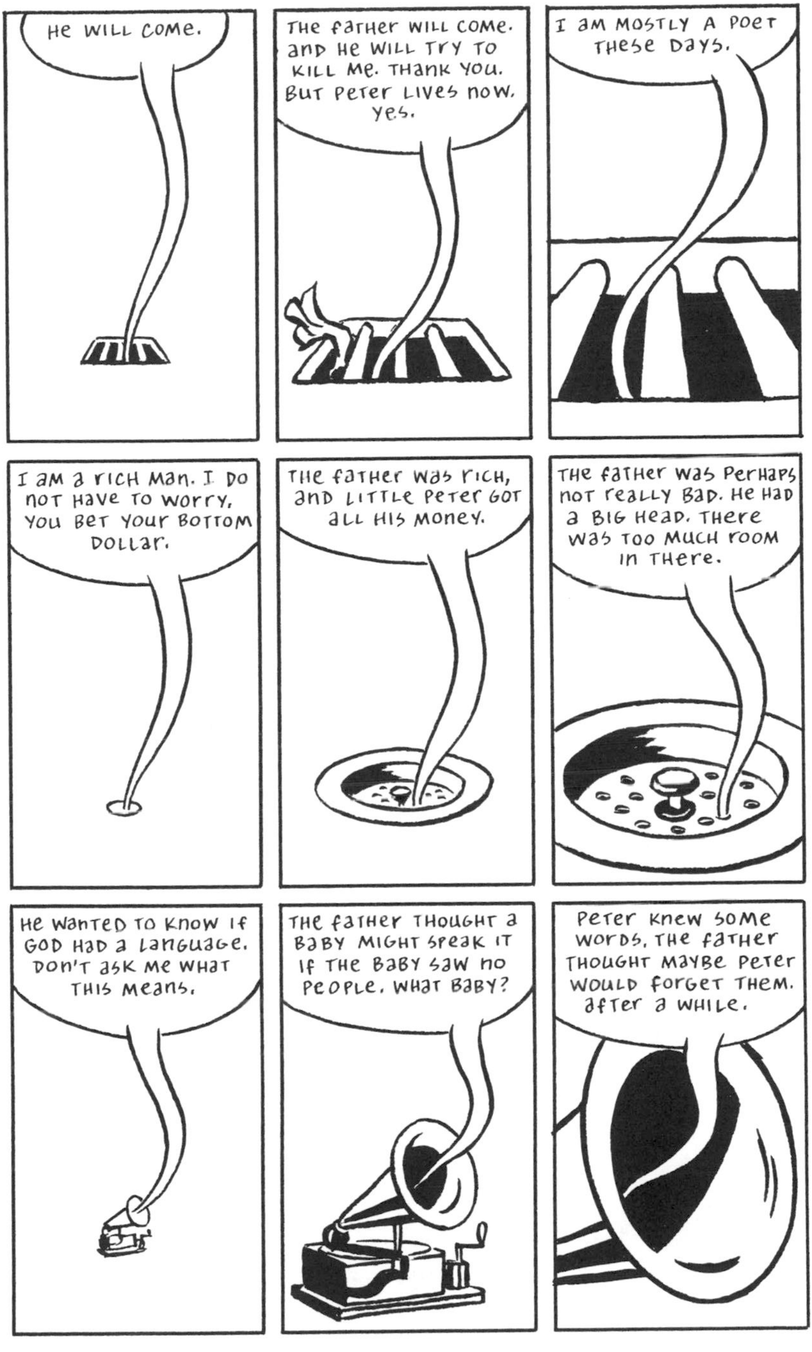
HE WILL COME.
THE FATHER WILL COME. AND HE WILL TRY TO KILL ME. THANK YOU. BUT PETER LIVES NOW. YES.
I AM MOSTLY A POET THESE DAYS.
I AM A RICH MAN. I DO NOT HAVE TO WORRY. YOU BET YOUR BOTTOM DOLLAR.
THE FATHER WAS RICH, AND LITTLE PETER GOT ALL HIS MONEY.
THE FATHER WAS PERHAPS NOT REALLY BAD. HE HAD A BIG HEAD. THERE WAS TOO MUCH ROOM IN THERE.
HE WANTED TO KNOW IF GOD HAD A LANGUAGE. DON'T ASK ME WHAT THIS MEANS.
THE FATHER THOUGHT A BABY MIGHT SPEAK IT IF THE BABY SAW NO PEOPLE. WHAT BABY?
PETER KNEW SOME WORDS. THE FATHER THOUGHT MAYBE PETER WOULD FORGET THEM. AFTER A WHILE.

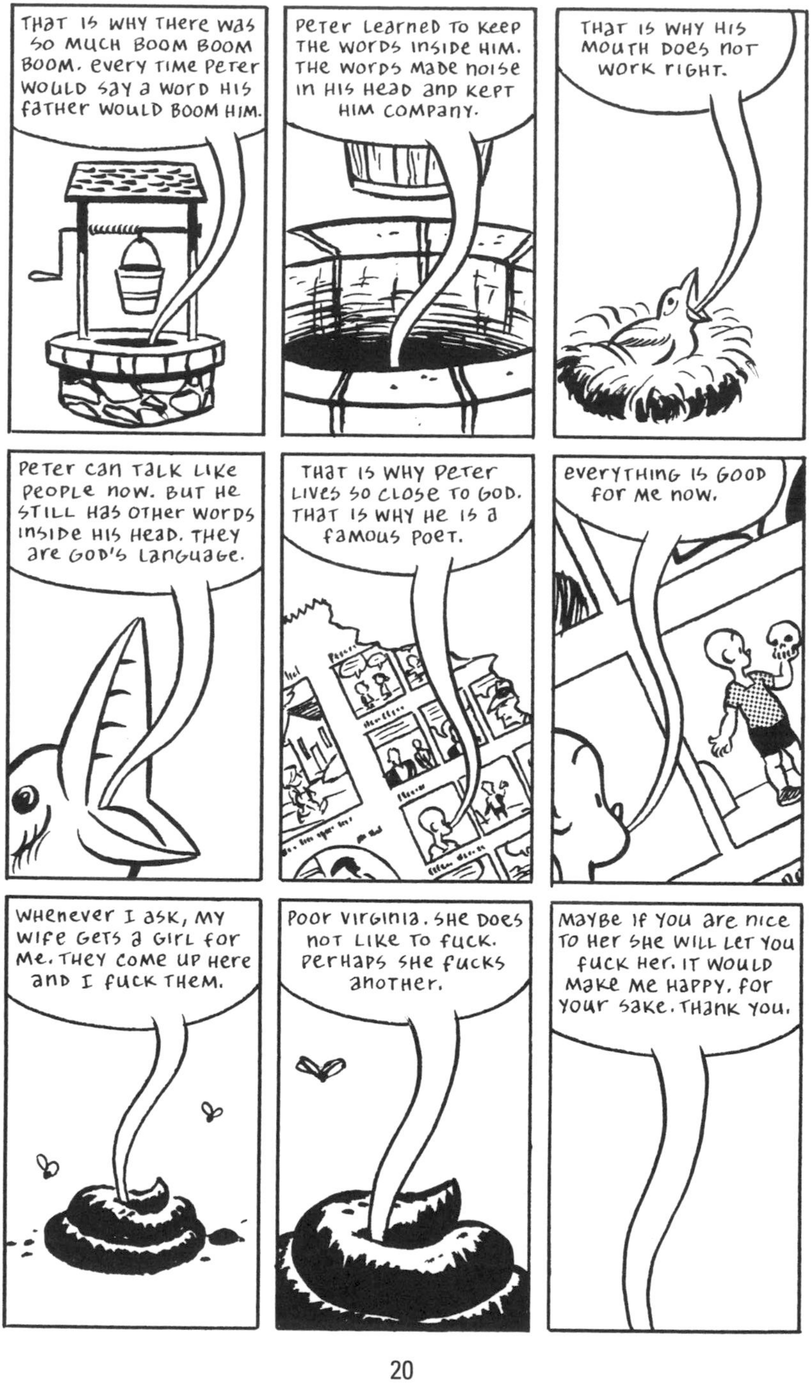
THAT IS WHY THERE WAS SO MUCH BOOM BOOM BOOM. EVERY TIME PETER WOULD SAY A WORD HIS FATHER WOULD BOOM HIM.
PETER LEARNED TO KEEP THE WORDS INSIDE HIM. THE WORDS MADE NOISE IN HIS HEAD AND KEPT HIM COMPANY.
THAT IS WHY HIS MOUTH DOES NOT WORK RIGHT.
PETER CAN TALK LIKE PEOPLE NOW. BUT HE STILL HAS OTHER WORDS INSIDE HIS HEAD. THEY ARE GOD'S LANGUAGE.
THAT IS WHY PETER LIVES SO CLOSE TO GOD. THAT IS WHY HE IS A FAMOUS POET.
EVERYTHING IS GOOD FOR ME NOW.
WHENEVER I ASK, MY WIFE GETS A GIRL FOR ME. THEY COME UP HERE AND I FUCK THEM.
POOR VIRGINIA. SHE DOES NOT LIKE TO FUCK. PERHAPS SHE FUCKS ANOTHER.
MAYBE IF YOU ARE NICE TO HER SHE WILL LET YOU FUCK HER. IT WOULD MAKE ME HAPPY. FOR YOUR SAKE. THANK YOU.

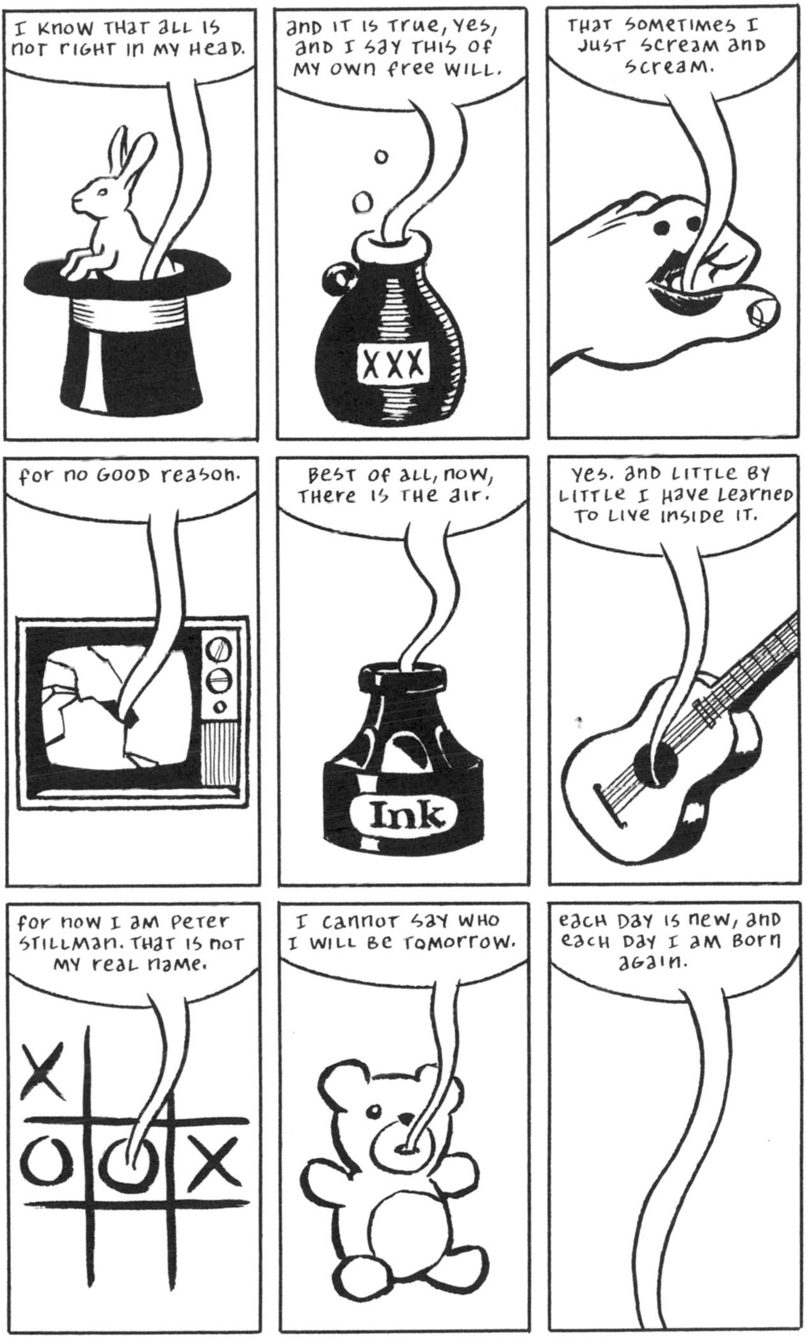
I KNOW THAT ALL IS NOT RIGHT IN MY HEAD.
AND IT IS TRUE, YES, AND I SAY THIS OF MY OWN FREE WILL.
THAT SOMETIMES I JUST SCREAM AND SCREAM.
XXX
FOR NO GOOD REASON.
BEST OF ALL, NOW, THERE IS THE AIR.
Ink
YES. AND LITTLE BY LITTLE I HAVE LEARNED TO LIVE INSIDE IT.
FOR NOW I AM PETER STILLMAN. THAT IS NOT MY REAL NAME.
I CANNOT SAY WHO I WILL BE TOMORROW.
EACH DAY IS NEW, AND EACH DAY I AM BORN AGAIN.

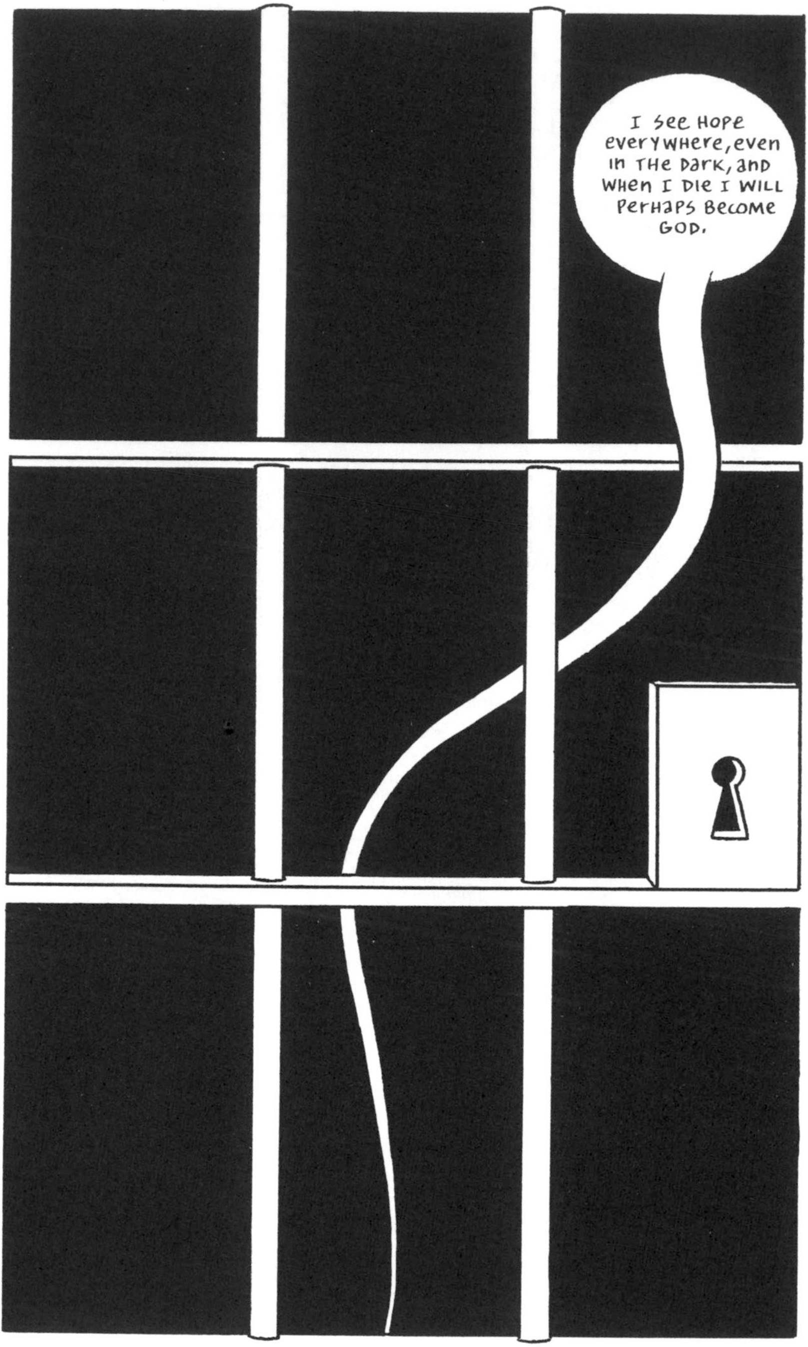
I see hope everywhere, even in the dark, and when I die I will perhaps become God.

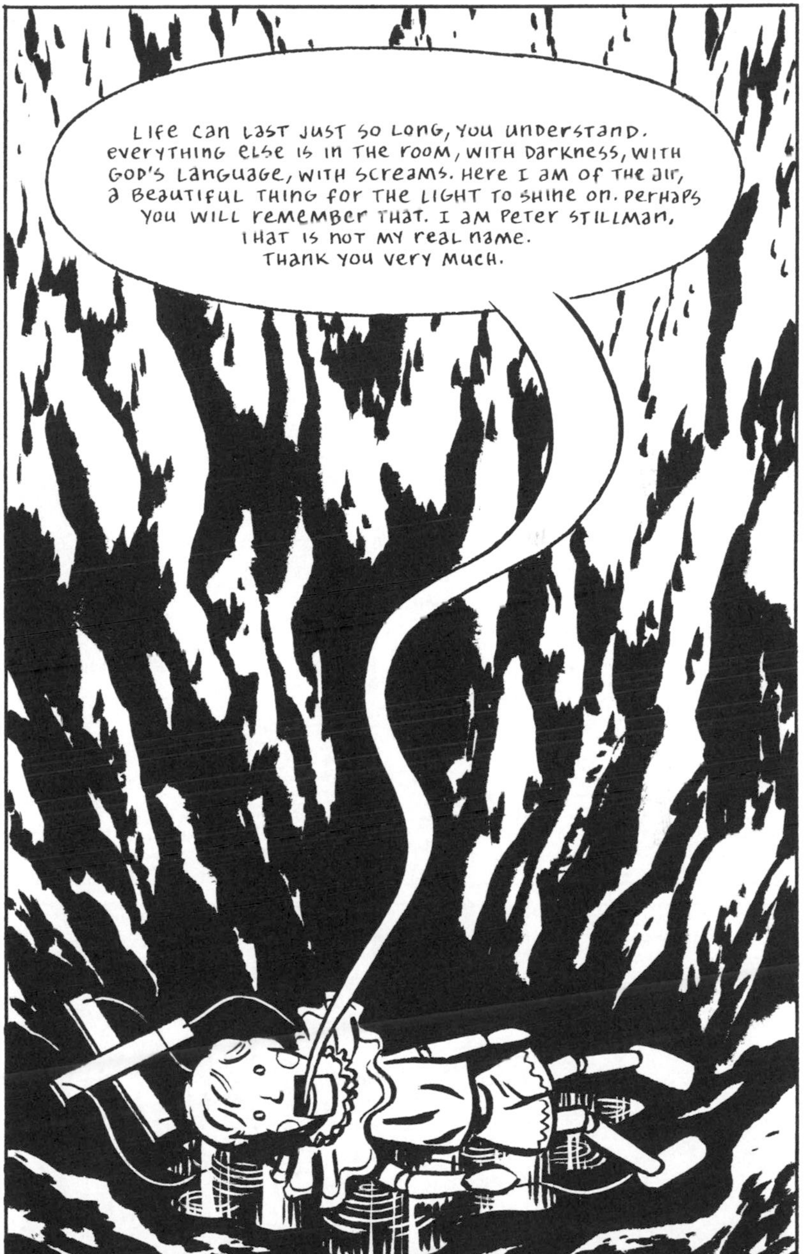
LIFE CAN LAST JUST SO LONG, YOU UNDERSTAND. EVERYTHING ELSE IS IN THE ROOM, WITH DARKNESS, WITH GOD'S LANGUAGE, WITH SCREAMS. HERE I AM OF THE AIR, A BEAUTIFUL THING FOR THE LIGHT TO SHINE ON. PERHAPS YOU WILL REMEMBER THAT. I AM PETER STILLMAN, THAT IS NOT MY REAL NAME. THANK YOU VERY MUCH.

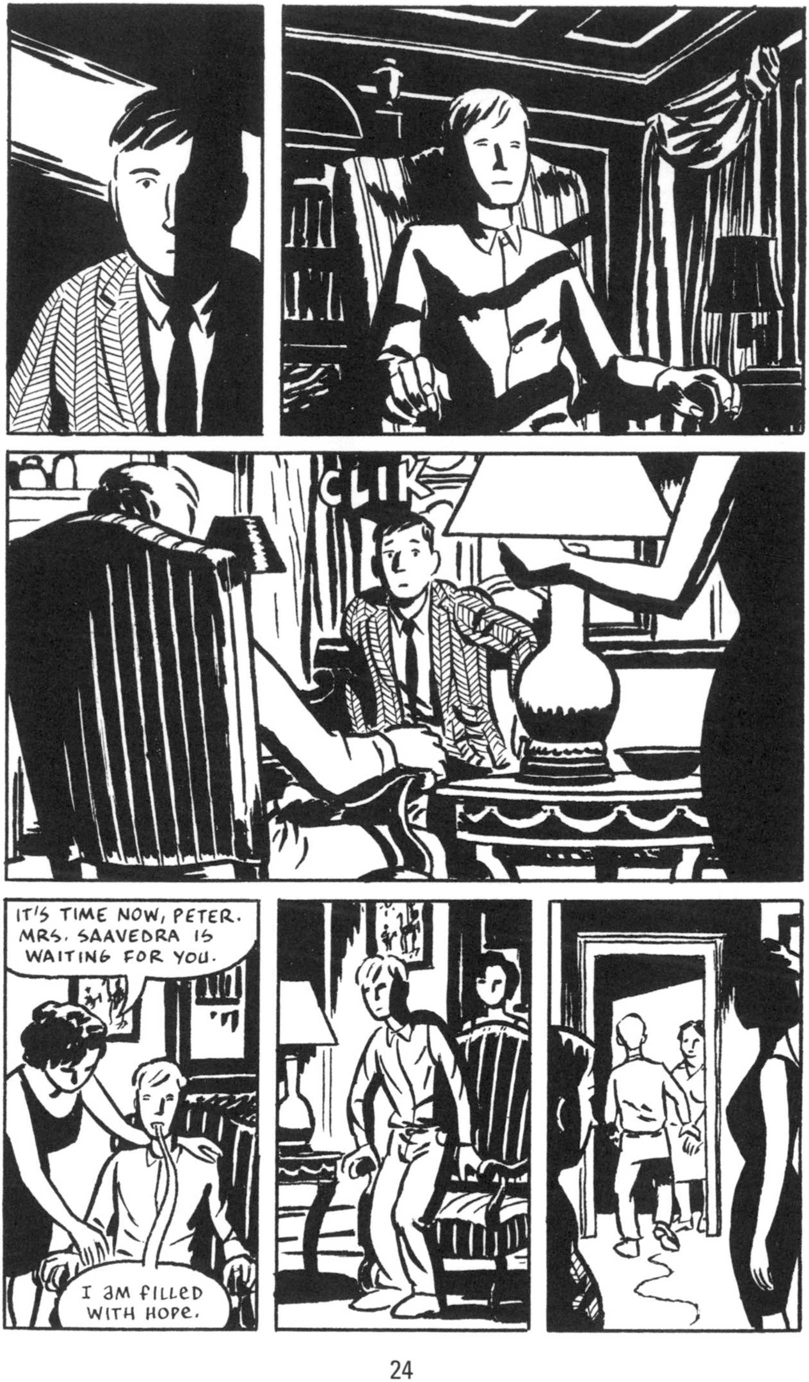
CLIK
IT'S TIME NOW, PETER. MRS. SAAVEDRA IS WAITING FOR YOU.
I AM FILLED WITH HOPE.

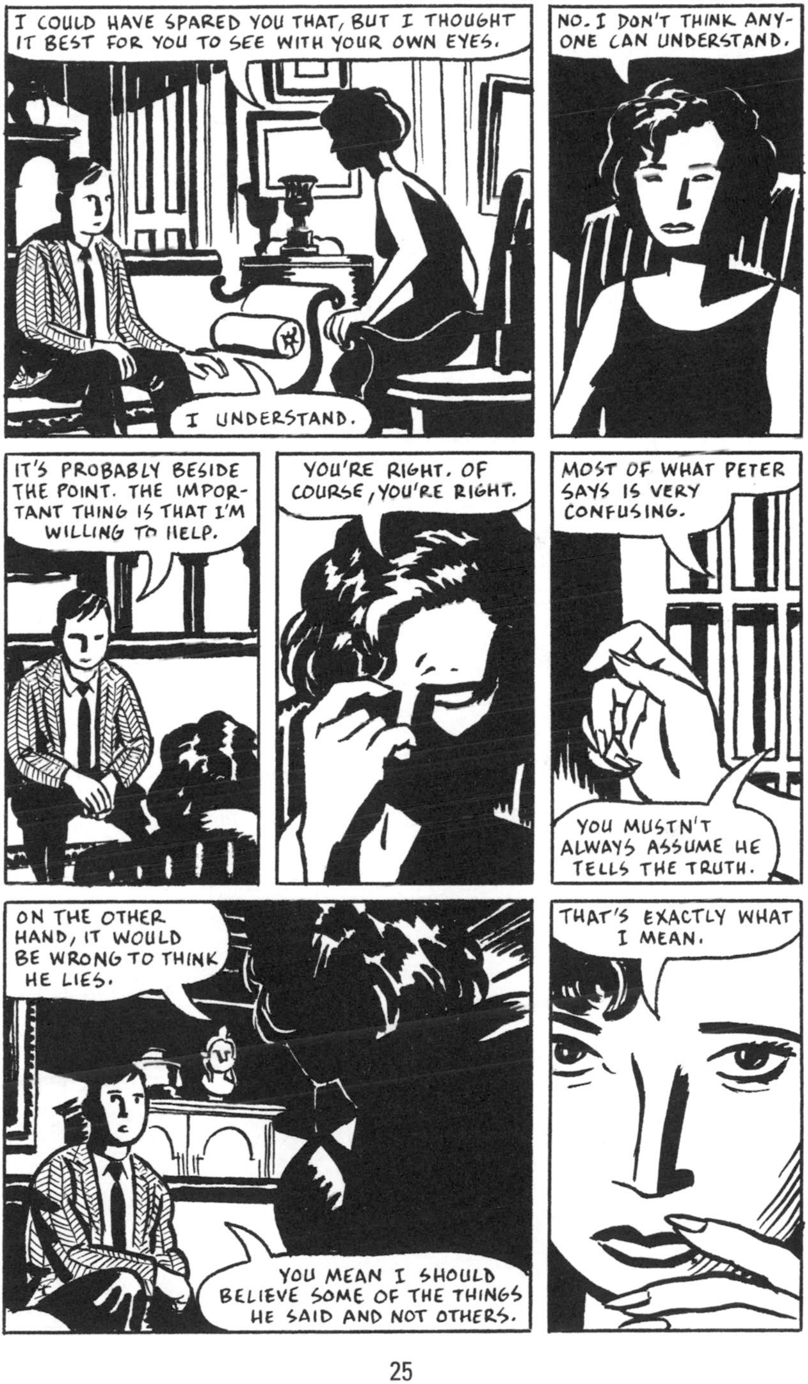
I COULD HAVE SPARED YOU THAT, BUT I THOUGHT IT BEST FOR YOU TO SEE WITH YOUR OWN EYES.
I UNDERSTAND.
NO. I DON'T THINK ANYONE CAN UNDERSTAND.
IT'S PROBABLY BESIDE THE POINT. THE IMPORTANT THING IS THAT I'M WILLING TO HELP.
YOU'RE RIGHT. OF COURSE, YOU'RE RIGHT.
MOST OF WHAT PETER SAYS IS VERY CONFUSING.
YOU MUSTN'T ALWAYS ASSUME HE TELLS THE TRUTH.
ON THE OTHER HAND, IT WOULD BE WRONG TO THINK HE LIES.
YOU MEAN I SHOULD BELIEVE SOME OF THE THINGS HE SAID AND NOT OTHERS.
THAT'S EXACTLY WHAT I MEAN.

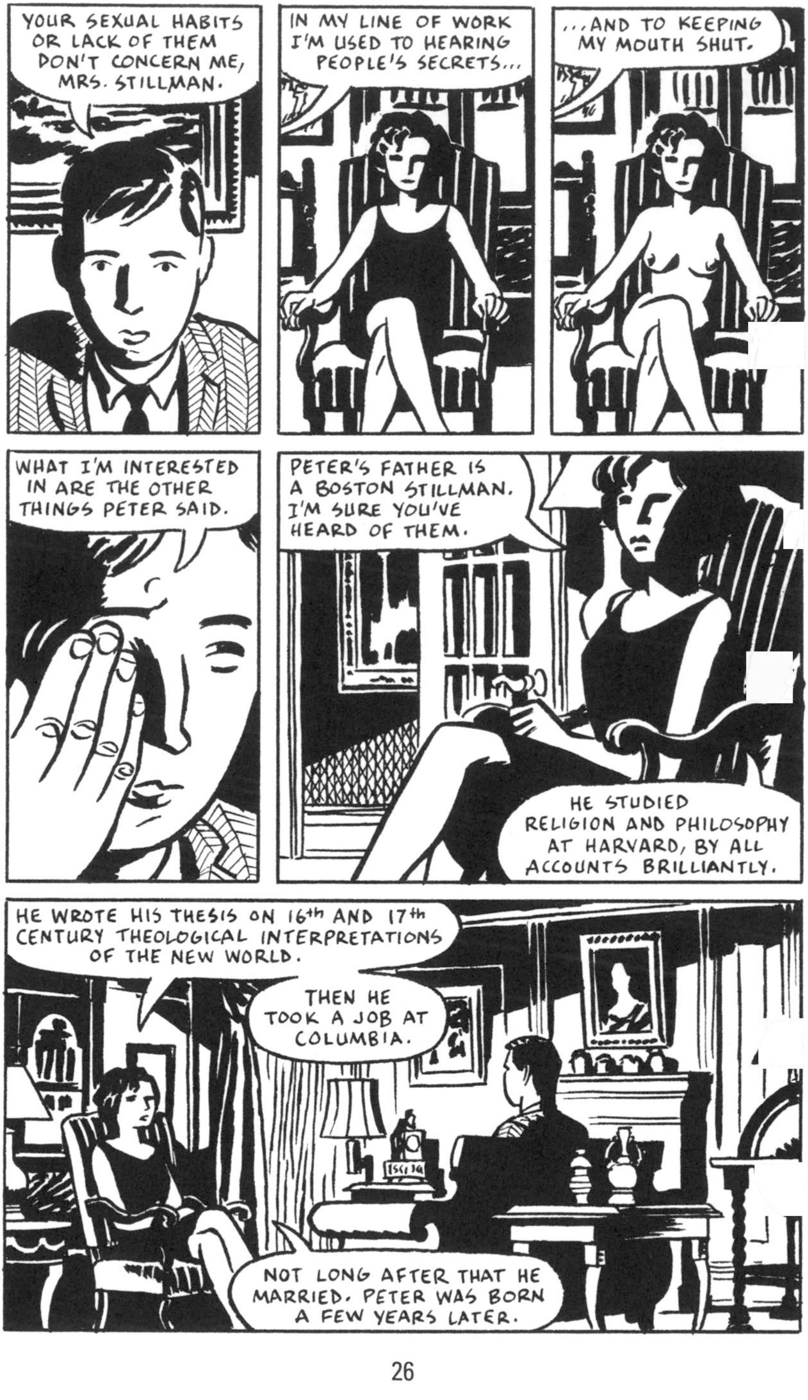
YOUR SEXUAL HABITS OR LACK OF THEM DON'T CONCERN ME, MRS. STILLMAN.
IN MY LINE OF WORK I'M USED TO HEARING PEOPLE'S SECRETS...
...AND TO KEEPING MY MOUTH SHUT.
WHAT I'M INTERESTED IN ARE THE OTHER THINGS PETER SAID.
PETER'S FATHER IS A BOSTON STILLMAN. I'M SURE YOU'VE HEARD OF THEM.
HE STUDIED RELIGION AND PHILOSOPHY AT HARVARD, BY ALL ACCOUNTS BRILLIANTLY.
HE WROTE HIS THESIS ON 16th AND 17th CENTURY THEOLOGICAL INTERPRETATIONS OF THE NEW WORLD.
THEN HE TOOK A JOB AT COLUMBIA.
NOT LONG AFTER THAT HE MARRIED. PETER WAS BORN A FEW YEARS LATER.

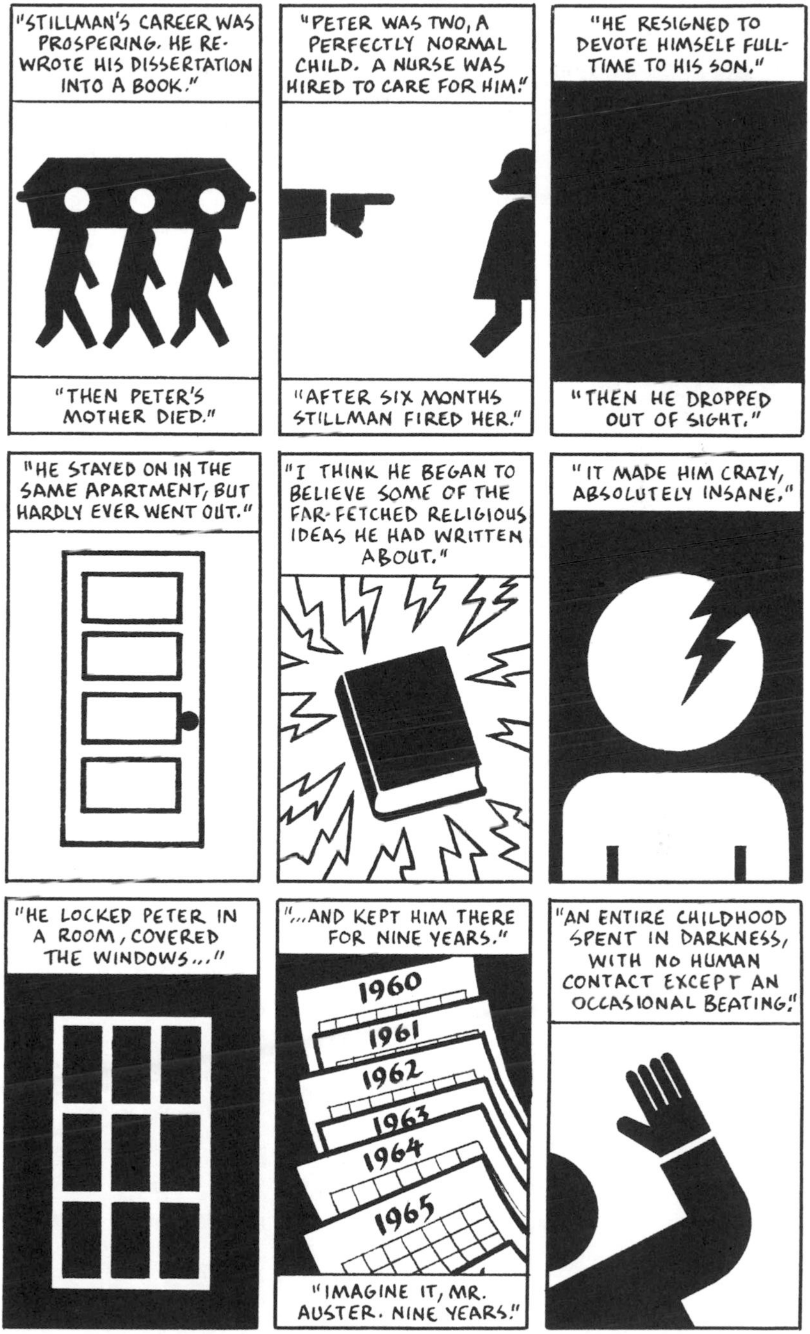
"STILLMAN'S CAREER WAS PROSPERING. HE RE-WROTE HIS DISSERTATION INTO A BOOK."
"THEN PETER'S MOTHER DIED."
"PETER WAS TWO, A PERFECTLY NORMAL CHILD. A NURSE WAS HIRED TO CARE FOR HIM."
"AFTER SIX MONTHS STILLMAN FIRED HER."
"HE RESIGNED TO DEVOTE HIMSELF FULL-TIME TO HIS SON."
"THEN HE DROPPED OUT OF SIGHT."
"HE STAYED ON IN THE SAME APARTMENT, BUT HARDLY EVER WENT OUT."
"I THINK HE BEGAN TO BELIEVE SOME OF THE FAR-FETCHED RELIGIOUS IDEAS HE HAD WRITTEN ABOUT."
"IT MADE HIM CRAZY, ABSOLUTELY INSANE."
"HE LOCKED PETER IN A ROOM, COVERED THE WINDOWS..."
"...AND KEPT HIM THERE FOR NINE YEARS."
1960
1961
1962
1963
1964
1965
"IMAGINE IT, MR. AUSTER. NINE YEARS."
"AN ENTIRE CHILDHOOD SPENT IN DARKNESS, WITH NO HUMAN CONTACT EXCEPT AN OCCASIONAL BEATING."

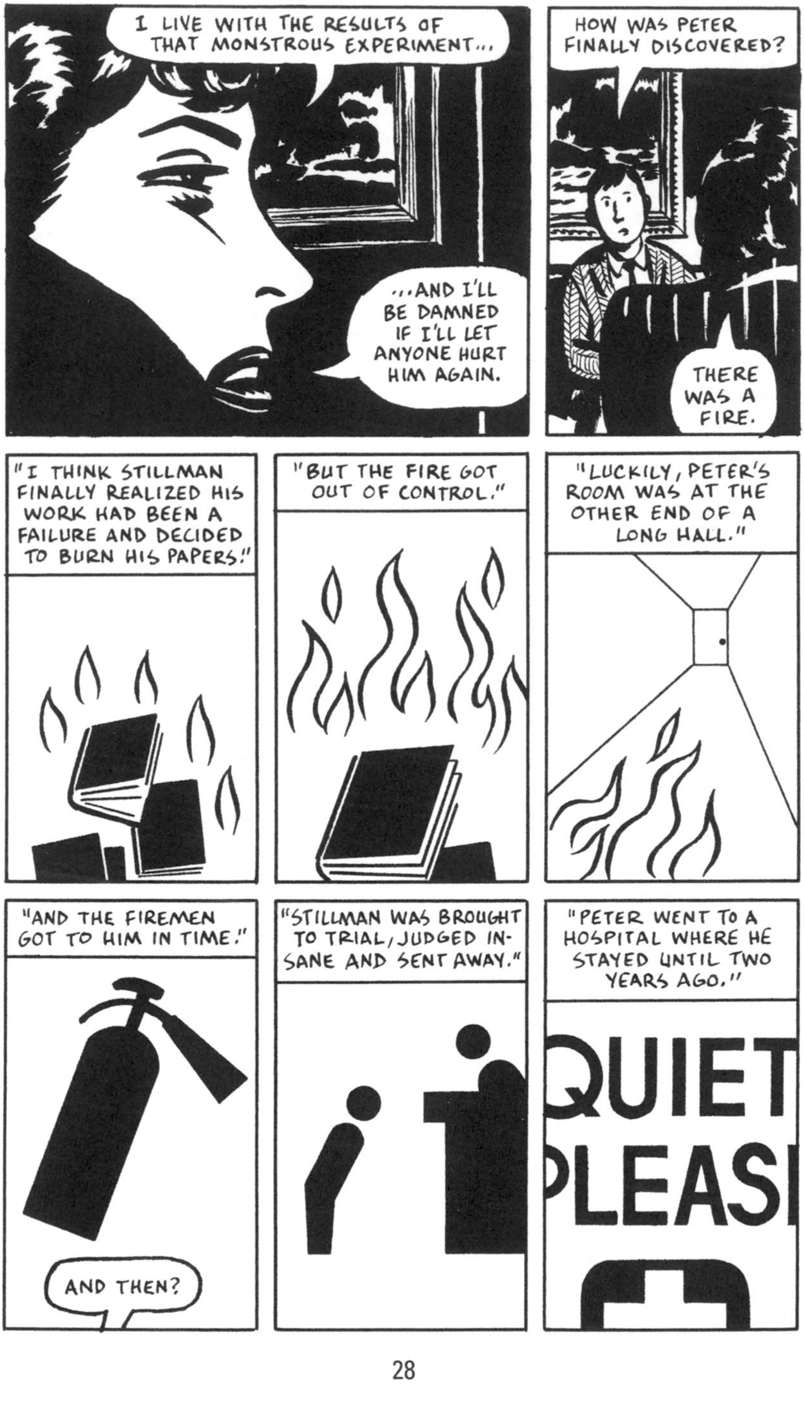
I LIVE WITH THE RESULTS OF THAT MONSTROUS EXPERIMENT...
...AND I'LL BE DAMNED IF I'LL LET ANYONE HURT HIM AGAIN.
HOW WAS PETER FINALLY DISCOVERED?
THERE WAS A FIRE.
"I THINK STILLMAN FINALLY REALIZED HIS WORK HAD BEEN A FAILURE AND DECIDED TO BURN HIS PAPERS."
"BUT THE FIRE GOT OUT OF CONTROL."
"LUCKILY, PETER'S ROOM WAS AT THE OTHER END OF A LONG HALL."
"AND THE FIREMEN GOT TO HIM IN TIME."
AND THEN?
"STILLMAN WAS BROUGHT TO TRIAL, JUDGED IN-SANE AND SENT AWAY."
"PETER WENT TO A HOSPITAL WHERE HE STAYED UNTIL TWO YEARS AGO."
QUIET PLEAS

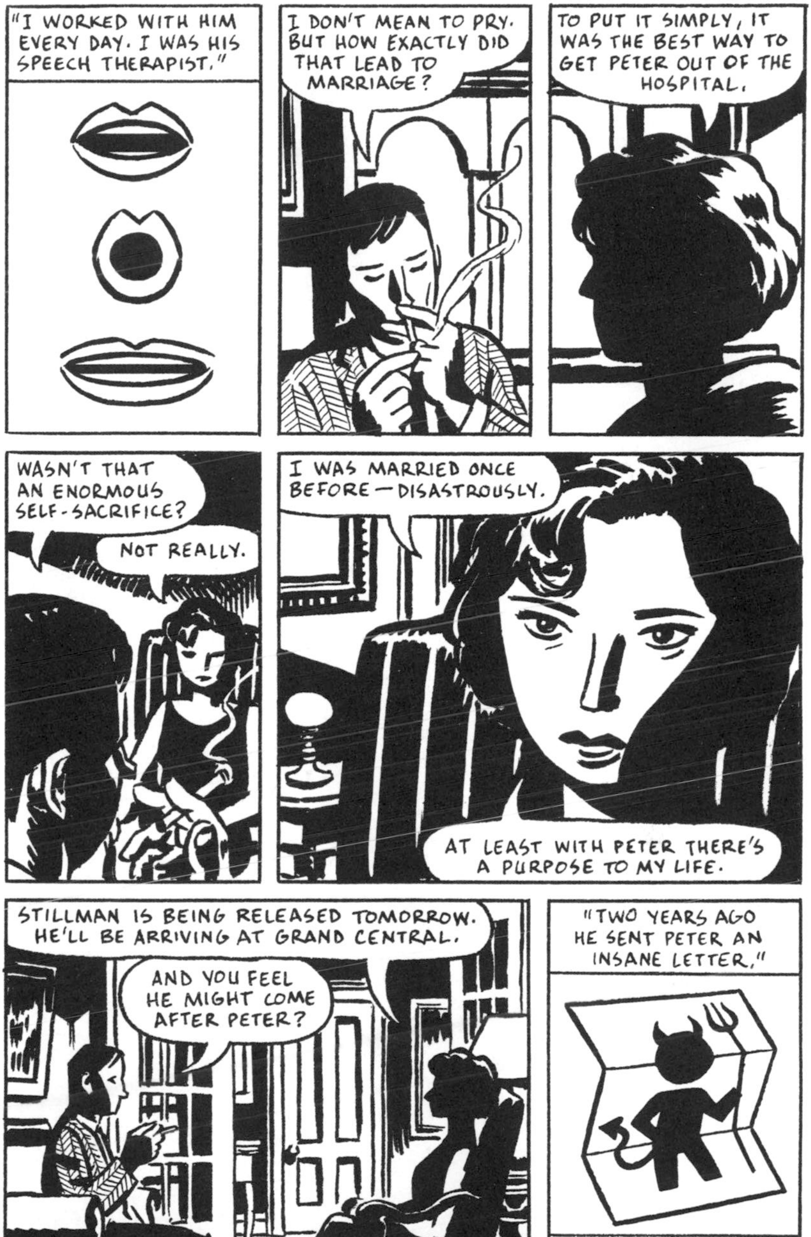

"I WORKED WITH HIM EVERY DAY. I WAS HIS SPEECH THERAPIST."
I DON'T MEAN TO PRY. BUT HOW EXACTLY DID THAT LEAD TO MARRIAGE?
TO PUT IT SIMPLY, IT WAS THE BEST WAY TO GET PETER OUT OF THE HOSPITAL.
WASN'T THAT AN ENORMOUS SELF-SACRIFICE?
NOT REALLY.
I WAS MARRIED ONCE BEFORE—DISASTROUSLY.
AT LEAST WITH PETER THERE'S A PURPOSE TO MY LIFE.
STILLMAN IS BEING RELEASED TOMORROW. HE'LL BE ARRIVING AT GRAND CENTRAL.
AND YOU FEEL HE MIGHT COME AFTER PETER?
"TWO YEARS AGO HE SENT PETER AN INSANE LETTER,"
"HE CALLED HIM A DEVIL BOY, AND SAID THERE WOULD BE A DAY OF RECKONING."

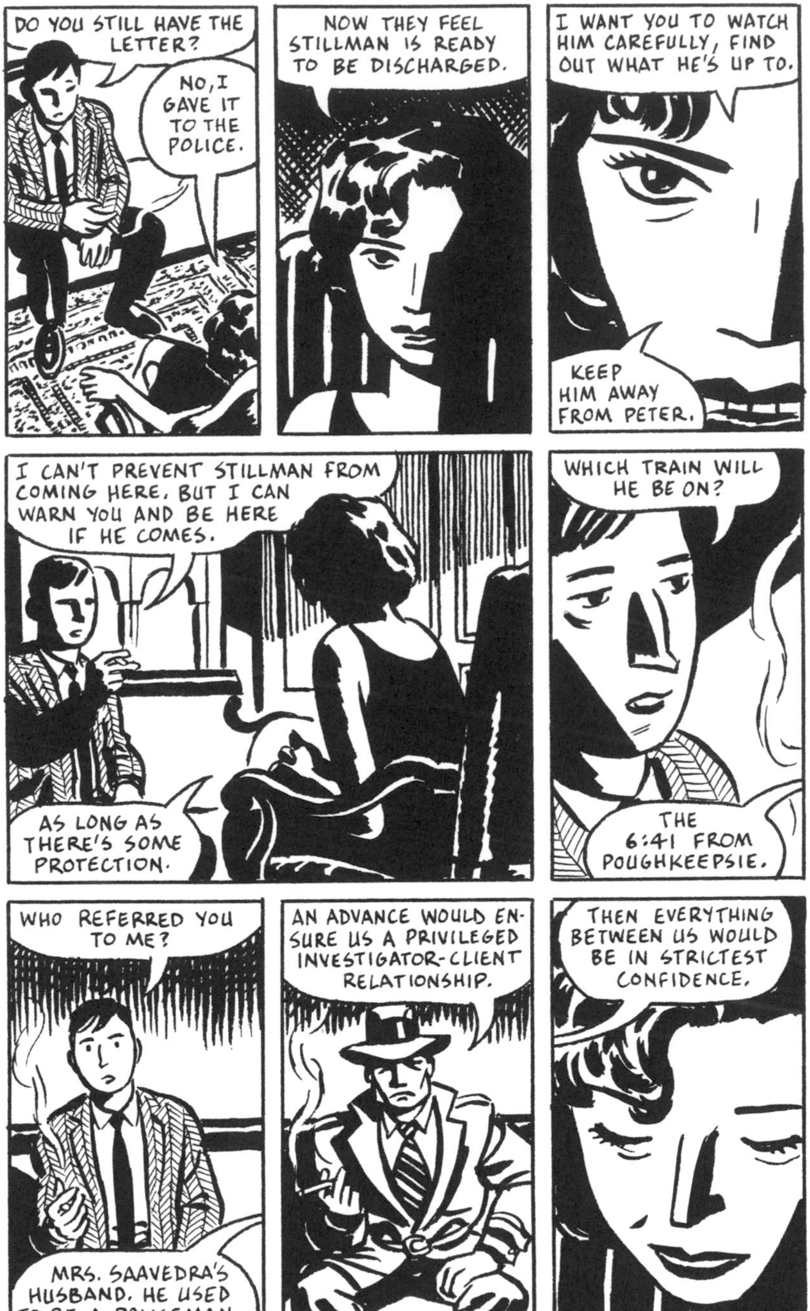
DO YOU STILL HAVE THE LETTER?
NO, I GAVE IT TO THE POLICE.
NOW THEY FEEL STILLMAN IS READY TO BE DISCHARGED.
I WANT YOU TO WATCH HIM CAREFULLY, FIND OUT WHAT HE'S UP TO.
KEEP HIM AWAY FROM PETER.
I CAN'T PREVENT STILLMAN FROM COMING HERE. BUT I CAN WARN YOU AND BE HERE IF HE COMES.
AS LONG AS THERE'S SOME PROTECTION.
WHICH TRAIN WILL HE BE ON?
THE 6:41 FROM POUGHKEEPSIE.
WHO REFERRED YOU TO ME?
MRS. SAAVEDRA'S HUSBAND. HE USED TO BE A POLICEMAN.
AN ADVANCE WOULD EN-SURE US A PRIVILEGED INVESTIGATOR-CLIENT RELATIONSHIP.
THEN EVERYTHING BETWEEN US WOULD BE IN STRICTEST CONFIDENCE.

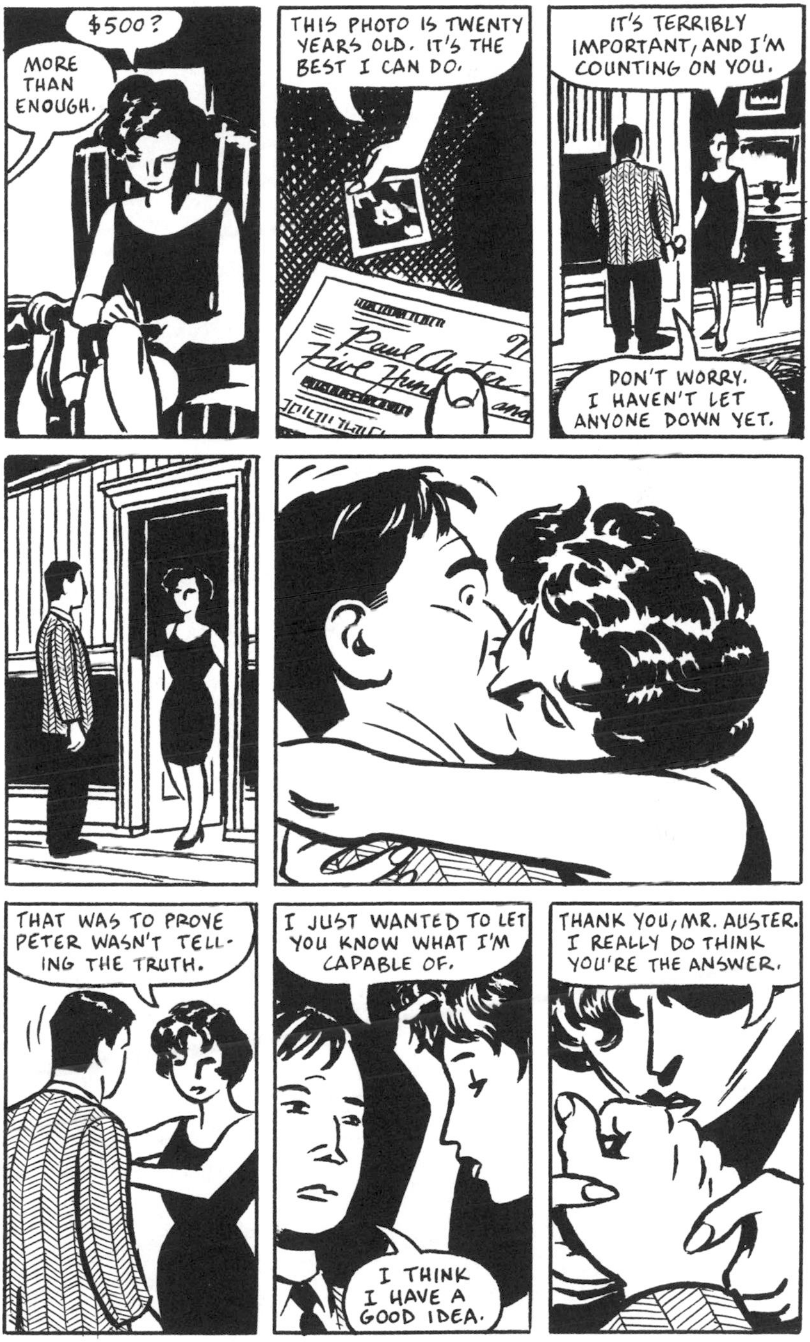
$500?
MORE THAN ENOUGH.
THIS PHOTO IS TWENTY YEARS OLD. IT'S THE BEST I CAN DO.
IT'S TERRIBLY IMPORTANT, AND I'M COUNTING ON YOU.
DON'T WORRY. I HAVEN'T LET ANYONE DOWN YET.
THAT WAS TO PROVE PETER WASN'T TELLING THE TRUTH.
I JUST WANTED TO LET YOU KNOW WHAT I'M CAPABLE OF.
I THINK I HAVE A GOOD IDEA.
THANK YOU, MR. AUSTER. I REALLY DO THINK YOU'RE THE ANSWER.

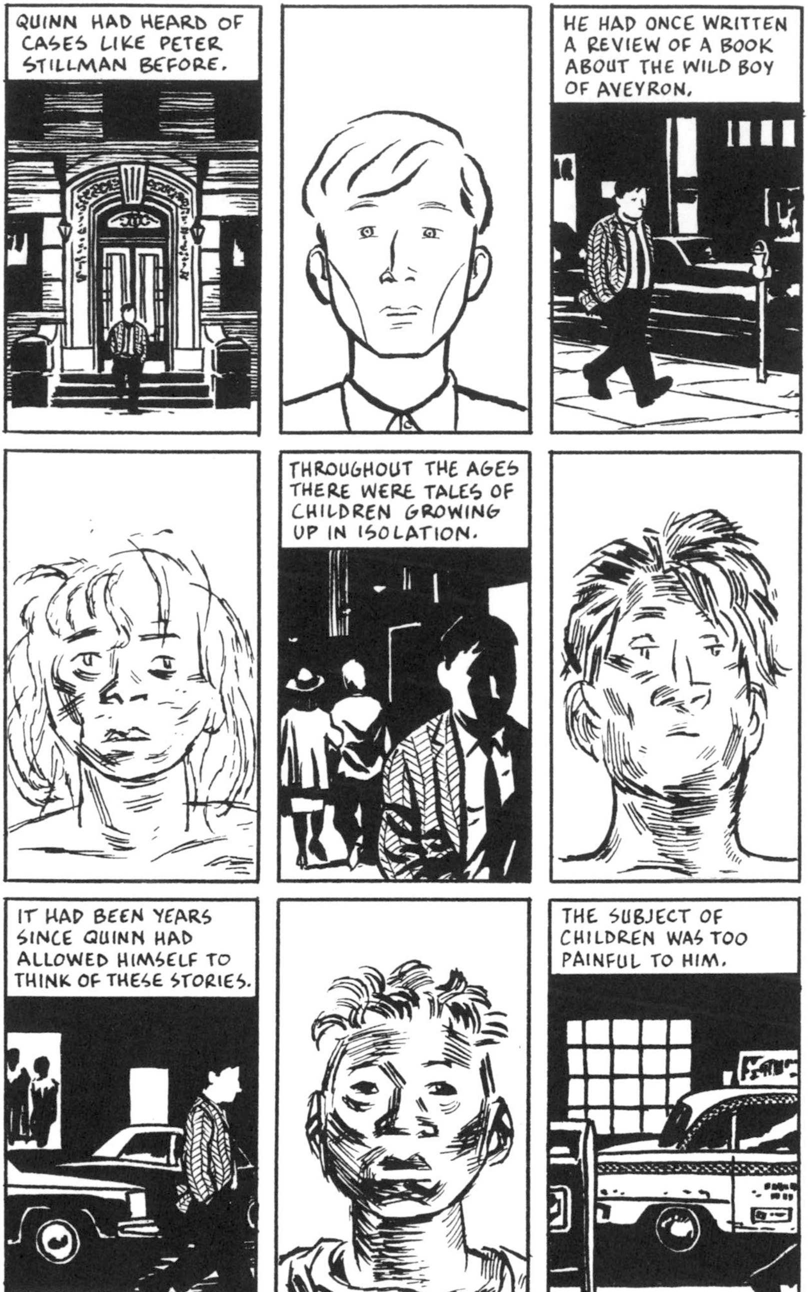
QUINN HAD HEARD OF CASES LIKE PETER STILLMAN BEFORE.
HE HAD ONCE WRITTEN A REVIEW OF A BOOK ABOUT THE WILD BOY OF AVEYRON.
THROUGHOUT THE AGES THERE WERE TALES OF CHILDREN GROWING UP IN ISOLATION.
IT HAD BEEN YEARS SINCE QUINN HAD ALLOWED HIMSELF TO THINK OF THESE STORIES.
THE SUBJECT OF CHILDREN WAS TOO PAINFUL TO HIM.

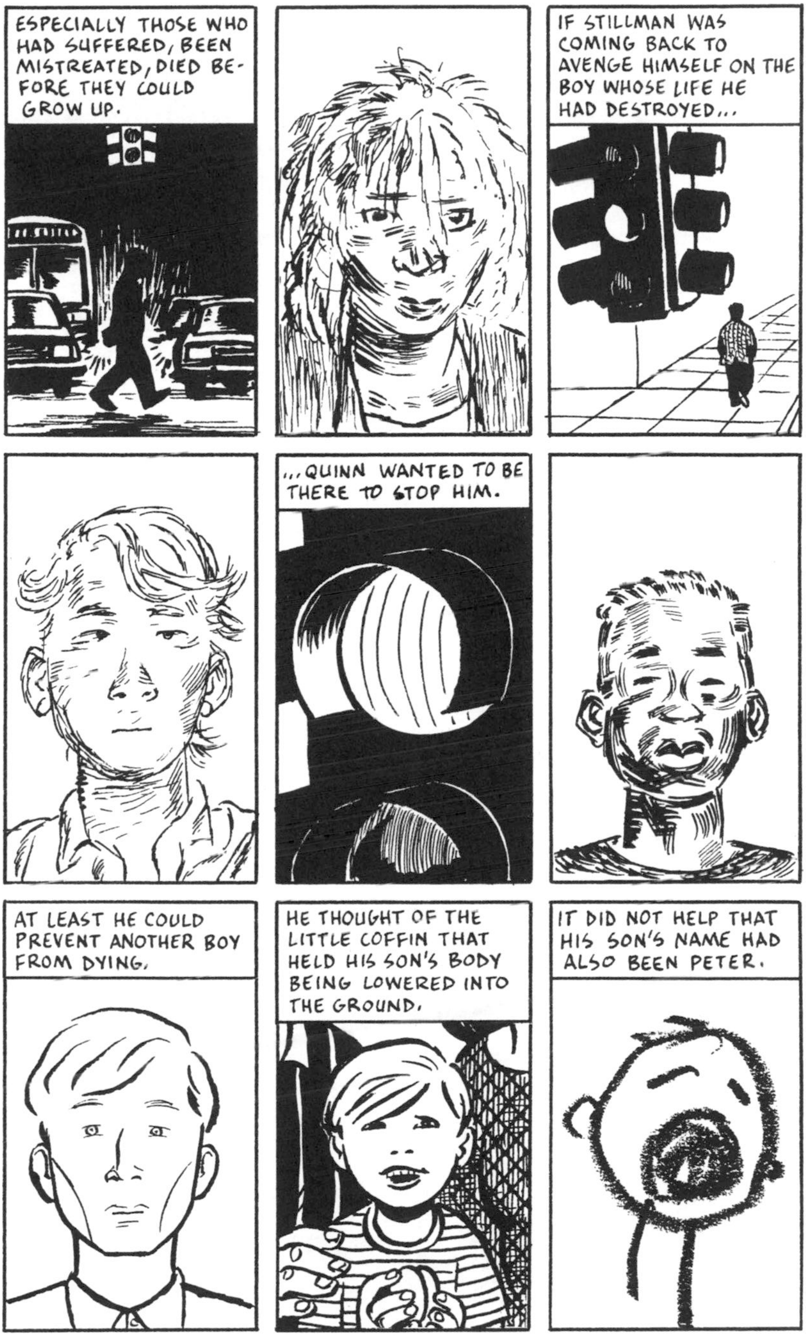
ESPECIALLY THOSE WHO HAD SUFFERED, BEEN MISTREATED, DIED BEFORE THEY COULD GROW UP.
IF STILLMAN WAS COMING BACK TO AVENGE HIMSELF ON THE BOY WHOSE LIFE HE HAD DESTROYED...
...QUINN WANTED TO BE THERE TO STOP HIM.
AT LEAST HE COULD PREVENT ANOTHER BOY FROM DYING.
HE THOUGHT OF THE LITTLE COFFIN THAT HELD HIS SON'S BODY BEING LOWERED INTO THE GROUND.
IT DID NOT HELP THAT HIS SON'S NAME HAD ALSO BEEN PETER.

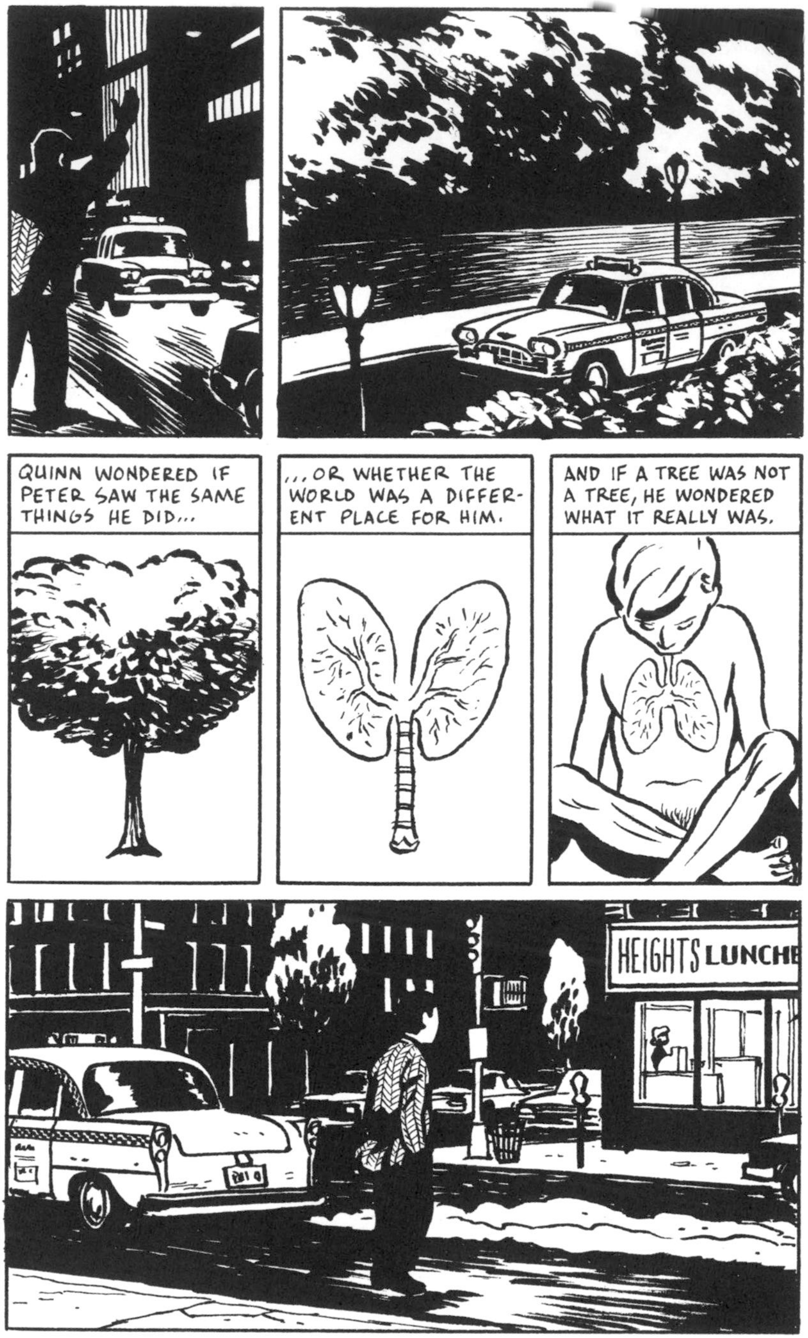
QUINN WONDERED IF PETER SAW THE SAME THINGS HE DID...
...OR WHETHER THE WORLD WAS A DIFFERENT PLACE FOR HIM.
AND IF A TREE WAS NOT A TREE, HE WONDERED WHAT IT REALLY WAS.
HEIGHTS LUNCHE

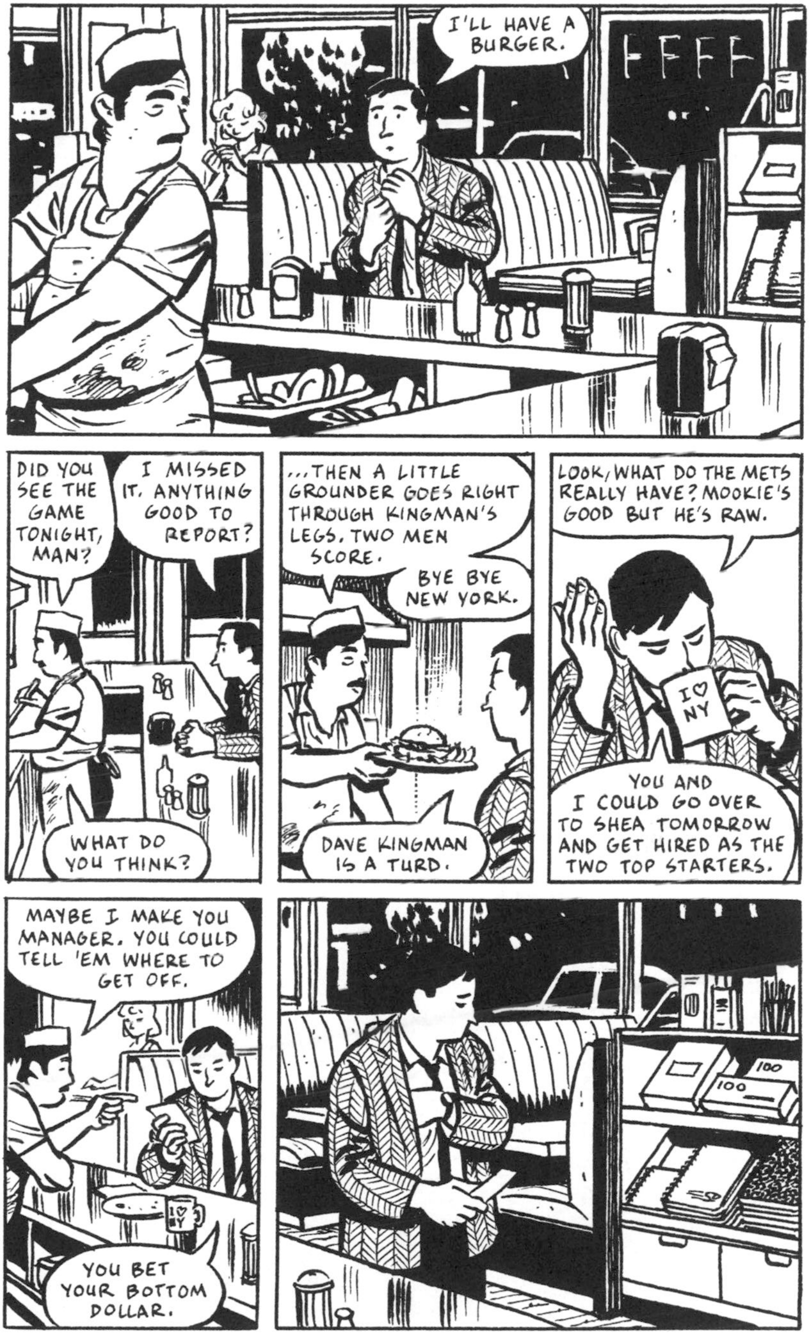
I'LL HAVE A BURGER.
DID YOU SEE THE GAME TONIGHT, MAN?
I MISSED IT. ANYTHING GOOD TO REPORT?
WHAT DO YOU THINK?
...THEN A LITTLE GROUNDER GOES RIGHT THROUGH KINGMAN'S LEGS. TWO MEN SCORE.
BYE BYE NEW YORK.
DAVE KINGMAN IS A TURD.
LOOK, WHAT DO THE METS REALLY HAVE? MOOKIE'S GOOD BUT HE'S RAW.
I ♡ NY
YOU AND I COULD GO OVER TO SHEA TOMORROW AND GET HIRED AS THE TWO TOP STARTERS.
MAYBE I MAKE YOU MANAGER. YOU COULD TELL 'EM WHERE TO GET OFF.
YOU BET YOUR BOTTOM DOLLAR.
100
100

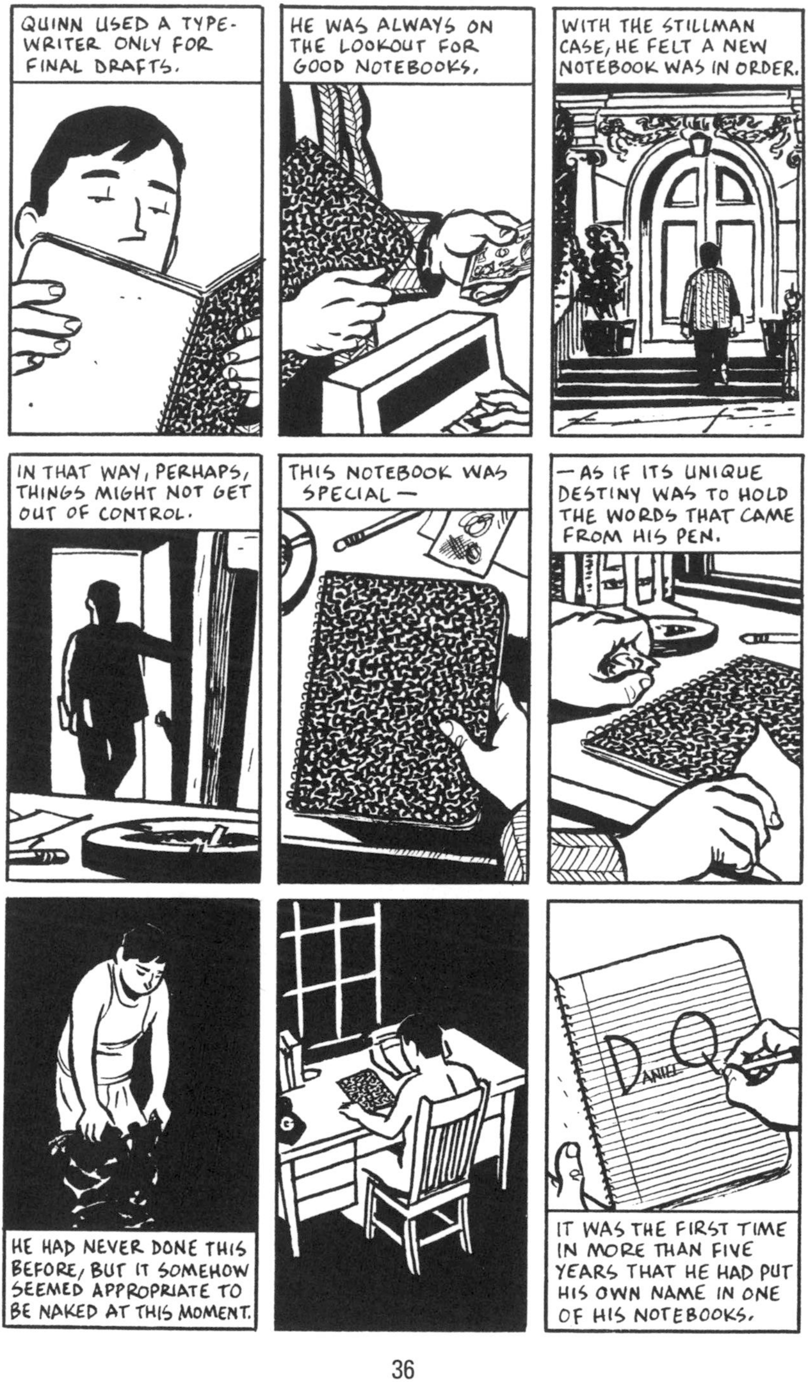
QUINN USED A TYPE-WRITER ONLY FOR FINAL DRAFTS.
HE WAS ALWAYS ON THE LOOKOUT FOR GOOD NOTEBOOKS.
WITH THE STILLMAN CASE, HE FELT A NEW NOTEBOOK WAS IN ORDER.
IN THAT WAY, PERHAPS, THINGS MIGHT NOT GET OUT OF CONTROL.
THIS NOTEBOOK WAS SPECIAL —
— AS IF ITS UNIQUE DESTINY WAS TO HOLD THE WORDS THAT CAME FROM HIS PEN.
HE HAD NEVER DONE THIS BEFORE, BUT IT SOMEHOW SEEMED APPROPRIATE TO BE NAKED AT THIS MOMENT.
IT WAS THE FIRST TIME IN MORE THAN FIVE YEARS THAT HE HAD PUT HIS OWN NAME IN ONE OF HIS NOTEBOOKS.

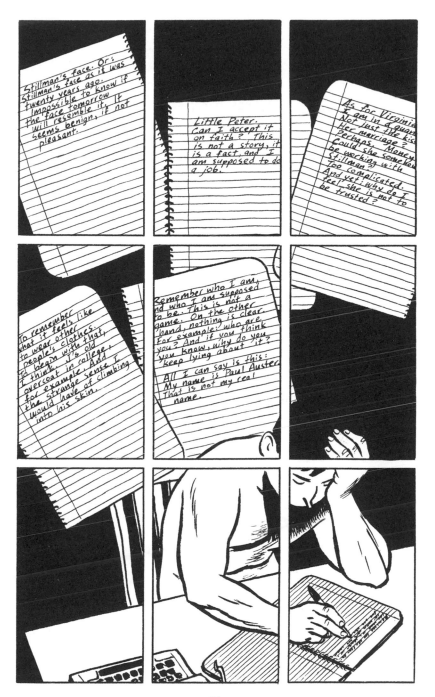

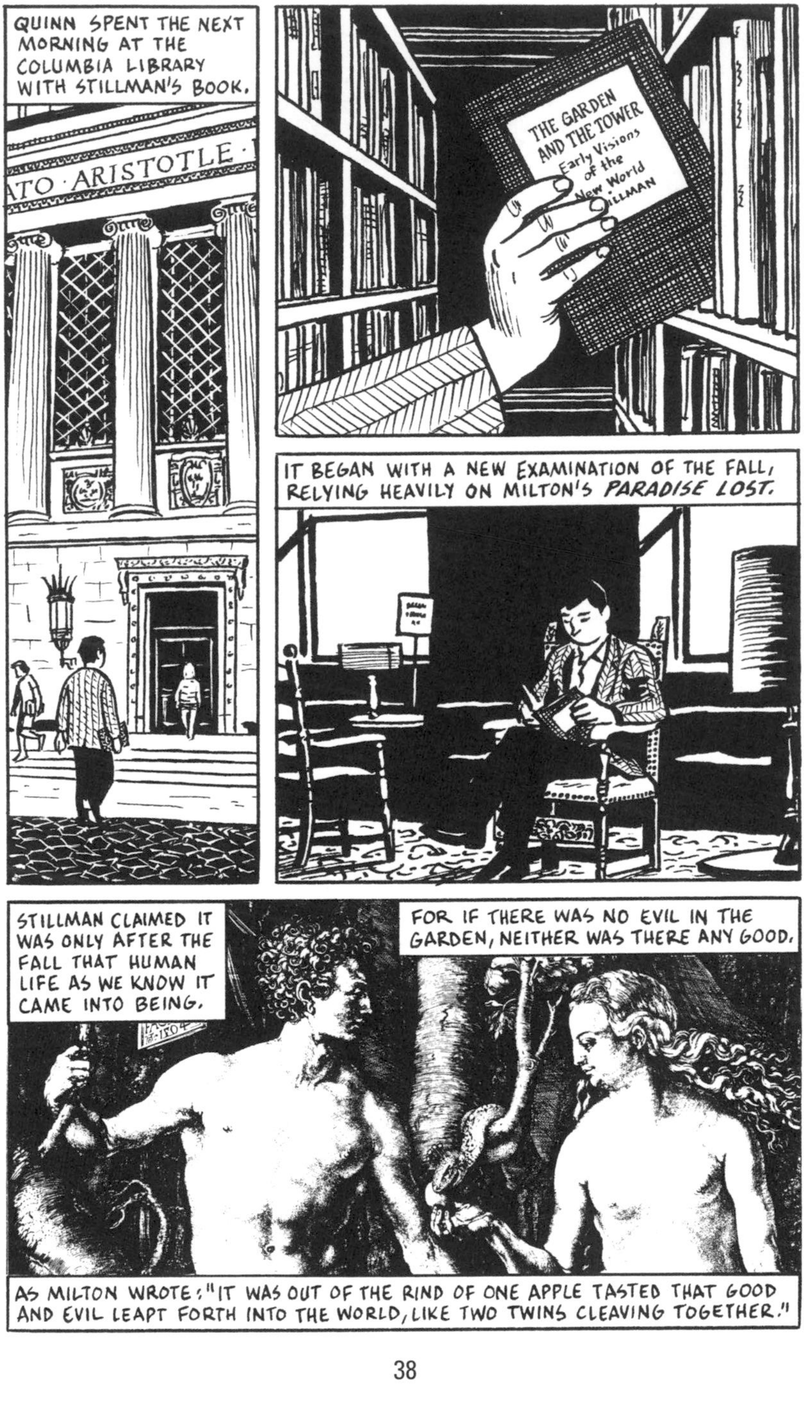
QUINN SPENT THE NEXT MORNING AT THE COLUMBIA LIBRARY WITH STILLMAN'S BOOK.
ATO · ARISTOTLE
THE GARDEN AND THE TOWER
Early Visions of the New World
IT BEGAN WITH A NEW EXAMINATION OF THE FALL, RELYING HEAVILY ON MILTON'S PARADISE LOST.
STILLMAN CLAIMED IT WAS ONLY AFTER THE FALL THAT HUMAN LIFE AS WE KNOW IT CAME INTO BEING.
FOR IF THERE WAS NO EVIL IN THE GARDEN, NEITHER WAS THERE ANY GOOD.
AS MILTON WROTE: "IT WAS OUT OF THE RIND OF ONE APPLE TASTED THAT GOOD AND EVIL LEAPT FORTH INTO THE WORLD, LIKE TWO TWINS CLEAVING TOGETHER."

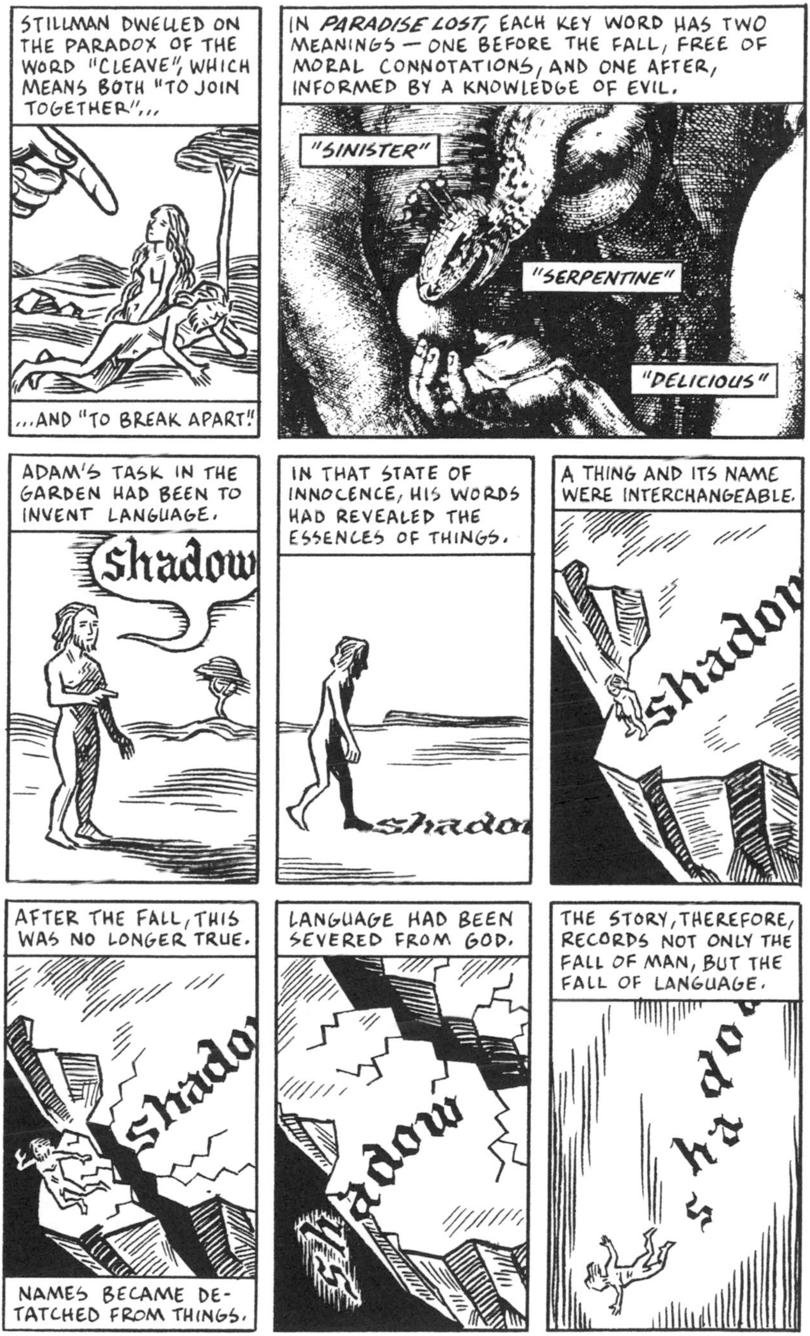
STILLMAN DWELLED ON THE PARADOX OF THE WORD "CLEAVE", WHICH MEANS BOTH "TO JOIN TOGETHER",..
...AND "TO BREAK APART."
IN *PARADISE LOST,* EACH KEY WORD HAS TWO MEANINGS — ONE BEFORE THE FALL, FREE OF MORAL CONNOTATIONS, AND ONE AFTER, INFORMED BY A KNOWLEDGE OF EVIL.
"SINISTER"
"SERPENTINE"
"DELICIOUS"
ADAM'S TASK IN THE GARDEN HAD BEEN TO INVENT LANGUAGE.
shadow
IN THAT STATE OF INNOCENCE, HIS WORDS HAD REVEALED THE ESSENCES OF THINGS.
A THING AND ITS NAME WERE INTERCHANGEABLE.
AFTER THE FALL, THIS WAS NO LONGER TRUE.
NAMES BECAME DE-TATCHED FROM THINGS.
LANGUAGE HAD BEEN SEVERED FROM GOD.
THE STORY, THEREFORE, RECORDS NOT ONLY THE FALL OF MAN, BUT THE FALL OF LANGUAGE.

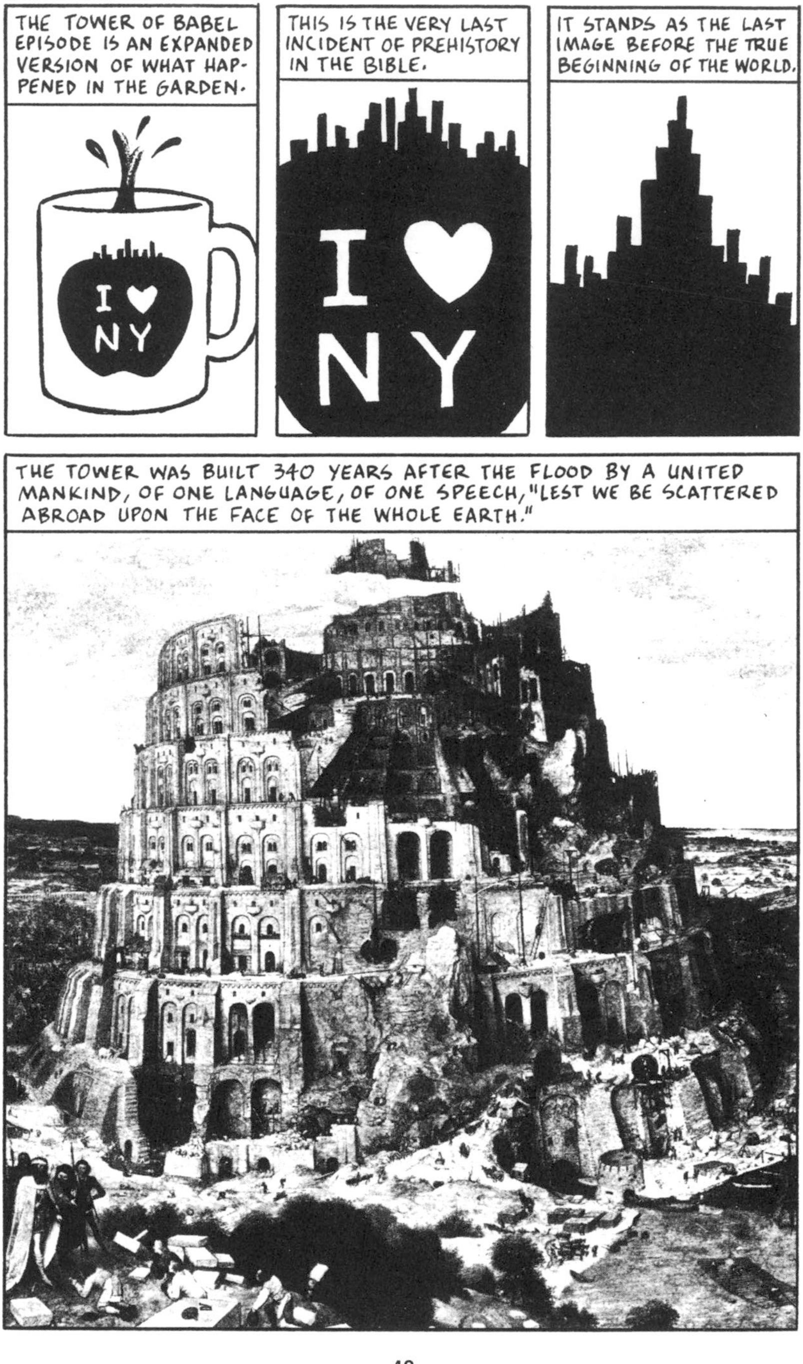
THE TOWER OF BABEL EPISODE IS AN EXPANDED VERSION OF WHAT HAPPENED IN THE GARDEN.
I ♥ NY
THIS IS THE VERY LAST INCIDENT OF PREHISTORY IN THE BIBLE.
I ♥ NY
IT STANDS AS THE LAST IMAGE BEFORE THE TRUE BEGINNING OF THE WORLD.
THE TOWER WAS BUILT 340 YEARS AFTER THE FLOOD BY A UNITED MANKIND, OF ONE LANGUAGE, OF ONE SPEECH, "LEST WE BE SCATTERED ABROAD UPON THE FACE OF THE WHOLE EARTH."

THIS DESIRE CONTRADICTED GOD'S COMMAND: "BE FERTILE...AND FILL THE EARTH."

AS DIVINE PUNISHMENT, ONE THIRD OF THE TOWER SANK INTO THE GROUND...

...AND ONE THIRD WAS DESTROYED BY FIRE.

STILL, A PERSON COULD WALK FOR THREE DAYS IN THE SHADOW OF THE PART LEFT STANDING.

AND WHOEVER LOOKED UPON THE RUINS OF THE TOWER...

...FORGOT EVERYTHING HE KNEW.

WHAT DOES ALL THIS HAVE TO DO WITH THE NEW WORLD?

THE GARDEN AND THE TOWER

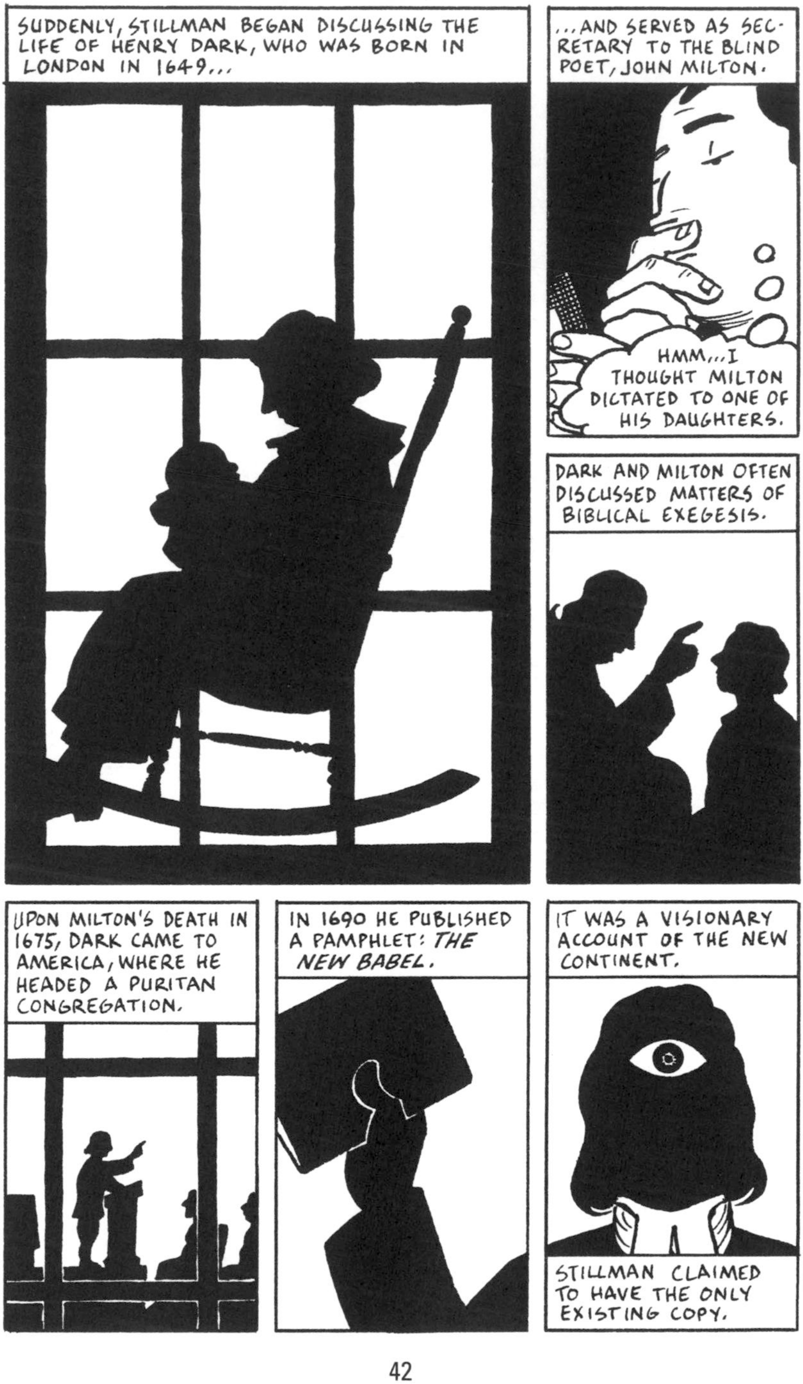
SUDDENLY, STILLMAN BEGAN DISCUSSING THE LIFE OF HENRY DARK, WHO WAS BORN IN LONDON IN 1649...
...AND SERVED AS SECRETARY TO THE BLIND POET, JOHN MILTON.
HMM... I THOUGHT MILTON DICTATED TO ONE OF HIS DAUGHTERS.
DARK AND MILTON OFTEN DISCUSSED MATTERS OF BIBLICAL EXEGESIS.
UPON MILTON'S DEATH IN 1675, DARK CAME TO AMERICA, WHERE HE HEADED A PURITAN CONGREGATION.
IN 1690 HE PUBLISHED A PAMPHLET: *THE NEW BABEL*.
IT WAS A VISIONARY ACCOUNT OF THE NEW CONTINENT.
STILLMAN CLAIMED TO HAVE THE ONLY EXISTING COPY.

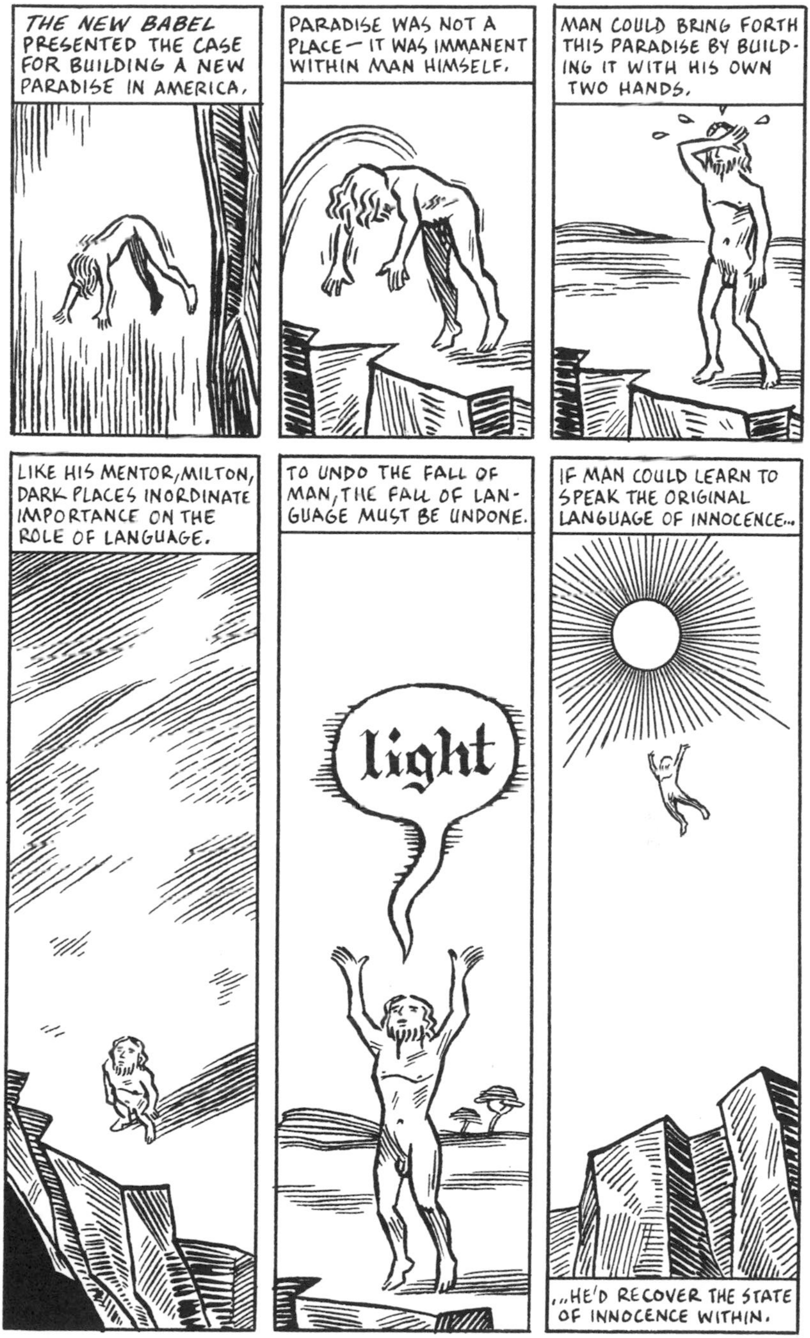
THE NEW BABEL PRESENTED THE CASE FOR BUILDING A NEW PARADISE IN AMERICA.
PARADISE WAS NOT A PLACE— IT WAS IMMANENT WITHIN MAN HIMSELF.
MAN COULD BRING FORTH THIS PARADISE BY BUILDING IT WITH HIS OWN TWO HANDS.
LIKE HIS MENTOR, MILTON, DARK PLACES INORDINATE IMPORTANCE ON THE ROLE OF LANGUAGE.
TO UNDO THE FALL OF MAN, THE FALL OF LANGUAGE MUST BE UNDONE.
light
IF MAN COULD LEARN TO SPEAK THE ORIGINAL LANGUAGE OF INNOCENCE...
...HE'D RECOVER THE STATE OF INNOCENCE WITHIN.

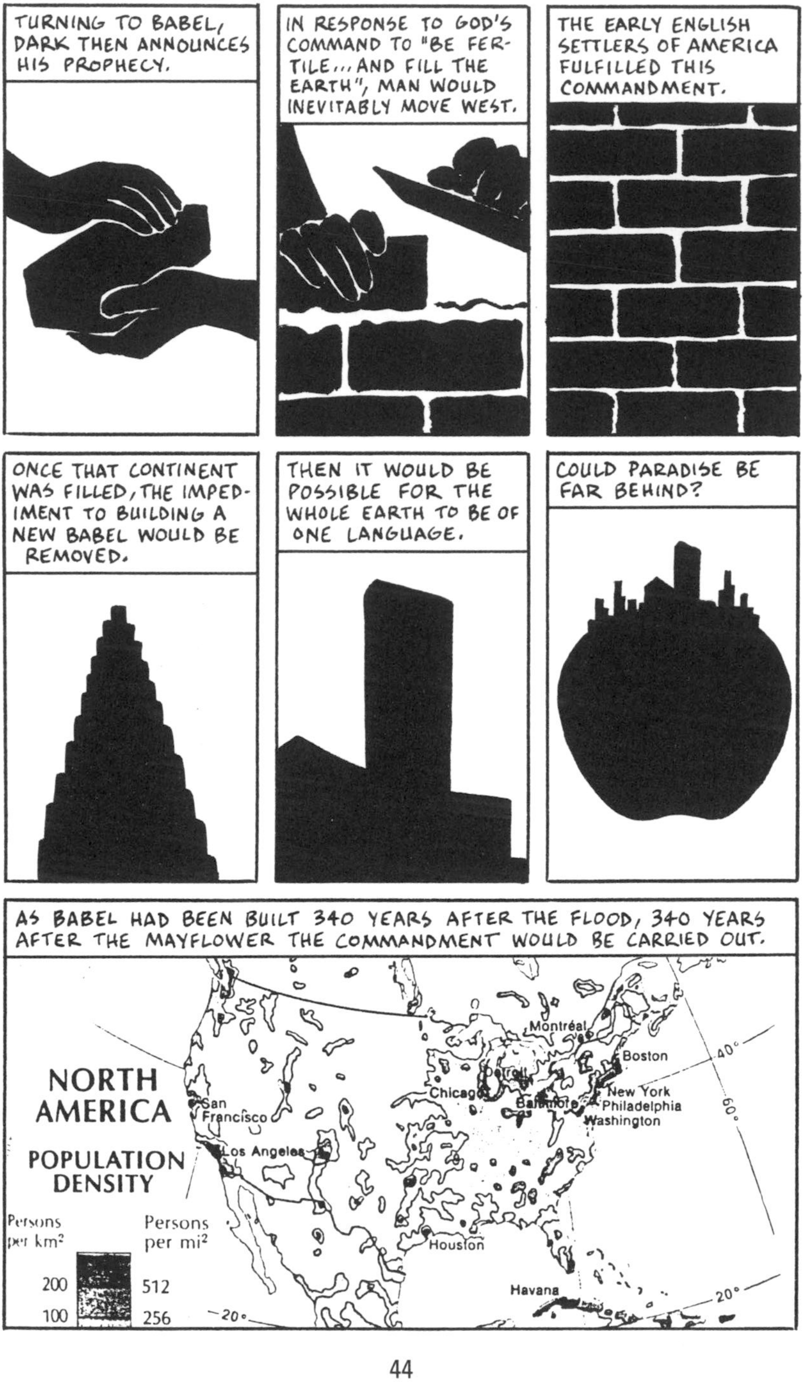
TURNING TO BABEL, DARK THEN ANNOUNCES HIS PROPHECY.
IN RESPONSE TO GOD'S COMMAND TO "BE FERTILE... AND FILL THE EARTH", MAN WOULD INEVITABLY MOVE WEST.
THE EARLY ENGLISH SETTLERS OF AMERICA FULFILLED THIS COMMANDMENT.
ONCE THAT CONTINENT WAS FILLED, THE IMPEDIMENT TO BUILDING A NEW BABEL WOULD BE REMOVED.
THEN IT WOULD BE POSSIBLE FOR THE WHOLE EARTH TO BE OF ONE LANGUAGE.
COULD PARADISE BE FAR BEHIND?
AS BABEL HAD BEEN BUILT 340 YEARS AFTER THE FLOOD, 340 YEARS AFTER THE MAYFLOWER THE COMMANDMENT WOULD BE CARRIED OUT.
NORTH AMERICA
POPULATION DENSITY
Persons per km²
Persons per mi²
200
512
100
256
Montréal
Boston
Chicago
New York
Philadelphia
Washington
San Francisco
Los Angeles
Houston
Havana
40°
60°
20°
20°

45

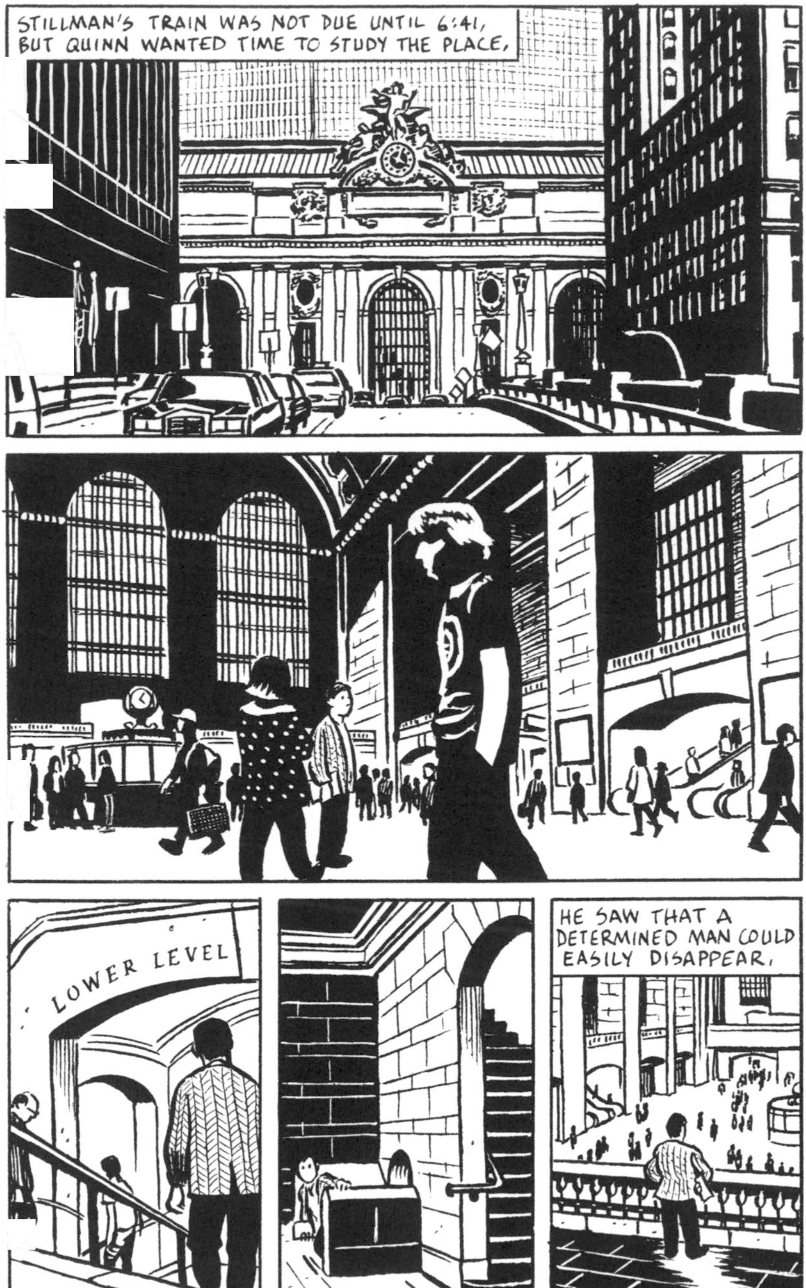
STILLMAN'S TRAIN WAS NOT DUE UNTIL 6:41, BUT QUINN WANTED TIME TO STUDY THE PLACE.
LOWER LEVEL
HE SAW THAT A DETERMINED MAN COULD EASILY DISAPPEAR.

47

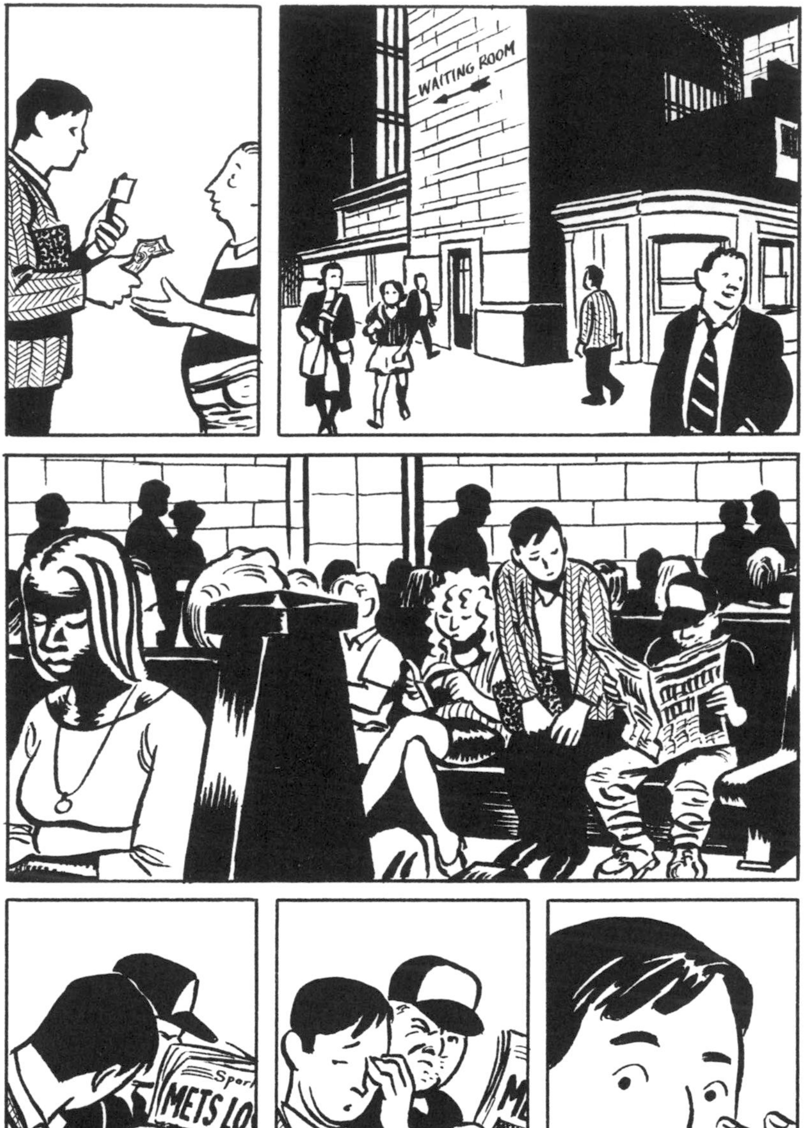
WAITING ROOM
Sport
METS LOS
MOOKIE HOMERS IN A LOSING CAUSE

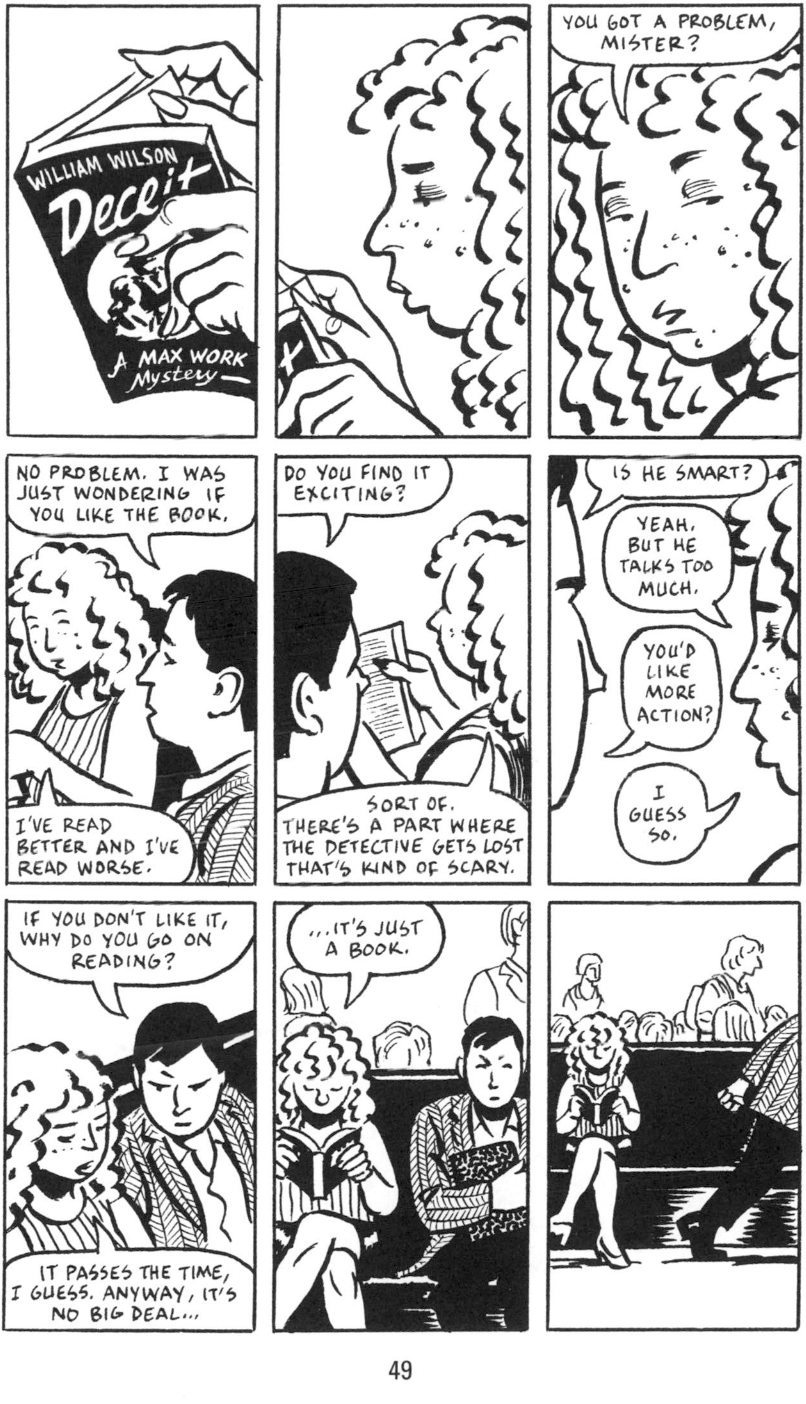
WILLIAM WILSON
Deceit
A MAX WORK Mystery
YOU GOT A PROBLEM, MISTER?
NO PROBLEM. I WAS JUST WONDERING IF YOU LIKE THE BOOK.
I'VE READ BETTER AND I'VE READ WORSE.
DO YOU FIND IT EXCITING?
SORT OF. THERE'S A PART WHERE THE DETECTIVE GETS LOST THAT'S KIND OF SCARY.
IS HE SMART?
YEAH. BUT HE TALKS TOO MUCH.
YOU'D LIKE MORE ACTION?
I GUESS SO.
IF YOU DON'T LIKE IT, WHY DO YOU GO ON READING?
IT PASSES THE TIME, I GUESS. ANYWAY, IT'S NO BIG DEAL...
...IT'S JUST A BOOK.

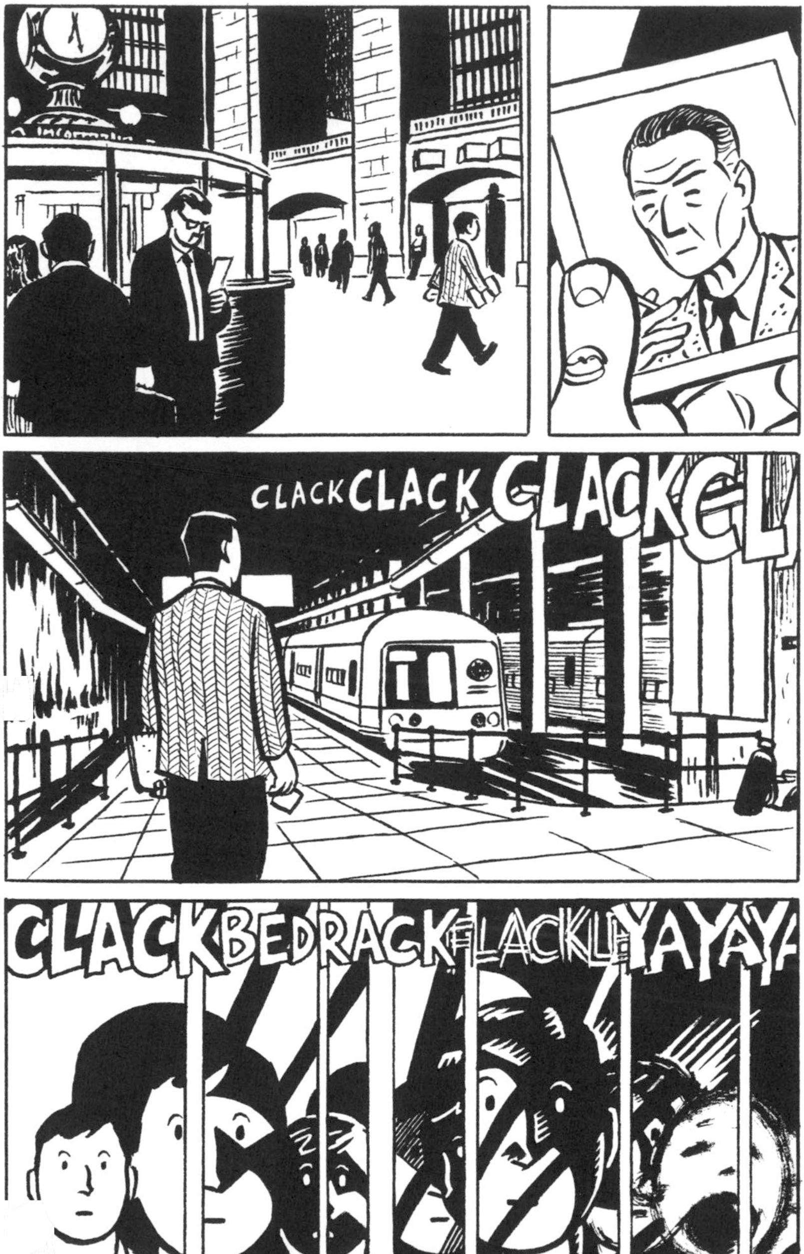
CLACK CLACK CLACK CL
CLACK BEDRACK FLACK LI YAYAYA

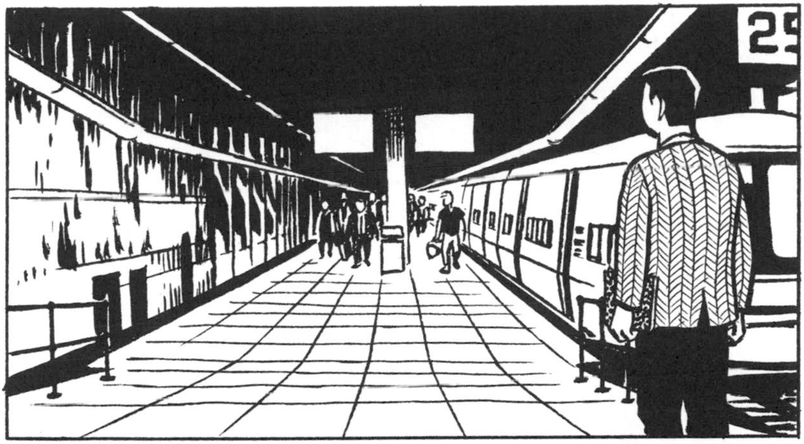
25

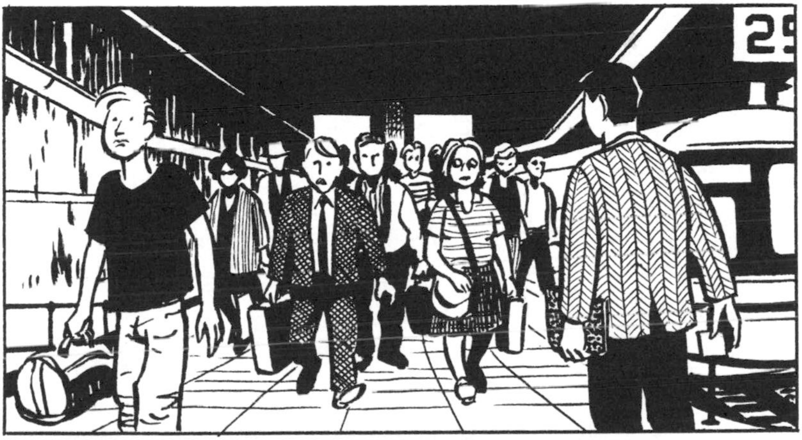
25

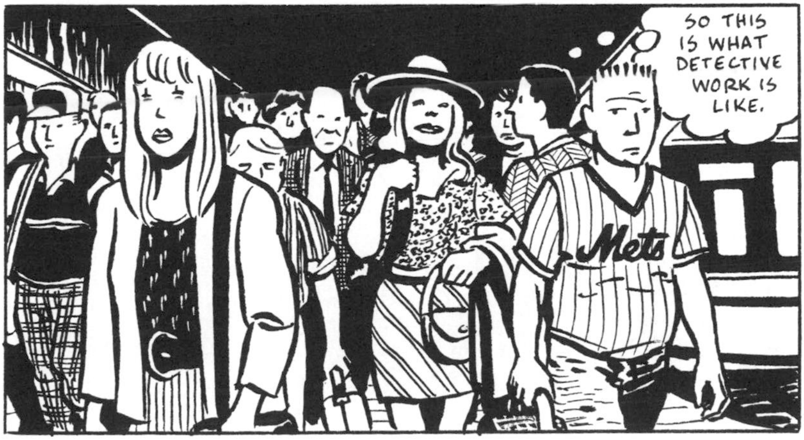
SO THIS IS WHAT DETECTIVE WORK IS LIKE.
Mets

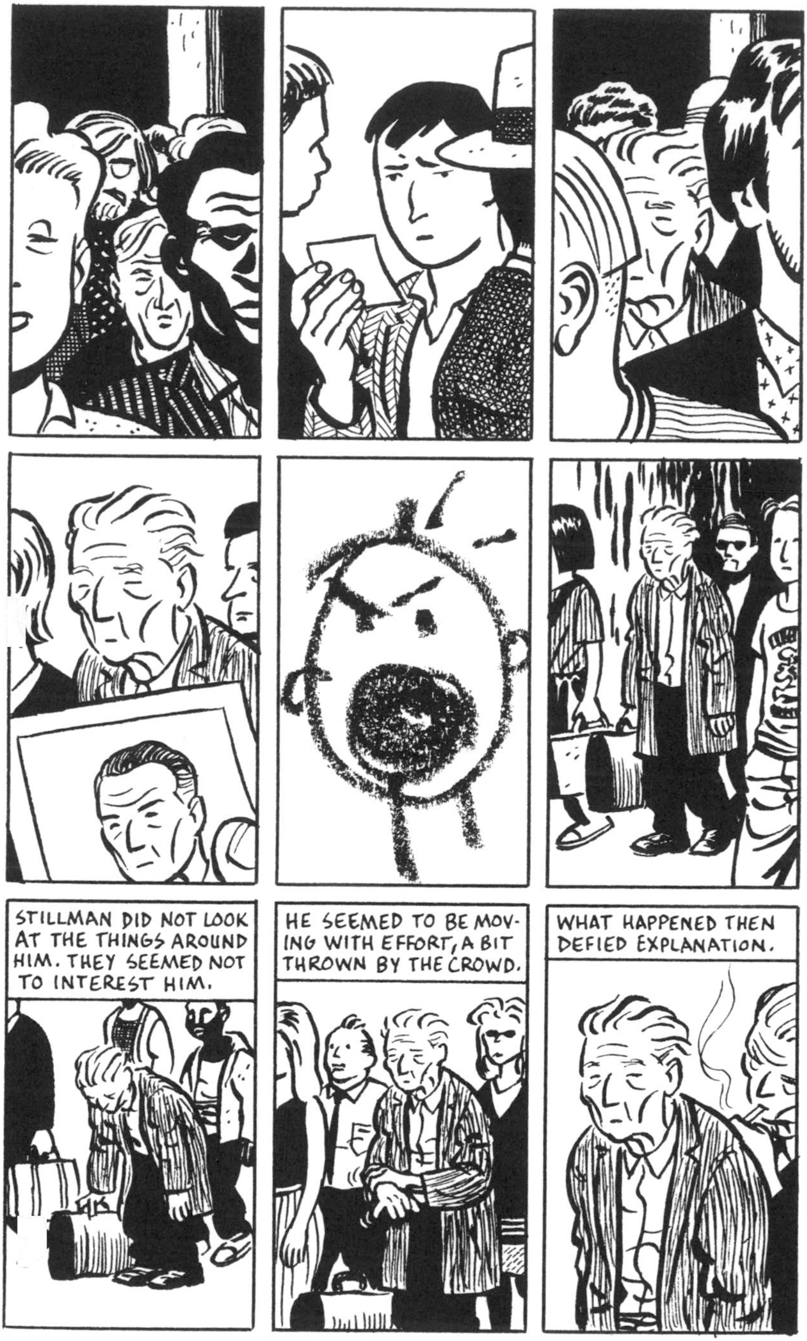
STILLMAN DID NOT LOOK AT THE THINGS AROUND HIM. THEY SEEMED NOT TO INTEREST HIM.
HE SEEMED TO BE MOVING WITH EFFORT, A BIT THROWN BY THE CROWD.
WHAT HAPPENED THEN DEFIED EXPLANATION.

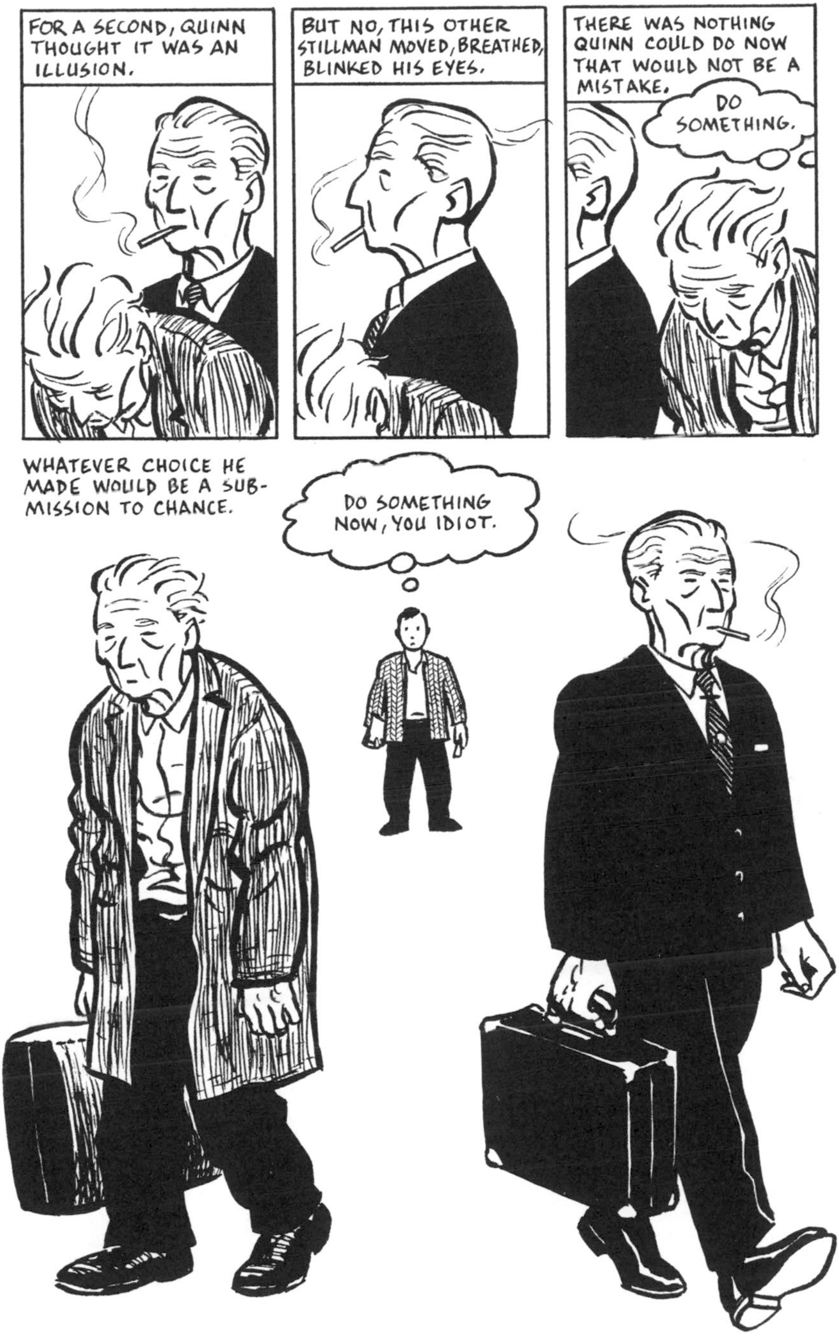
FOR A SECOND, QUINN THOUGHT IT WAS AN ILLUSION.
BUT NO, THIS OTHER STILLMAN MOVED, BREATHED, BLINKED HIS EYES.
THERE WAS NOTHING QUINN COULD DO NOW THAT WOULD NOT BE A MISTAKE.
DO SOMETHING.
WHATEVER CHOICE HE MADE WOULD BE A SUB-MISSION TO CHANCE.
DO SOMETHING NOW, YOU IDIOT.

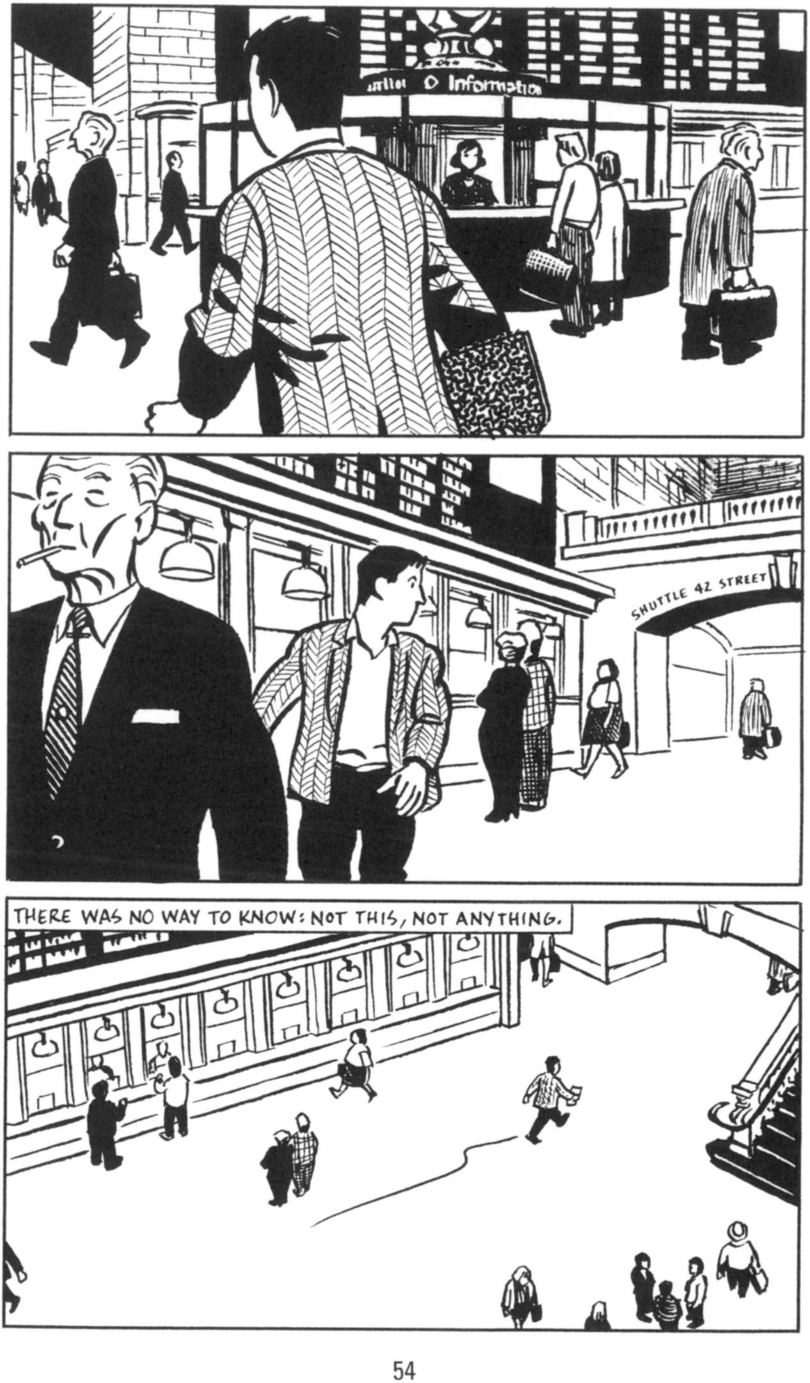
Information
SHUTTLE 42 STREET
THERE WAS NO WAY TO KNOW: NOT THIS, NOT ANYTHING.

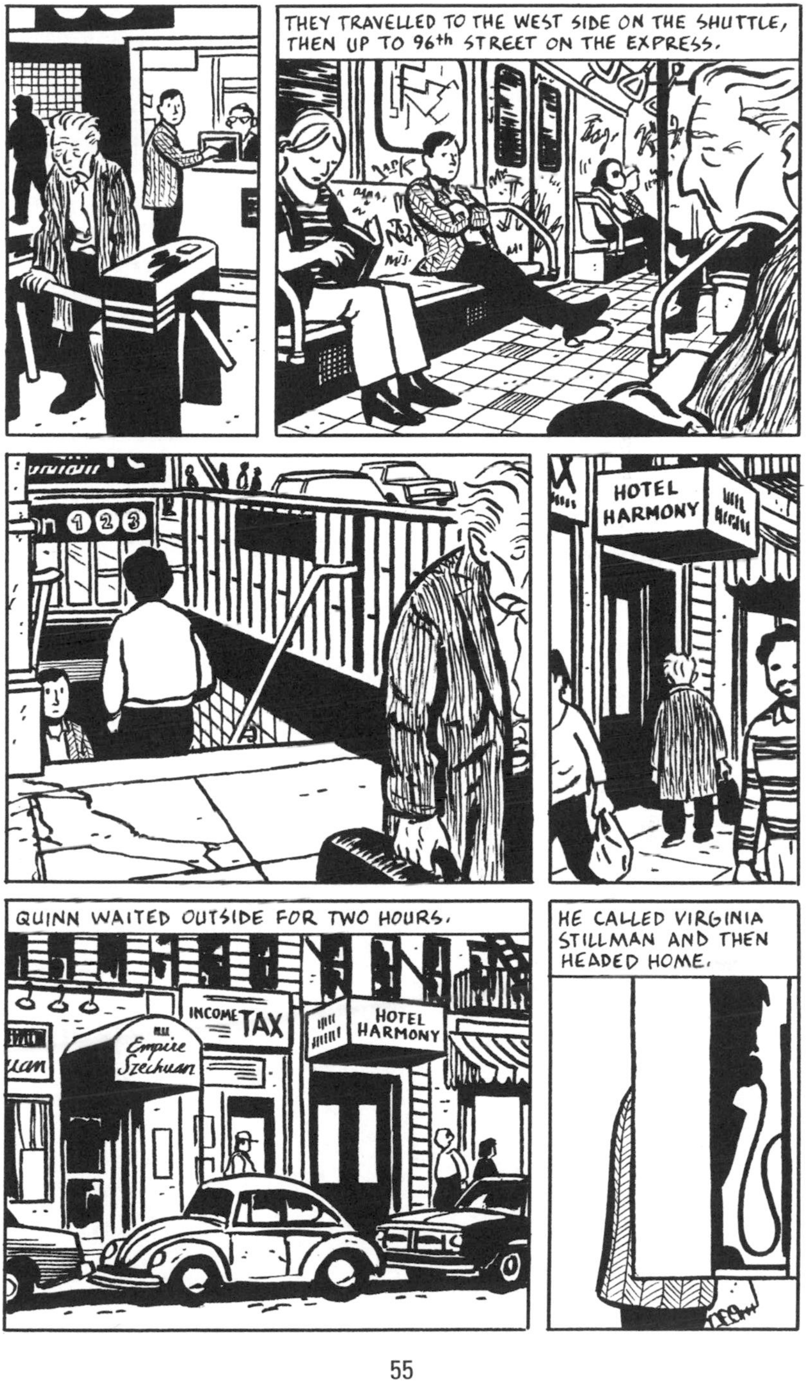
THEY TRAVELLED TO THE WEST SIDE ON THE SHUTTLE, THEN UP TO 96th STREET ON THE EXPRESS.
1 2 3
HOTEL HARMONY
QUINN WAITED OUTSIDE FOR TWO HOURS.
INCOME TAX
Empire Szechuan
HOTEL HARMONY
HE CALLED VIRGINIA STILLMAN AND THEN HEADED HOME.

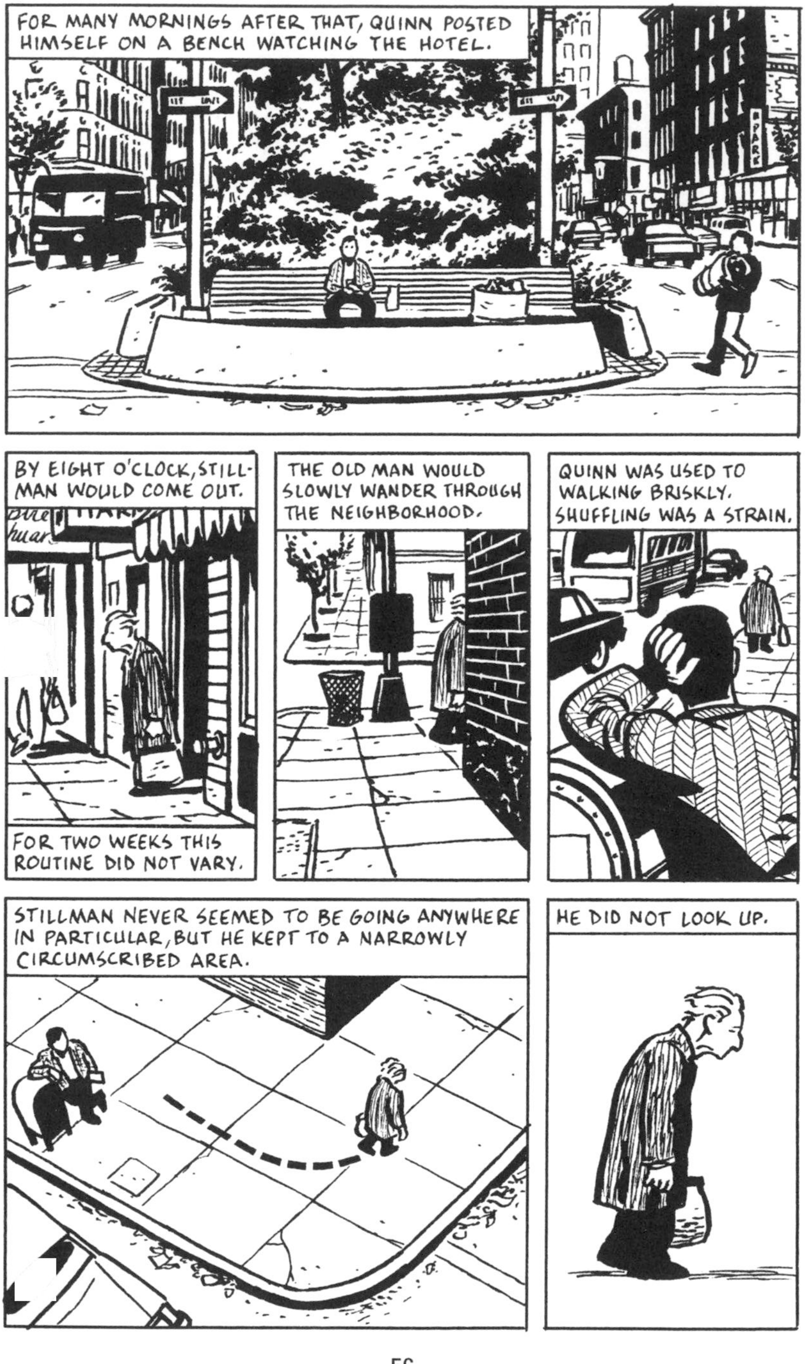
FOR MANY MORNINGS AFTER THAT, QUINN POSTED HIMSELF ON A BENCH WATCHING THE HOTEL.
BY EIGHT O'CLOCK, STILLMAN WOULD COME OUT.
FOR TWO WEEKS THIS ROUTINE DID NOT VARY.
THE OLD MAN WOULD SLOWLY WANDER THROUGH THE NEIGHBORHOOD.
QUINN WAS USED TO WALKING BRISKLY. SHUFFLING WAS A STRAIN.
STILLMAN NEVER SEEMED TO BE GOING ANYWHERE IN PARTICULAR, BUT HE KEPT TO A NARROWLY CIRCUMSCRIBED AREA.
HE DID NOT LOOK UP.

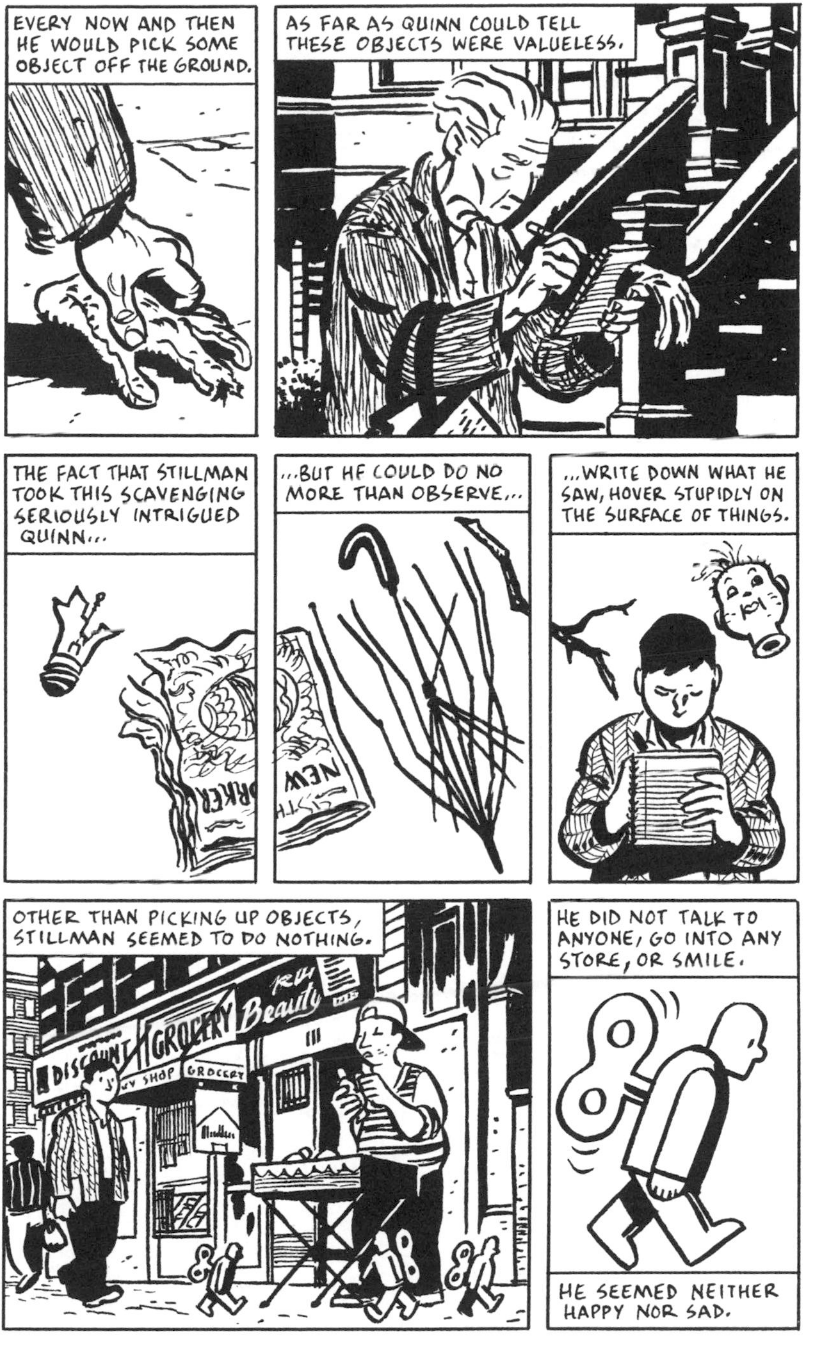
EVERY NOW AND THEN HE WOULD PICK SOME OBJECT OFF THE GROUND.
AS FAR AS QUINN COULD TELL THESE OBJECTS WERE VALUELESS.
THE FACT THAT STILLMAN TOOK THIS SCAVENGING SERIOUSLY INTRIGUED QUINN...
...BUT HE COULD DO NO MORE THAN OBSERVE...
...WRITE DOWN WHAT HE SAW, HOVER STUPIDLY ON THE SURFACE OF THINGS.
OTHER THAN PICKING UP OBJECTS, STILLMAN SEEMED TO DO NOTHING.
DISCOUNT
GROCERY
Beauty
SHOP
GROCERY
HE DID NOT TALK TO ANYONE, GO INTO ANY STORE, OR SMILE.
HE SEEMED NEITHER HAPPY NOR SAD.

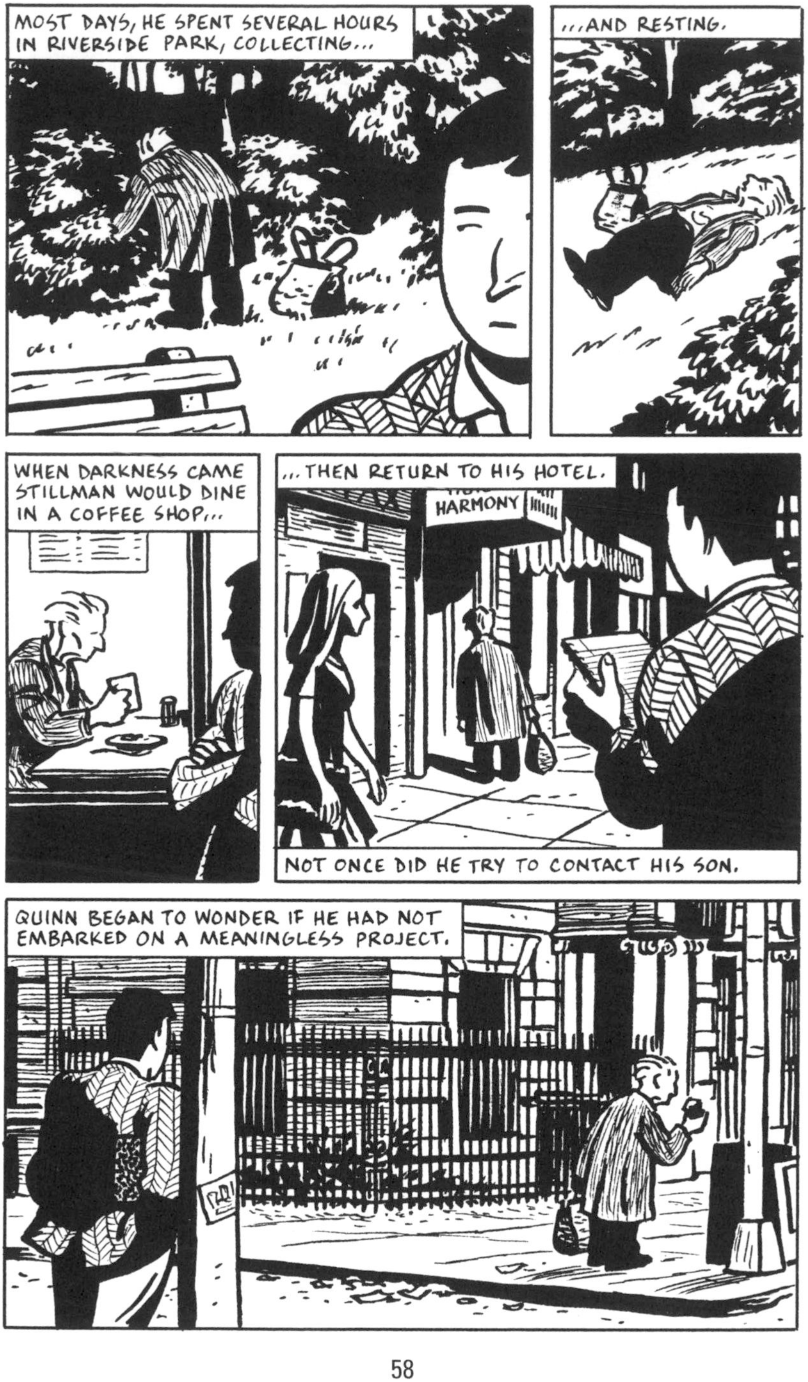
MOST DAYS, HE SPENT SEVERAL HOURS IN RIVERSIDE PARK, COLLECTING...
...AND RESTING.
WHEN DARKNESS CAME STILLMAN WOULD DINE IN A COFFEE SHOP...
...THEN RETURN TO HIS HOTEL.
HARMONY
NOT ONCE DID HE TRY TO CONTACT HIS SON.
QUINN BEGAN TO WONDER IF HE HAD NOT EMBARKED ON A MEANINGLESS PROJECT.

IT WAS POSSIBLE THAT STILLMAN WAS MERELY BIDING HIS TIME.

QUINN PREFERRED TO THINK THAT STILLMAN HAD A PLAN.

IT JUSTIFIED HIS TAILING HIM.

BUT TIME AND AGAIN HIS THOUGHTS WOULD BEGIN TO DRIFT.

THIS MEANT HE WAS CONSTANTLY IN DANGER OF OVERTAKING STILLMAN.

HE DECIDED TO RECORD EVERY DETAIL ABOUT STILLMAN HE POSSIBLY COULD.

THIS KEPT HIM OCCUPIED, AND SLOWED HIM DOWN.

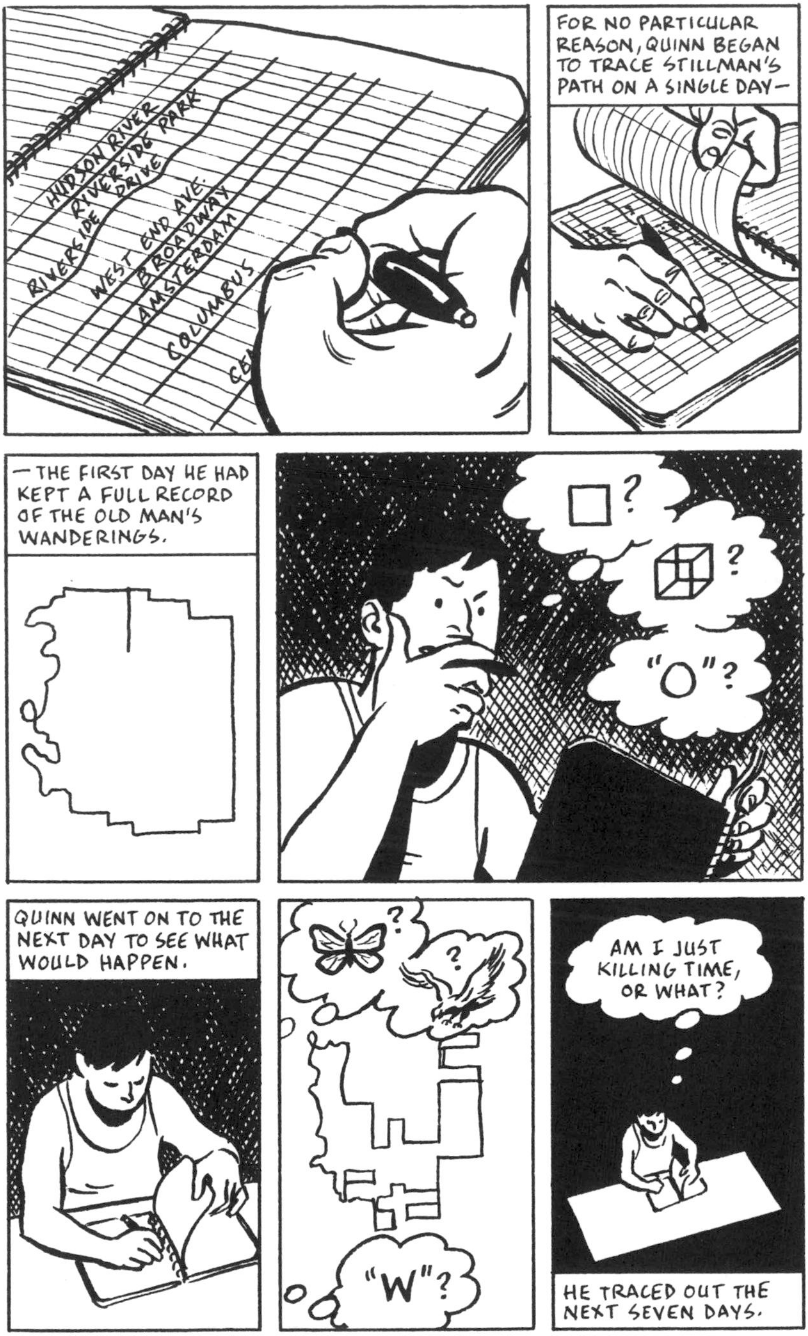
HUDSON RIVER
RIVERSIDE PARK
RIVERSIDE DRIVE
WEST END AVE.
BROADWAY
AMSTERDAM
COLUMBUS
FOR NO PARTICULAR REASON, QUINN BEGAN TO TRACE STILLMAN'S PATH ON A SINGLE DAY—
—THE FIRST DAY HE HAD KEPT A FULL RECORD OF THE OLD MAN'S WANDERINGS.
?
?
"O"?
QUINN WENT ON TO THE NEXT DAY TO SEE WHAT WOULD HAPPEN.
?
?
"W"?
AM I JUST KILLING TIME, OR WHAT?
HE TRACED OUT THE NEXT SEVEN DAYS.

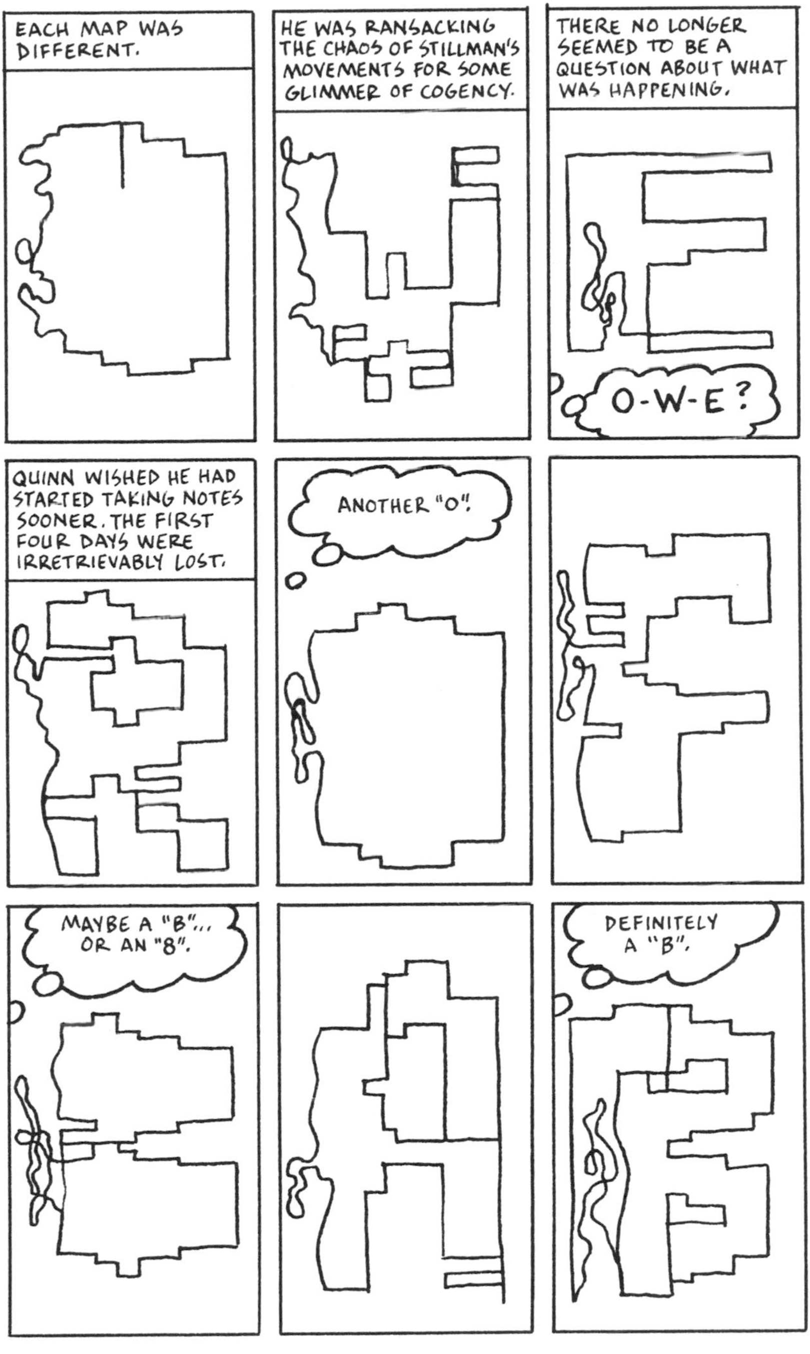
EACH MAP WAS DIFFERENT.
HE WAS RANSACKING THE CHAOS OF STILLMAN'S MOVEMENTS FOR SOME GLIMMER OF COGENCY.
THERE NO LONGER SEEMED TO BE A QUESTION ABOUT WHAT WAS HAPPENING.
O-W-E?
QUINN WISHED HE HAD STARTED TAKING NOTES SOONER. THE FIRST FOUR DAYS WERE IRRETRIEVABLY LOST.
ANOTHER "O".
MAYBE A "B"... OR AN "8".
DEFINITELY A "B".

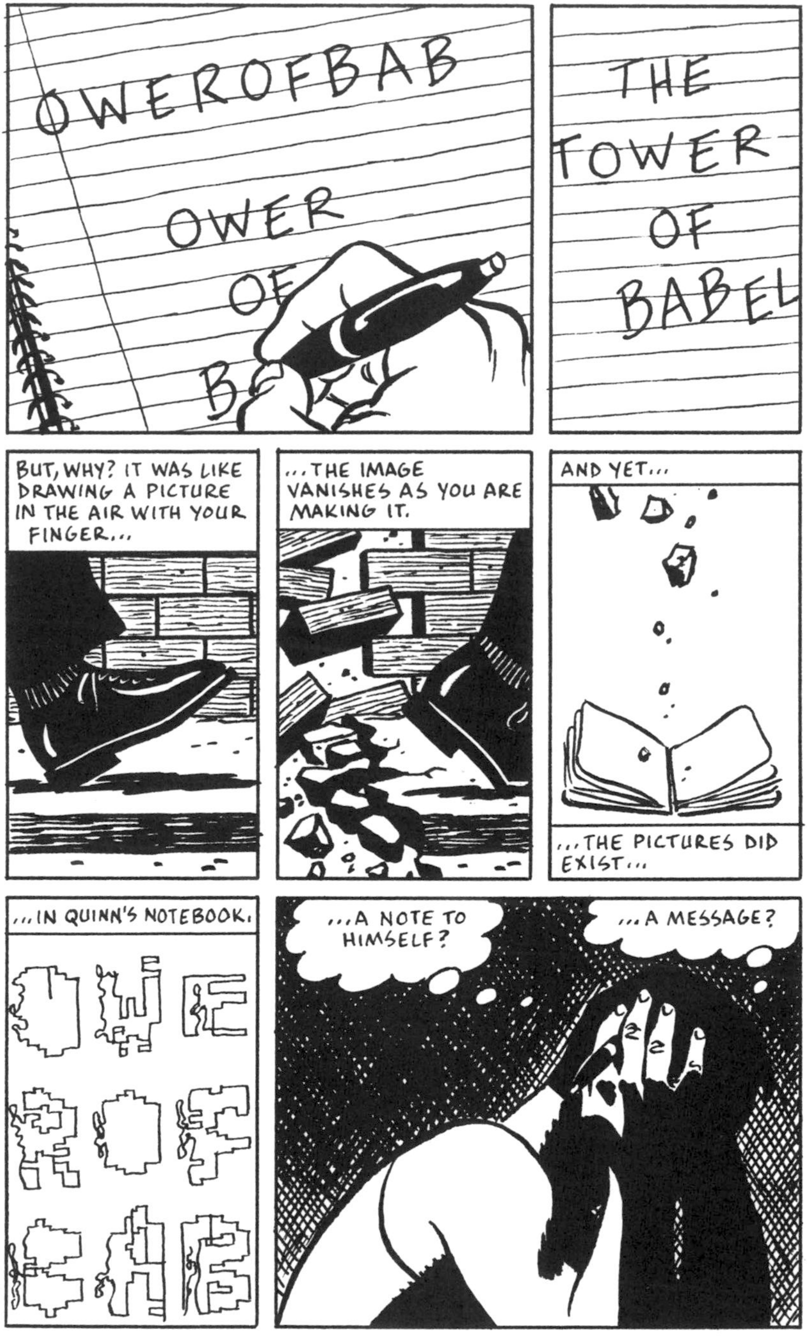
OWEROFBAB
OWER
OF
B
THE
TOWER
OF
BABEL
BUT, WHY? IT WAS LIKE DRAWING A PICTURE IN THE AIR WITH YOUR FINGER...
...THE IMAGE VANISHES AS YOU ARE MAKING IT.
AND YET...
...THE PICTURES DID EXIST...
...IN QUINN'S NOTEBOOK.
...A NOTE TO HIMSELF?
...A MESSAGE?

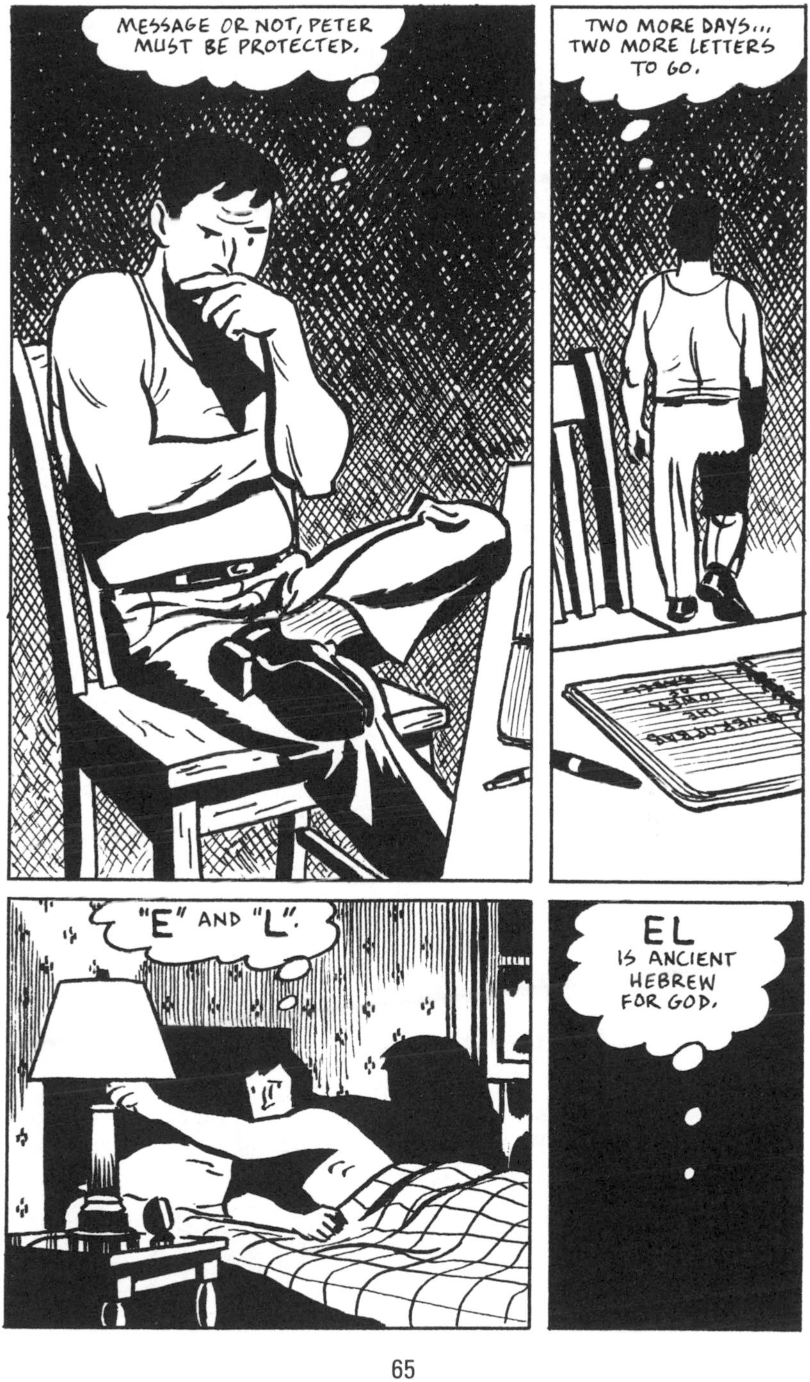
MESSAGE OR NOT, PETER MUST BE PROTECTED.
TWO MORE DAYS... TWO MORE LETTERS TO GO.
"E" AND "L".
EL IS ANCIENT HEBREW FOR GOD.

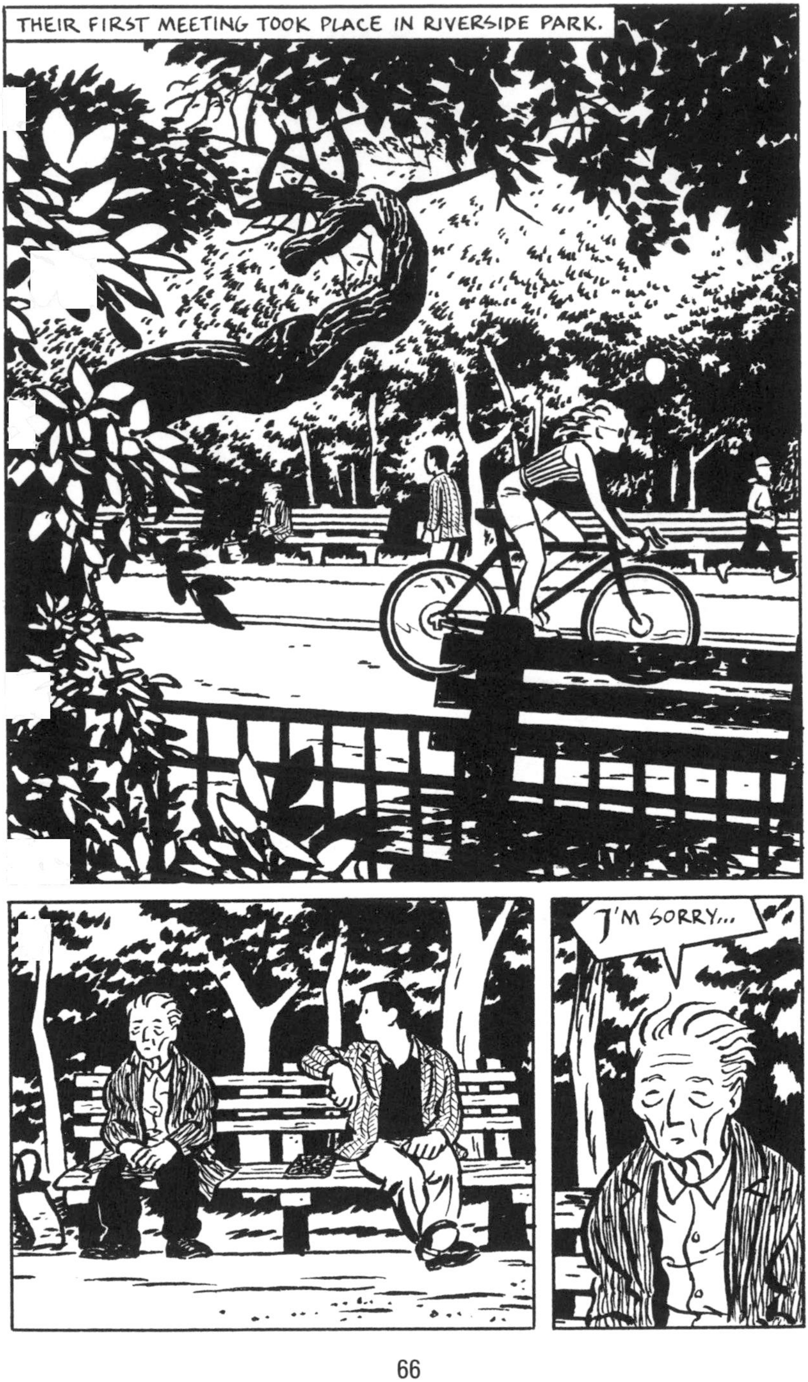
THEIR FIRST MEETING TOOK PLACE IN RIVERSIDE PARK.
I'M SORRY...

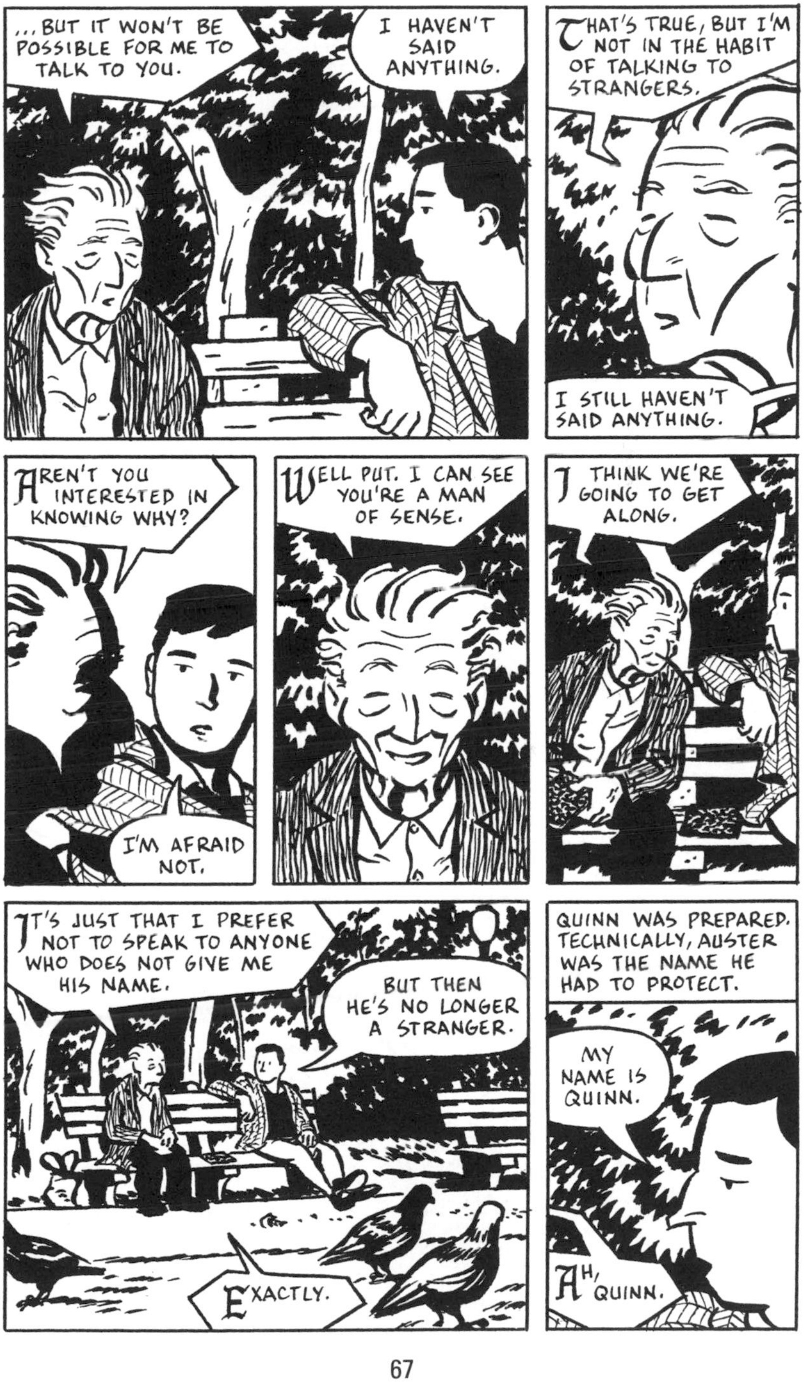
...BUT IT WON'T BE POSSIBLE FOR ME TO TALK TO YOU.
I HAVEN'T SAID ANYTHING.
THAT'S TRUE, BUT I'M NOT IN THE HABIT OF TALKING TO STRANGERS.
I STILL HAVEN'T SAID ANYTHING.
AREN'T YOU INTERESTED IN KNOWING WHY?
I'M AFRAID NOT.
WELL PUT. I CAN SEE YOU'RE A MAN OF SENSE.
I THINK WE'RE GOING TO GET ALONG.
IT'S JUST THAT I PREFER NOT TO SPEAK TO ANYONE WHO DOES NOT GIVE ME HIS NAME.
BUT THEN HE'S NO LONGER A STRANGER.
EXACTLY.
QUINN WAS PREPARED. TECHNICALLY, AUSTER WAS THE NAME HE HAD TO PROTECT.
MY NAME IS QUINN.
AH, QUINN.

71

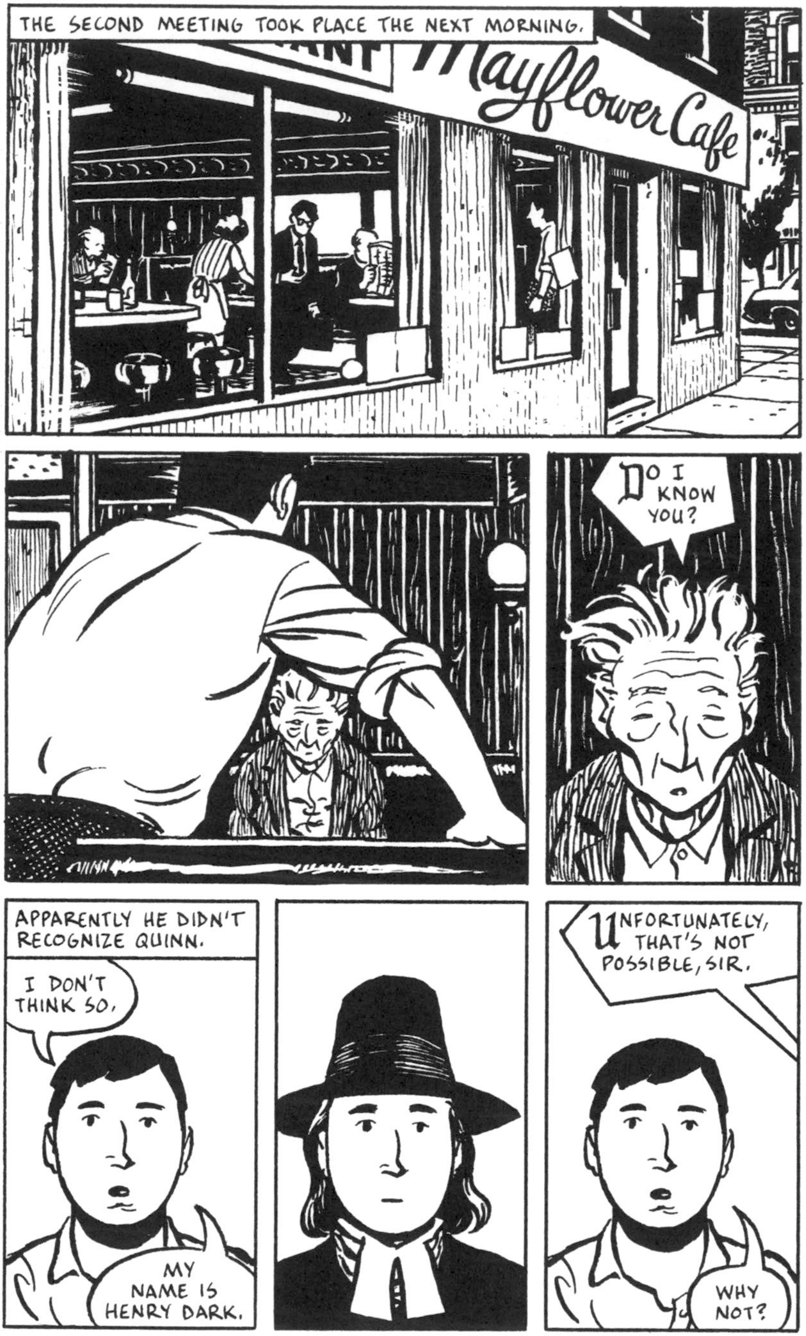
THE SECOND MEETING TOOK PLACE THE NEXT MORNING.
Mayflower Cafe
DO I KNOW YOU?
APPARENTLY HE DIDN'T RECOGNIZE QUINN.
I DON'T THINK SO.
MY NAME IS HENRY DARK.
UNFORTUNATELY, THAT'S NOT POSSIBLE, SIR.
WHY NOT?

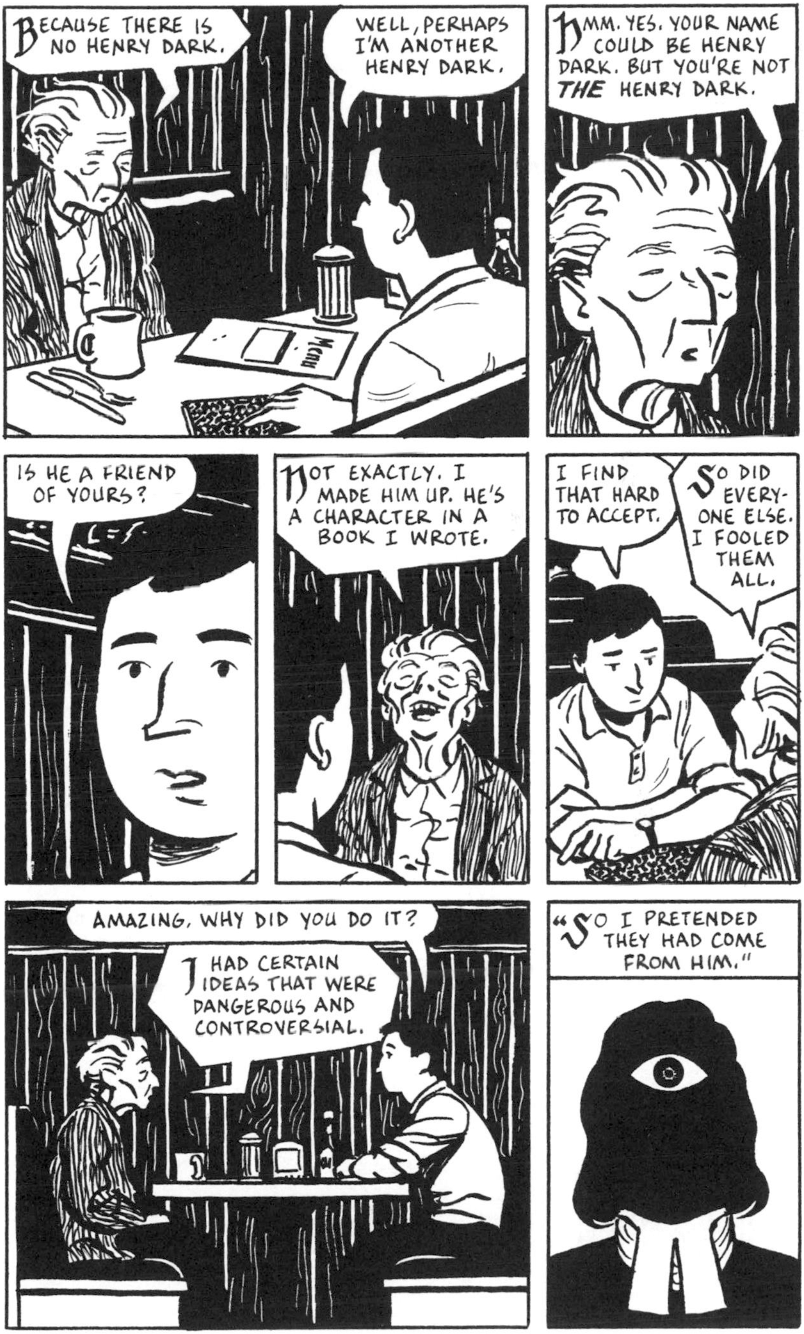
BECAUSE THERE IS NO HENRY DARK.
WELL, PERHAPS I'M ANOTHER HENRY DARK.
MENU
HMM. YES. YOUR NAME COULD BE HENRY DARK. BUT YOU'RE NOT *THE* HENRY DARK.
IS HE A FRIEND OF YOURS?
NOT EXACTLY. I MADE HIM UP. HE'S A CHARACTER IN A BOOK I WROTE.
I FIND THAT HARD TO ACCEPT.
SO DID EVERYONE ELSE. I FOOLED THEM ALL.
AMAZING. WHY DID YOU DO IT?
I HAD CERTAIN IDEAS THAT WERE DANGEROUS AND CONTROVERSIAL.
"SO I PRETENDED THEY HAD COME FROM HIM."

74

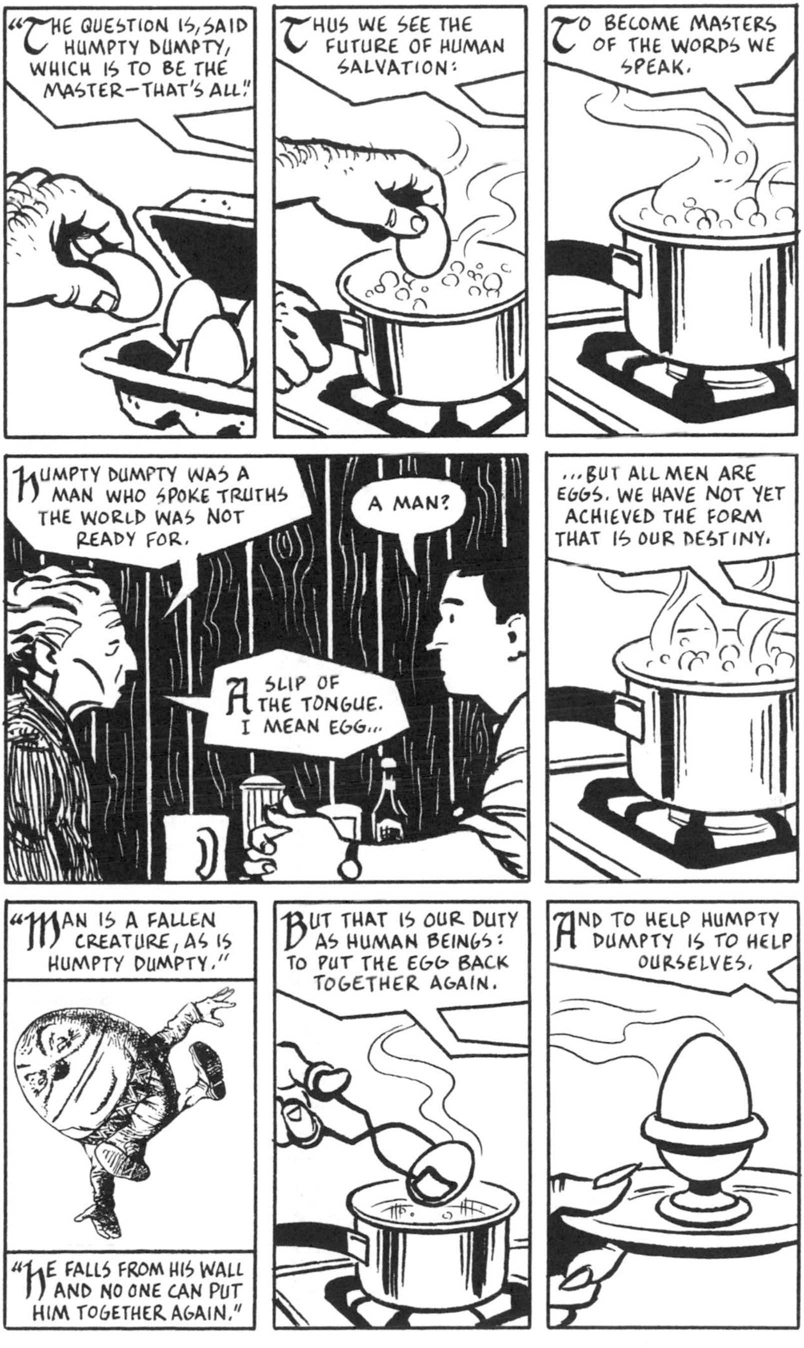
"THE QUESTION IS, SAID HUMPTY DUMPTY, WHICH IS TO BE THE MASTER—THAT'S ALL."
THUS WE SEE THE FUTURE OF HUMAN SALVATION:
TO BECOME MASTERS OF THE WORDS WE SPEAK.
HUMPTY DUMPTY WAS A MAN WHO SPOKE TRUTHS THE WORLD WAS NOT READY FOR.
A MAN?
A SLIP OF THE TONGUE. I MEAN EGG...
...BUT ALL MEN ARE EGGS. WE HAVE NOT YET ACHIEVED THE FORM THAT IS OUR DESTINY.
"MAN IS A FALLEN CREATURE, AS IS HUMPTY DUMPTY."
"HE FALLS FROM HIS WALL AND NO ONE CAN PUT HIM TOGETHER AGAIN."
BUT THAT IS OUR DUTY AS HUMAN BEINGS: TO PUT THE EGG BACK TOGETHER AGAIN.
AND TO HELP HUMPTY DUMPTY IS TO HELP OURSELVES.

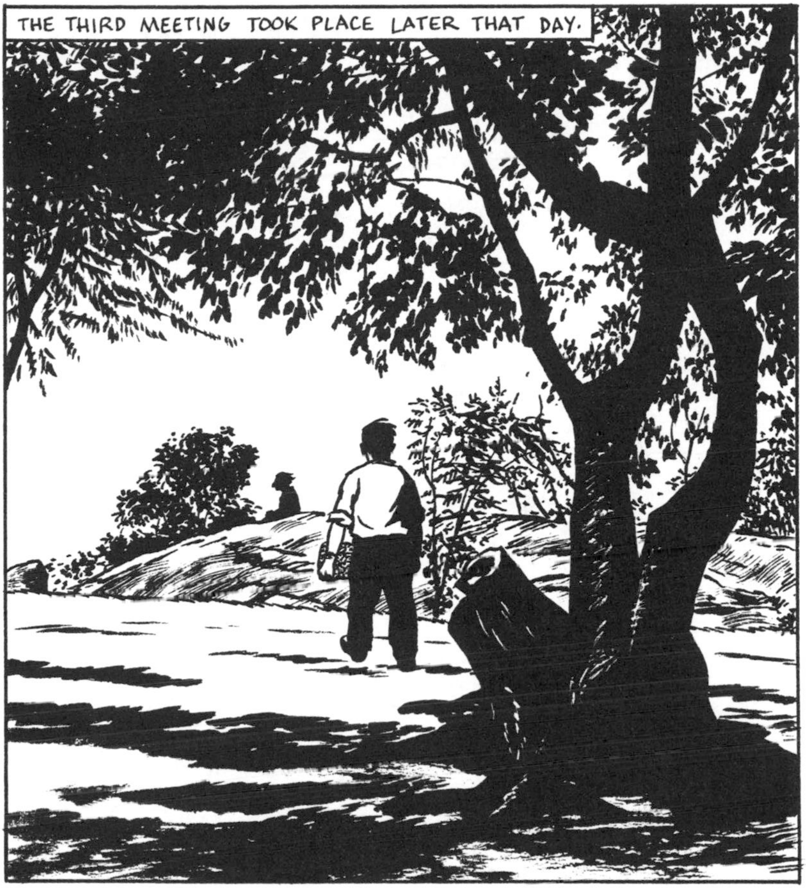
THE THIRD MEETING TOOK PLACE LATER THAT DAY.

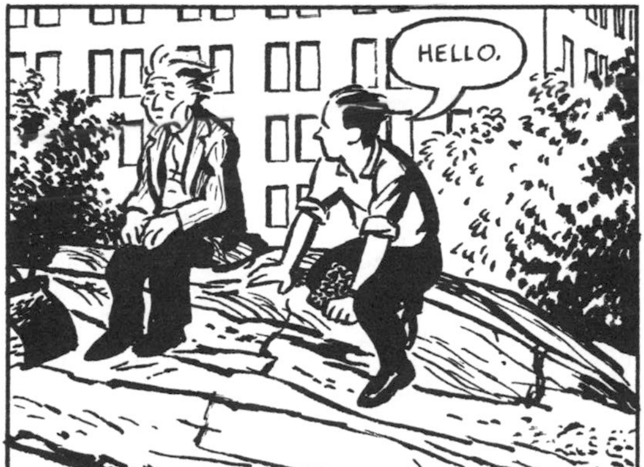
HELLO.

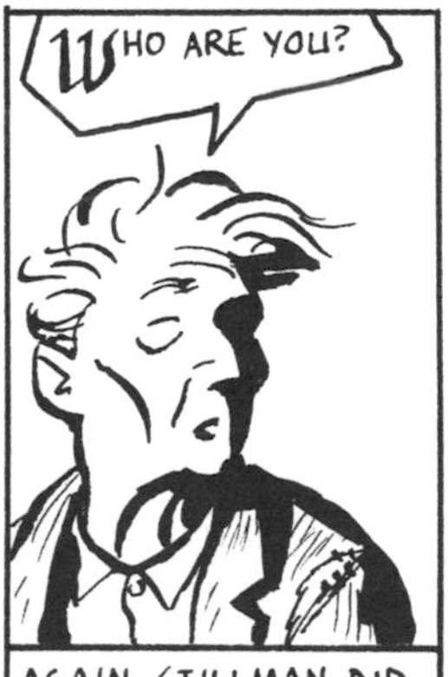
WHO ARE YOU?
AGAIN, STILLMAN DID NOT RECOGNIZE HIM.

78

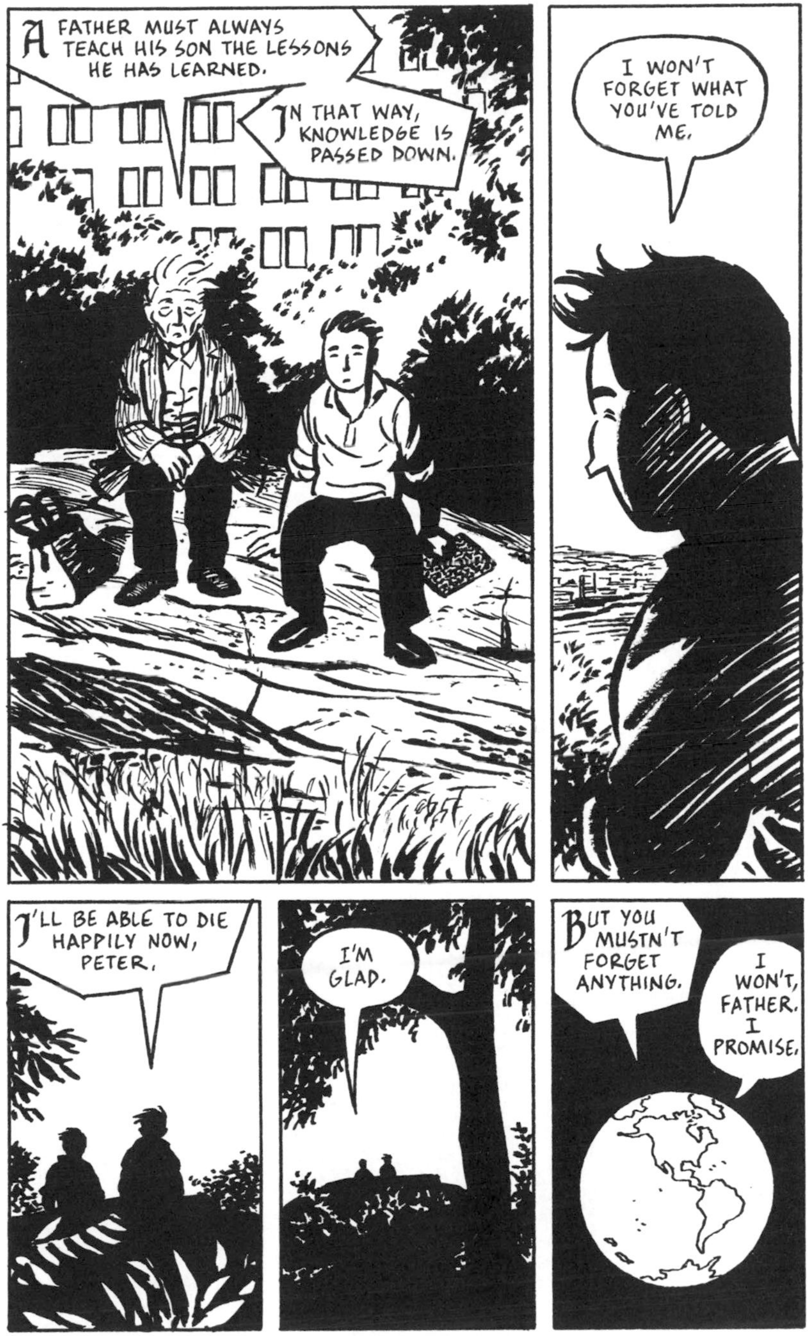
A FATHER MUST ALWAYS TEACH HIS SON THE LESSONS HE HAS LEARNED.
IN THAT WAY, KNOWLEDGE IS PASSED DOWN.
I WON'T FORGET WHAT YOU'VE TOLD ME.
I'LL BE ABLE TO DIE HAPPILY NOW, PETER.
I'M GLAD.
BUT YOU MUSTN'T FORGET ANYTHING.
I WON'T, FATHER. I PROMISE.

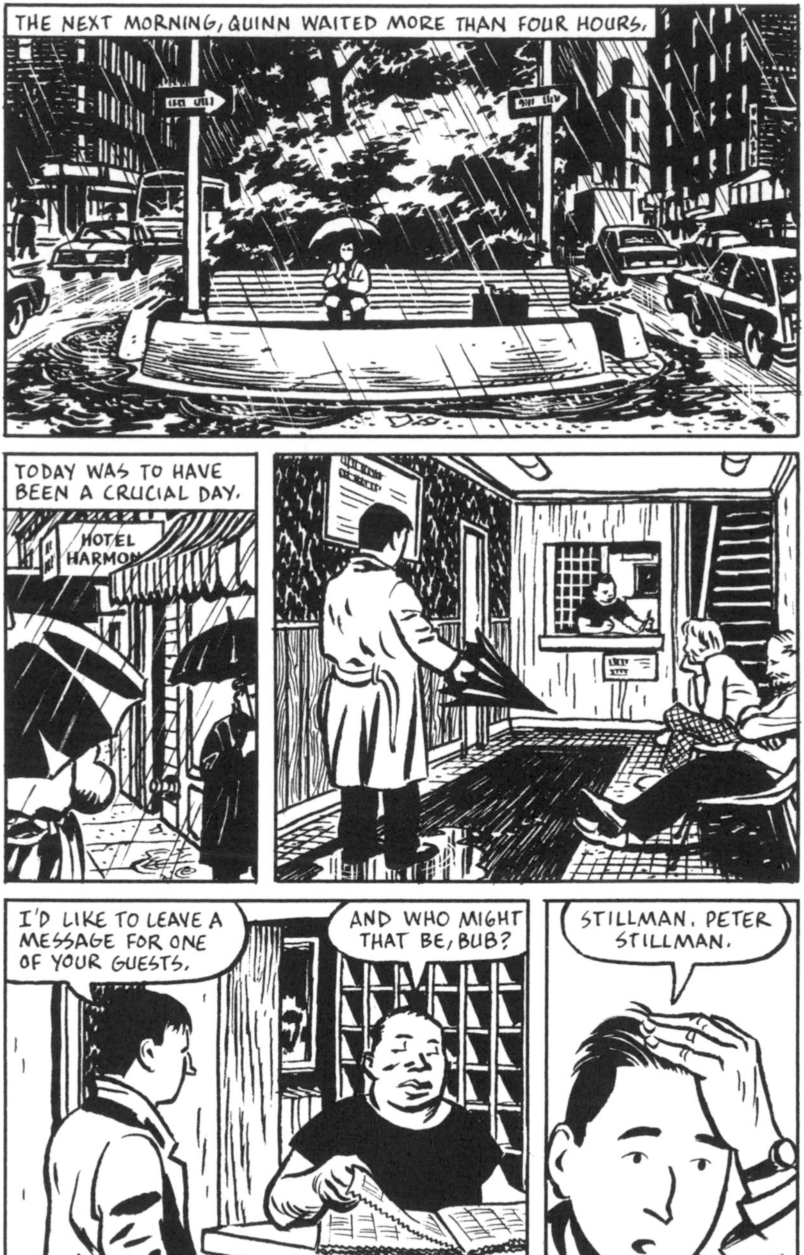
THE NEXT MORNING, QUINN WAITED MORE THAN FOUR HOURS.
TODAY WAS TO HAVE BEEN A CRUCIAL DAY.
HOTEL HARMON
I'D LIKE TO LEAVE A MESSAGE FOR ONE OF YOUR GUESTS.
AND WHO MIGHT THAT BE, BUB?
STILLMAN. PETER STILLMAN.

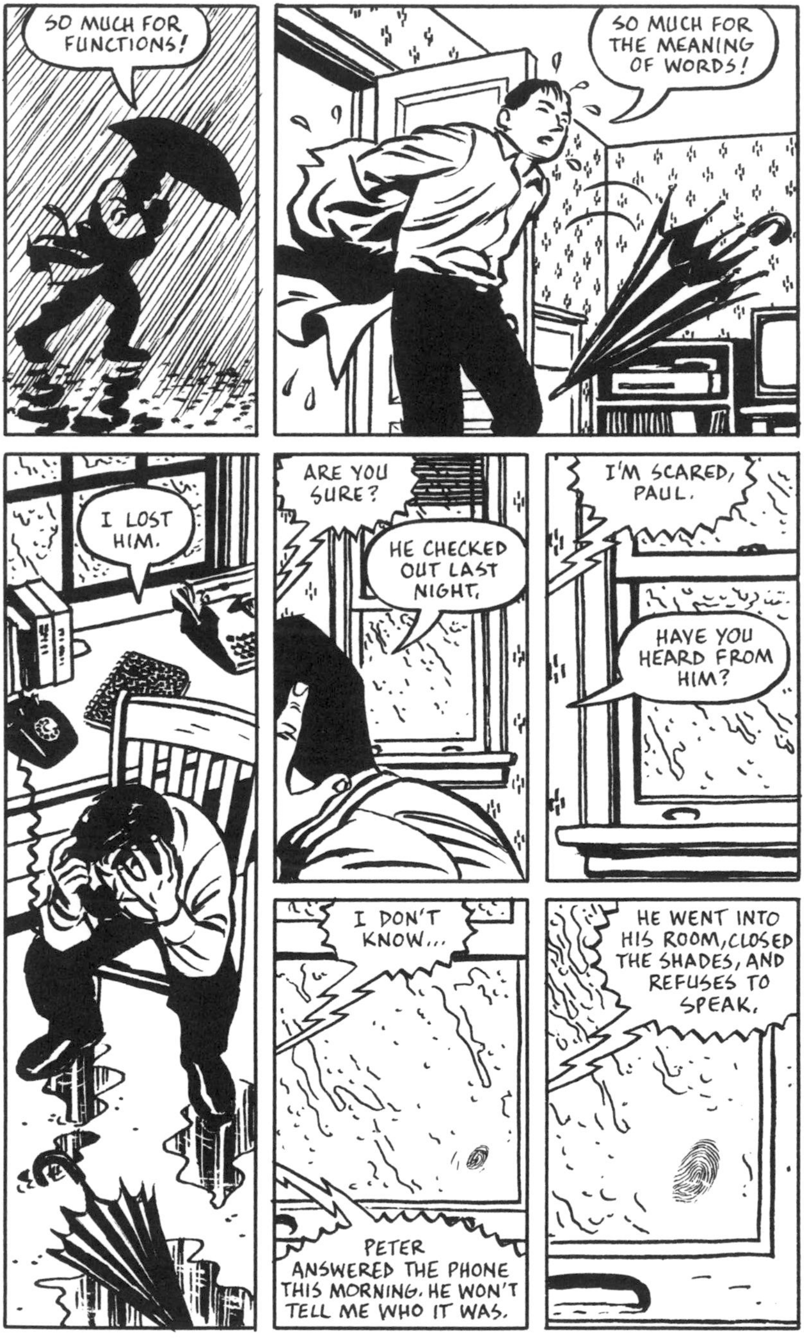
SO MUCH FOR FUNCTIONS!
SO MUCH FOR THE MEANING OF WORDS!
I LOST HIM.
ARE YOU SURE?
HE CHECKED OUT LAST NIGHT.
I'M SCARED, PAUL.
HAVE YOU HEARD FROM HIM?
I DON'T KNOW...
PETER ANSWERED THE PHONE THIS MORNING. HE WON'T TELL ME WHO IT WAS.
HE WENT INTO HIS ROOM, CLOSED THE SHADES, AND REFUSES TO SPEAK.

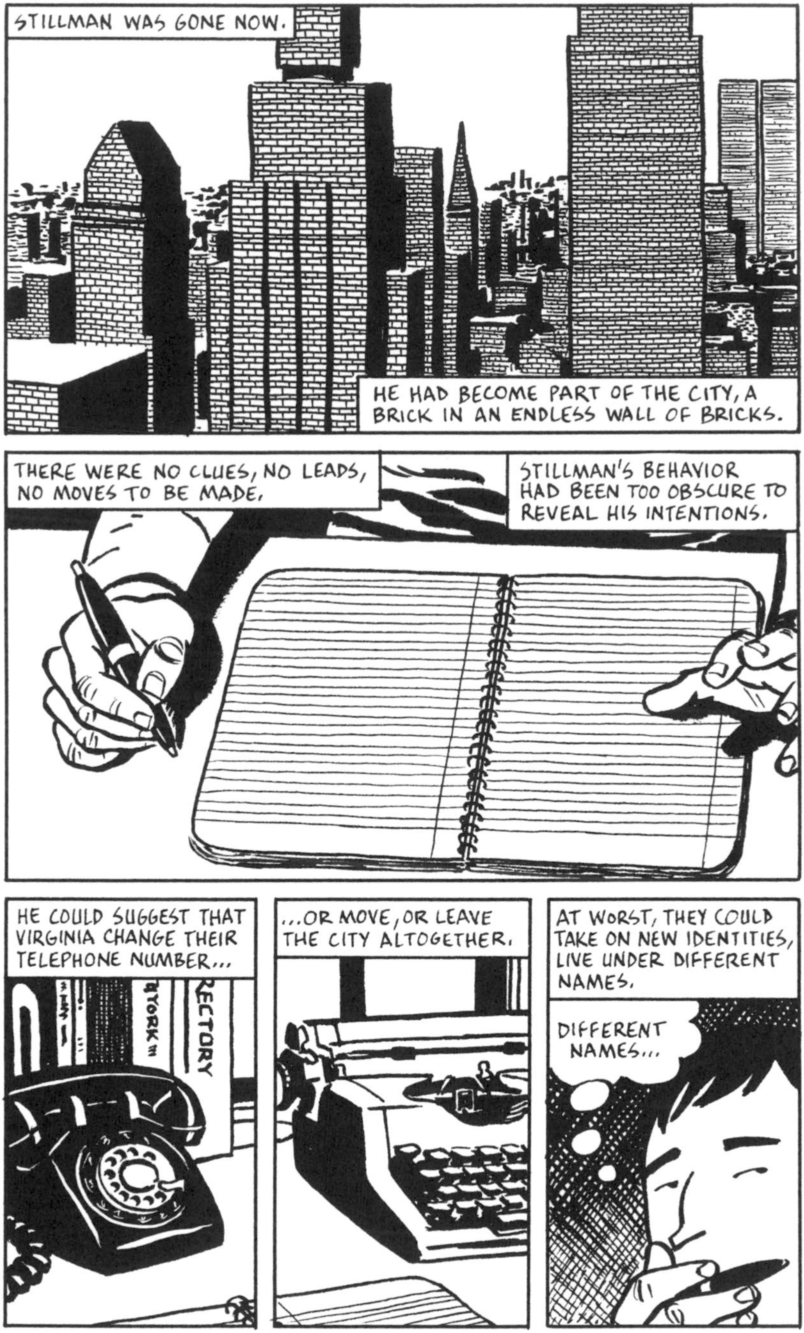
STILLMAN WAS GONE NOW.
HE HAD BECOME PART OF THE CITY, A BRICK IN AN ENDLESS WALL OF BRICKS.
THERE WERE NO CLUES, NO LEADS, NO MOVES TO BE MADE.
STILLMAN'S BEHAVIOR HAD BEEN TOO OBSCURE TO REVEAL HIS INTENTIONS.
HE COULD SUGGEST THAT VIRGINIA CHANGE THEIR TELEPHONE NUMBER...
...OR MOVE, OR LEAVE THE CITY ALTOGETHER.
AT WORST, THEY COULD TAKE ON NEW IDENTITIES, LIVE UNDER DIFFERENT NAMES.
DIFFERENT NAMES...

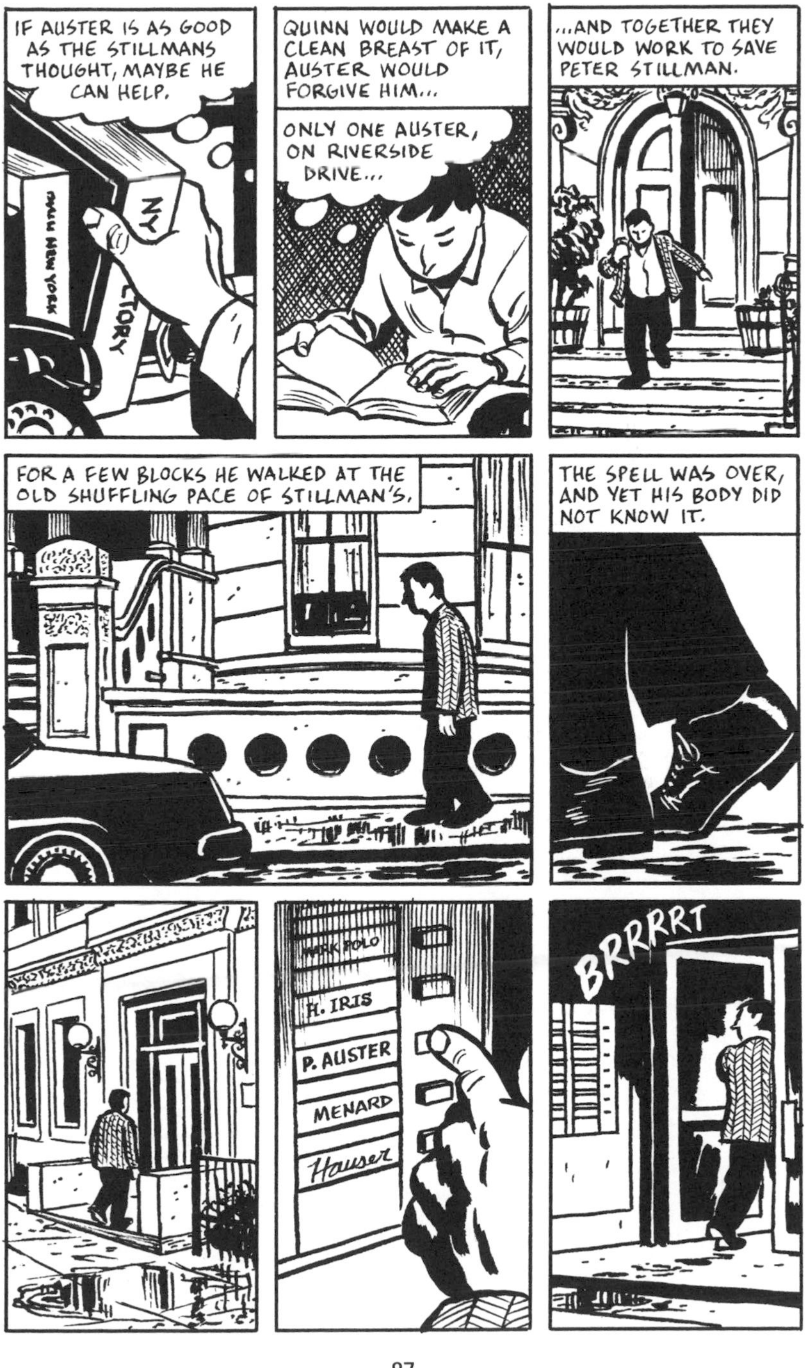
IF AUSTER IS AS GOOD AS THE STILLMANS THOUGHT, MAYBE HE CAN HELP.
NY
NEW YORK
CTORY
QUINN WOULD MAKE A CLEAN BREAST OF IT, AUSTER WOULD FORGIVE HIM...
ONLY ONE AUSTER, ON RIVERSIDE DRIVE...
...AND TOGETHER THEY WOULD WORK TO SAVE PETER STILLMAN.
FOR A FEW BLOCKS HE WALKED AT THE OLD SHUFFLING PACE OF STILLMAN'S.
THE SPELL WAS OVER, AND YET HIS BODY DID NOT KNOW IT.
H. IRIS
P. AUSTER
MENARD
Hauser
BRRRRT

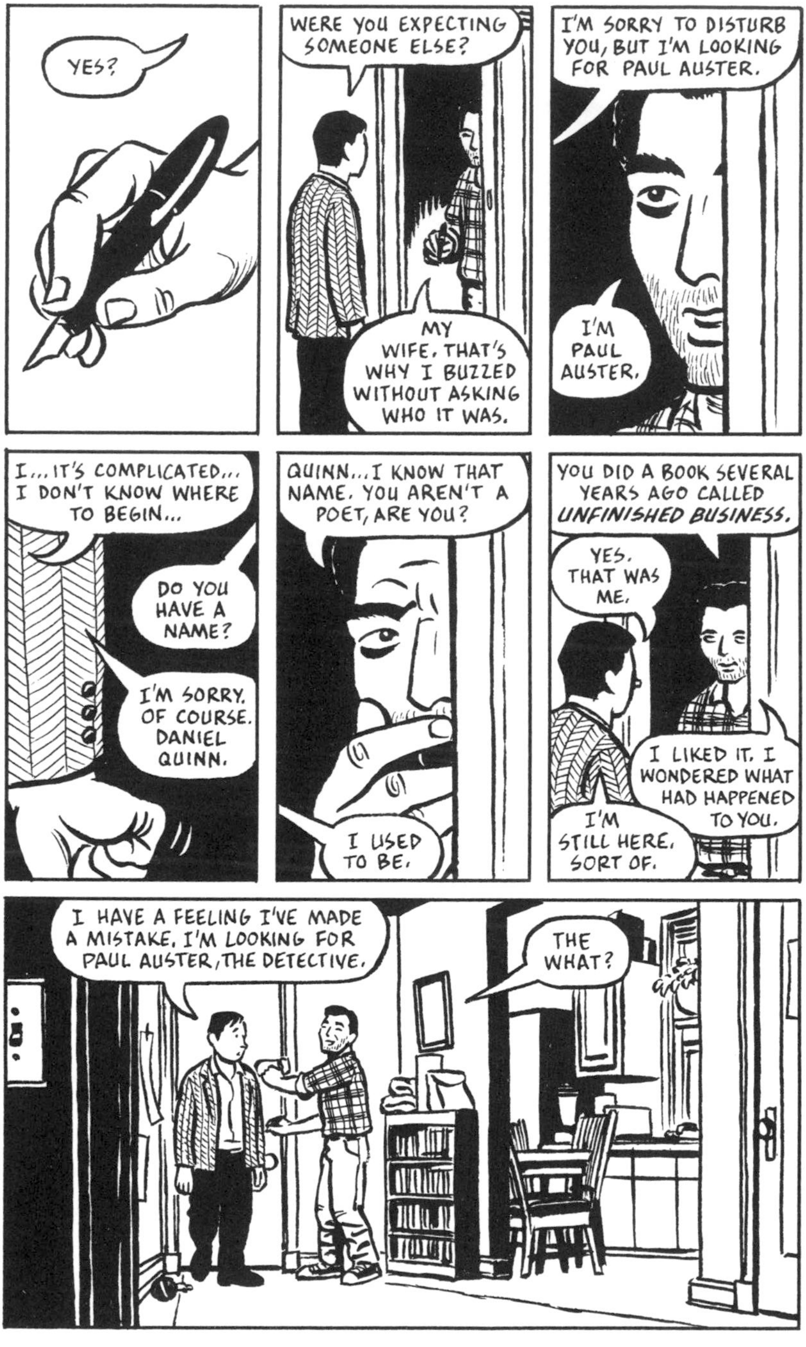
YES?
WERE YOU EXPECTING SOMEONE ELSE?
MY WIFE. THAT'S WHY I BUZZED WITHOUT ASKING WHO IT WAS.
I'M SORRY TO DISTURB YOU, BUT I'M LOOKING FOR PAUL AUSTER.
I'M PAUL AUSTER.
I... IT'S COMPLICATED... I DON'T KNOW WHERE TO BEGIN...
DO YOU HAVE A NAME?
I'M SORRY. OF COURSE. DANIEL QUINN.
QUINN... I KNOW THAT NAME. YOU AREN'T A POET, ARE YOU?
I USED TO BE.
YOU DID A BOOK SEVERAL YEARS AGO CALLED *UNFINISHED BUSINESS.*
YES. THAT WAS ME.
I LIKED IT. I WONDERED WHAT HAD HAPPENED TO YOU.
I'M STILL HERE. SORT OF.
I HAVE A FEELING I'VE MADE A MISTAKE. I'M LOOKING FOR PAUL AUSTER, THE DETECTIVE.
THE WHAT?

89

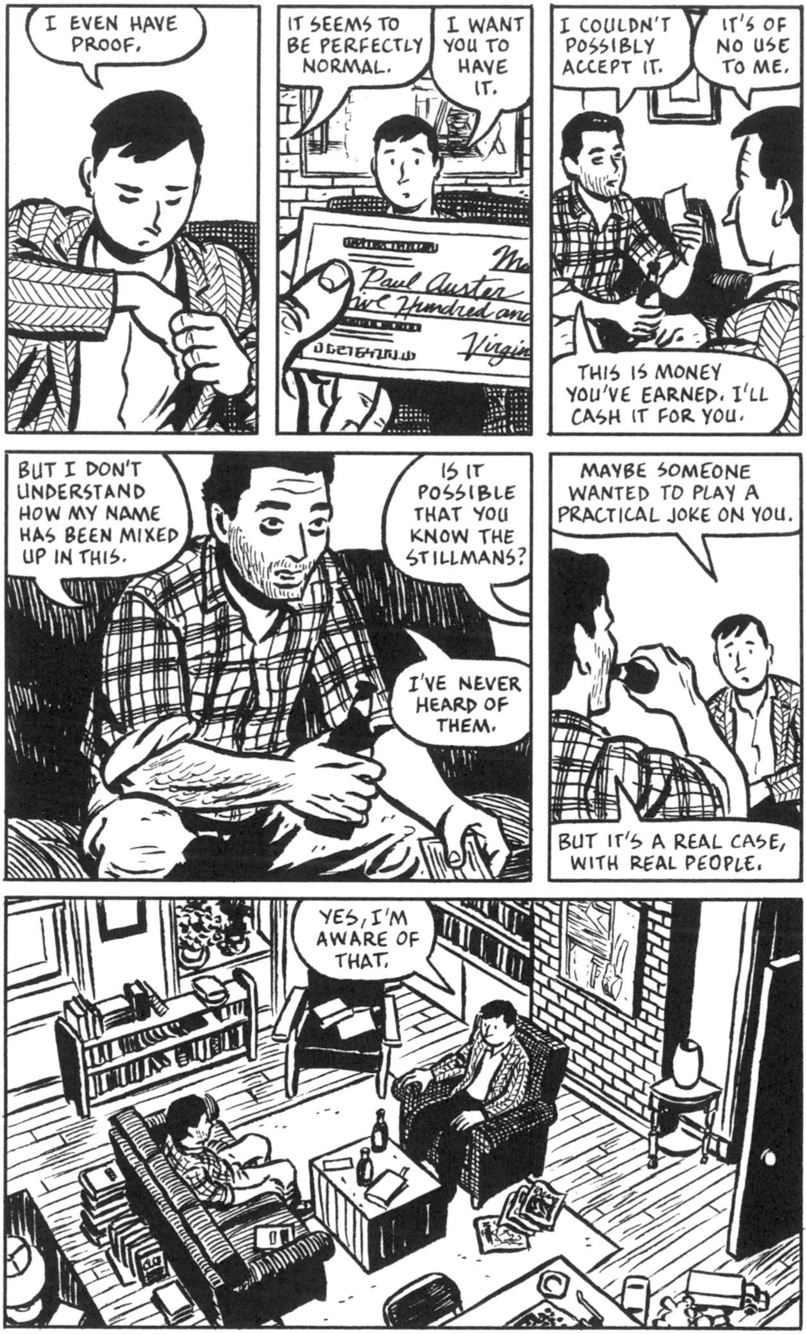
I EVEN HAVE PROOF.
IT SEEMS TO BE PERFECTLY NORMAL.
I WANT YOU TO HAVE IT.
Paul Auster
I COULDN'T POSSIBLY ACCEPT IT.
IT'S OF NO USE TO ME.
THIS IS MONEY YOU'VE EARNED. I'LL CASH IT FOR YOU.
BUT I DON'T UNDERSTAND HOW MY NAME HAS BEEN MIXED UP IN THIS.
IS IT POSSIBLE THAT YOU KNOW THE STILLMANS?
I'VE NEVER HEARD OF THEM.
MAYBE SOMEONE WANTED TO PLAY A PRACTICAL JOKE ON YOU.
BUT IT'S A REAL CASE, WITH REAL PEOPLE.
YES, I'M AWARE OF THAT.

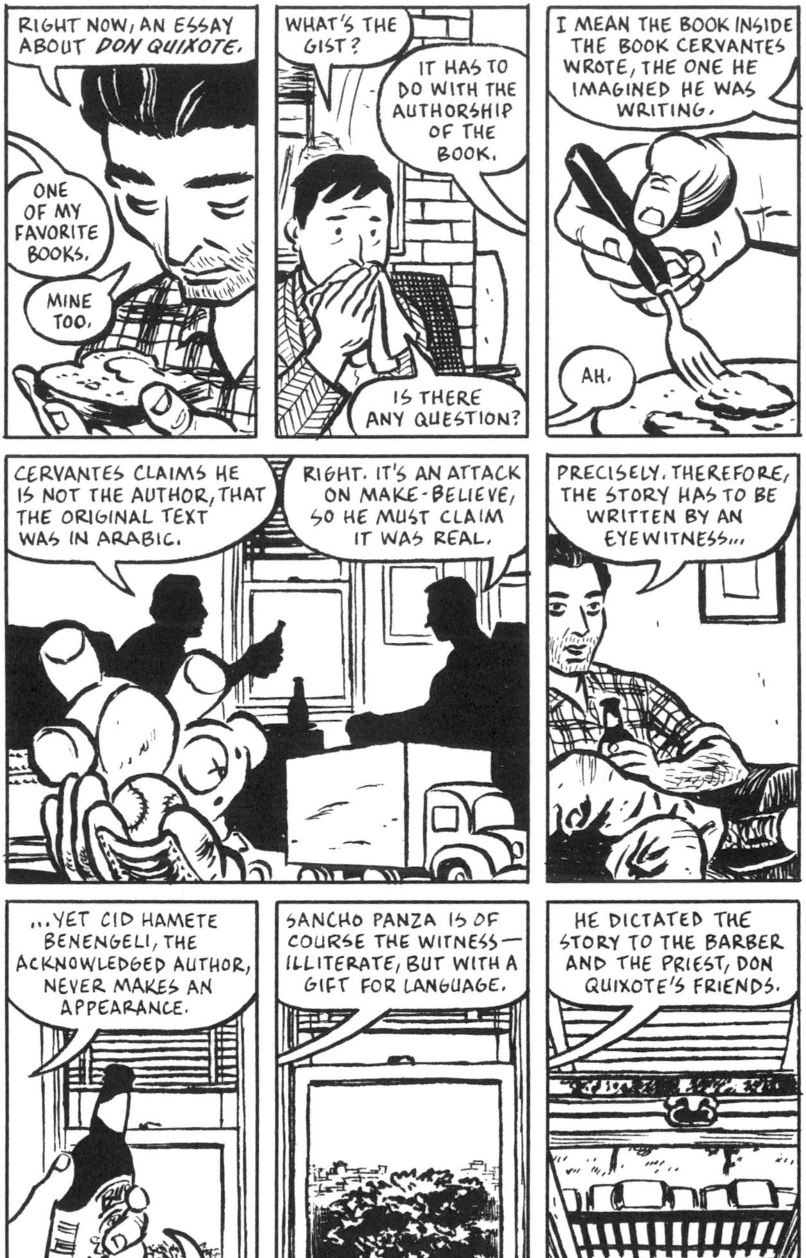
RIGHT NOW, AN ESSAY ABOUT *DON QUIXOTE*.
ONE OF MY FAVORITE BOOKS.
MINE TOO.
WHAT'S THE GIST?
IT HAS TO DO WITH THE AUTHORSHIP OF THE BOOK.
IS THERE ANY QUESTION?
I MEAN THE BOOK INSIDE THE BOOK CERVANTES WROTE, THE ONE HE IMAGINED HE WAS WRITING.
AH.
CERVANTES CLAIMS HE IS NOT THE AUTHOR, THAT THE ORIGINAL TEXT WAS IN ARABIC.
RIGHT. IT'S AN ATTACK ON MAKE-BELIEVE, SO HE MUST CLAIM IT WAS REAL.
PRECISELY. THEREFORE, THE STORY HAS TO BE WRITTEN BY AN EYEWITNESS...
...YET CID HAMETE BENENGELI, THE ACKNOWLEDGED AUTHOR, NEVER MAKES AN APPEARANCE.
SO, WHO IS HE?
SANCHO PANZA IS OF COURSE THE WITNESS— ILLITERATE, BUT WITH A GIFT FOR LANGUAGE.
HE DICTATED THE STORY TO THE BARBER AND THE PRIEST, DON QUIXOTE'S FRIENDS.

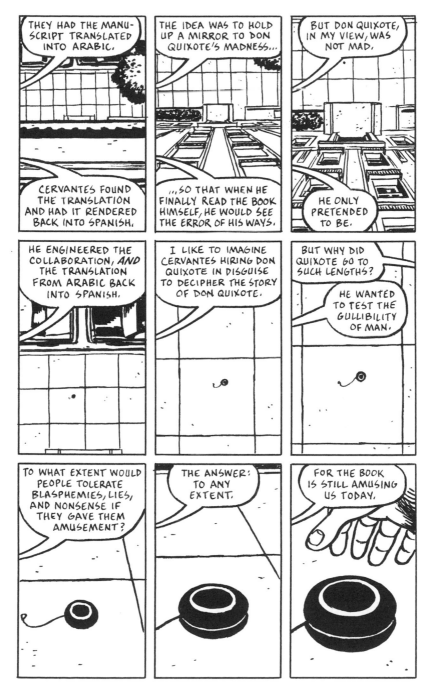

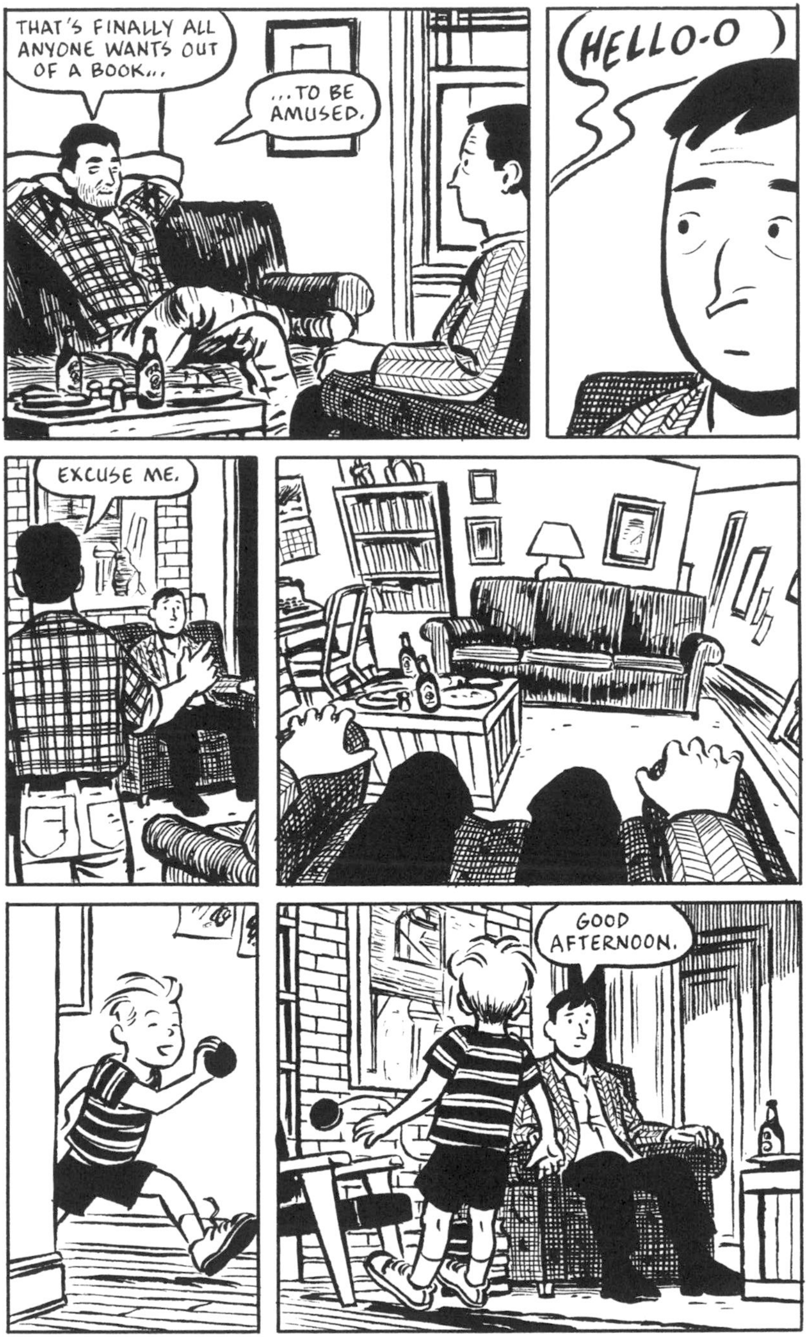
THAT'S FINALLY ALL ANYONE WANTS OUT OF A BOOK...
...TO BE AMUSED.
(HELLO-O)
EXCUSE ME.
GOOD AFTERNOON.

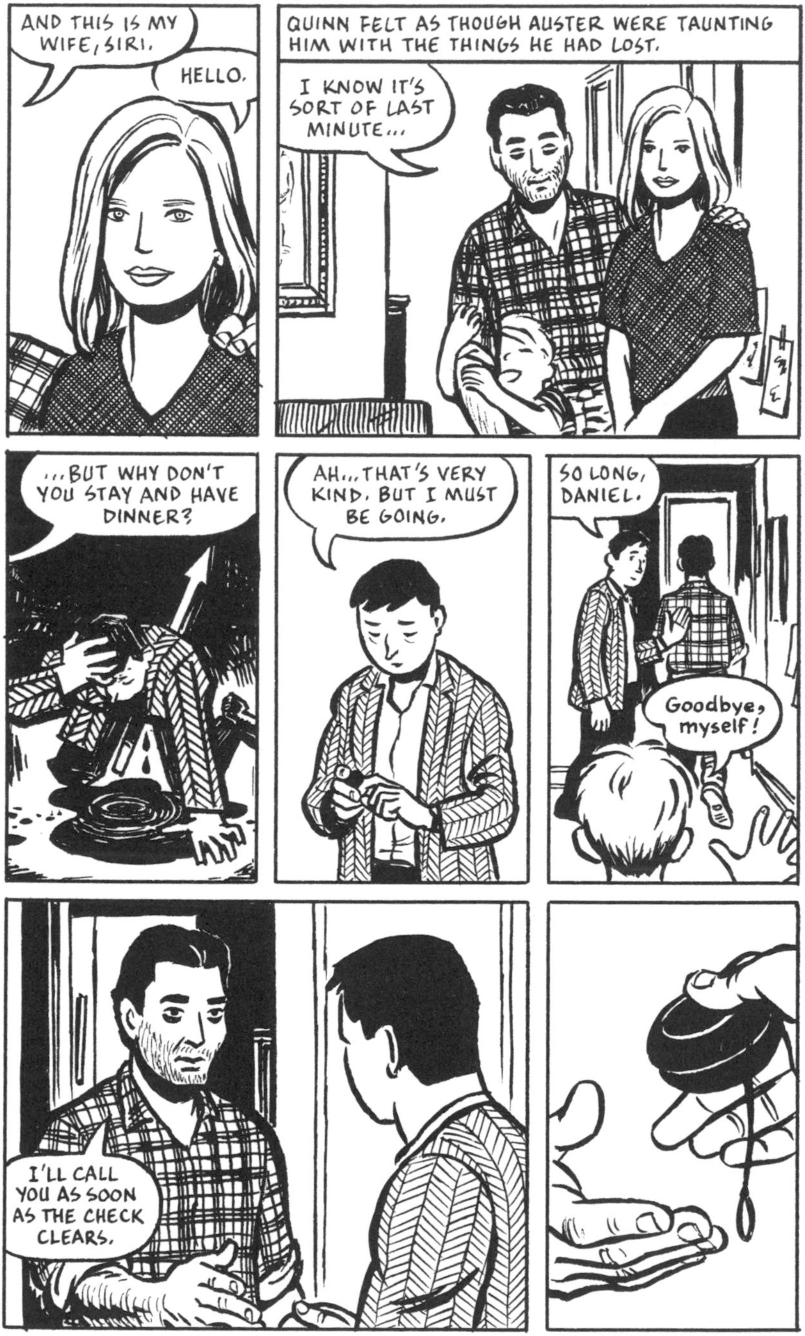
AND THIS IS MY WIFE, SIRI.
HELLO.
QUINN FELT AS THOUGH AUSTER WERE TAUNTING HIM WITH THE THINGS HE HAD LOST.
I KNOW IT'S SORT OF LAST MINUTE...
...BUT WHY DON'T YOU STAY AND HAVE DINNER?
AH... THAT'S VERY KIND. BUT I MUST BE GOING.
SO LONG, DANIEL.
Goodbye, myself!
I'LL CALL YOU AS SOON AS THE CHECK CLEARS.

QUINN WAS NOWHERE NOW.

IT'S JUNE SECOND.

HE HAD NOTHING, HE KNEW NOTHING.

THIS IS NEW YORK.

HE KNEW THAT HE KNEW NOTHING.

TOMORROW WILL BE JUNE THIRD.

BUT NOTHING IS CERTAIN.

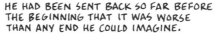

HE HAD BEEN SENT BACK SO FAR BEFORE THE BEGINNING THAT IT WAS WORSE THAN ANY END HE COULD IMAGINE.

I COULD FORGET ABOUT THE CASE...

...GET BACK TO MY ROUTINE...

...WRITE ANOTHER BOOK...

...TAKE A TRIP.

THE HOUR HAD PASSED FOR HIS CALL TO VIRGINIA.

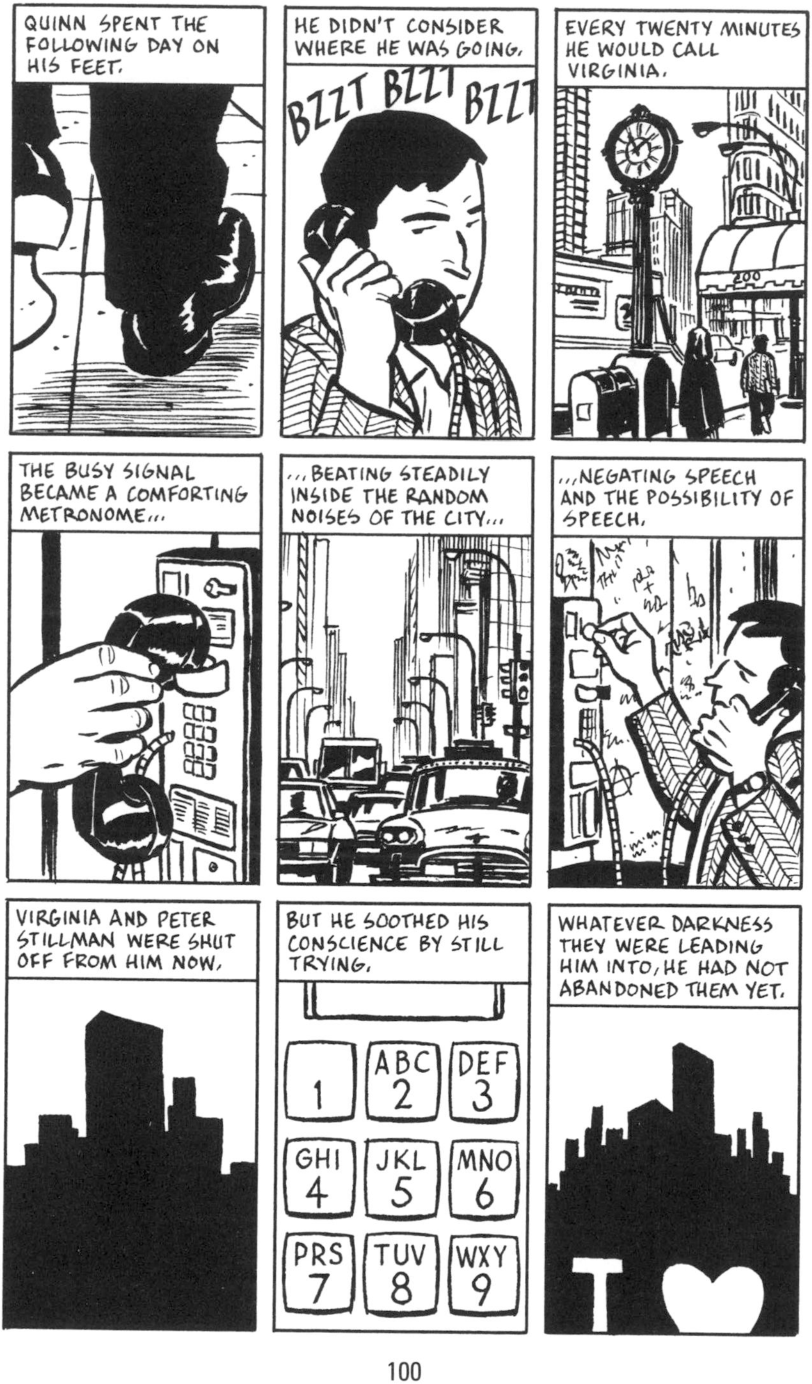
QUINN SPENT THE FOLLOWING DAY ON HIS FEET.
HE DIDN'T CONSIDER WHERE HE WAS GOING.
BZZT BZZT BZZT
EVERY TWENTY MINUTES HE WOULD CALL VIRGINIA.
200
THE BUSY SIGNAL BECAME A COMFORTING METRONOME...
...BEATING STEADILY INSIDE THE RANDOM NOISES OF THE CITY...
...NEGATING SPEECH AND THE POSSIBILITY OF SPEECH.
VIRGINIA AND PETER STILLMAN WERE SHUT OFF FROM HIM NOW.
BUT HE SOOTHED HIS CONSCIENCE BY STILL TRYING.
1
ABC 2
DEF 3
GHI 4
JKL 5
MNO 6
PRS 7
TUV 8
WXY 9
WHATEVER DARKNESS THEY WERE LEADING HIM INTO, HE HAD NOT ABANDONED THEM YET.

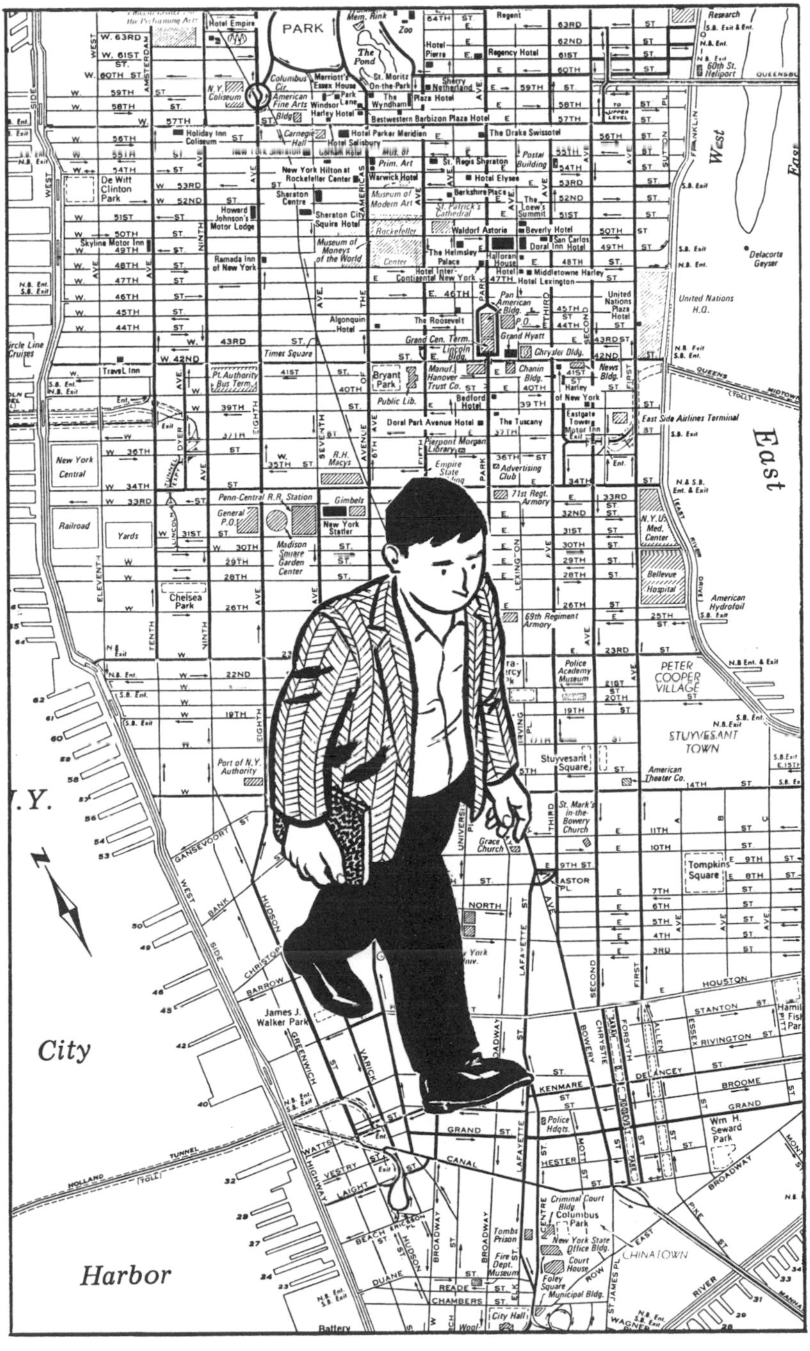
PARK
Zoo
The Pond
Hotel Empire
Columbus Cir.
N.Y. Coliseum
Carnegie Hall
Hotel Parker Meridien
The Drake Swissotel
Plaza Hotel
Bestwestern Barbizon Plaza Hotel
Holiday Inn Coliseum
New York Hilton at Rockefeller Center
Warwick Hotel
Museum of Modern Art
St. Regis Sheraton
Hotel Elysee
Berkshire Place
St. Patrick's Cathedral
The Lowe's Summit
Waldorf Astoria
Beverly Hotel
San Carlos
Doral Inn Hotel
De Witt Clinton Park
Howard Johnson's Motor Lodge
Sheraton Centre
Sheraton City Squire Hotel
Skyline Motor Inn
Museum of Moneys of the World
Rockefeller Center
The Helmsley Palace
Ramada Inn of New York
Hotel Inter-Continental New York
Hotel Lexington
Middletowne Harley
Pan American Bldg.
P.O.
Grand Hyatt
Chrysler Bldg.
United Nations Plaza Hotel
United Nations H.Q.
Delacorte Geyser
Algonquin Hotel
The Roosevelt
Grand Cen. Term.
Lincoln Bldg.
Times Square
Pt. Authority Bus Term.
Bryant Park
Public Lib.
Manuf. Hanover Trust Co.
Chanin Bldg.
News Bldg.
Harley of New York
Bedford Hotel
Doral Park Avenue Hotel
The Tuscany
Eastgate Tower Motor Inn
East Side Airlines Terminal
Pierpont Morgan Library
Empire State Bldg.
Advertising Club
R.H. Macy's
Gimbels
New York Central Railroad Yards
Penn-Central R.R. Station
General P.O.
Madison Square Garden Center
New York Statler
71st Regt. Armory
N.Y.U. Med. Center
Bellevue Hospital
American Hydrofoil
Chelsea Park
69th Regiment Armory
Police Academy Museum
PETER COOPER VILLAGE
STUYVESANT TOWN
Stuyvesant Square
American Theater Co.
Port of N.Y. Authority
St. Mark's in-the-Bowery Church
Grace Church
Tompkins Square
ASTOR PL.
James J. Walker Park
Police Hdqts.
Wm H. Seward Park
Criminal Court Bldg
Columbus Park
Tombs Prison
New York State Office Bldg.
Court House
Fire Dept. Museum
Foley Square
Municipal Bldg.
City Hall
CHINATOWN
Circle Line Cruises
TravelL Inn
HOLLAND TUNNEL
West
East
N.Y.
City
Harbor

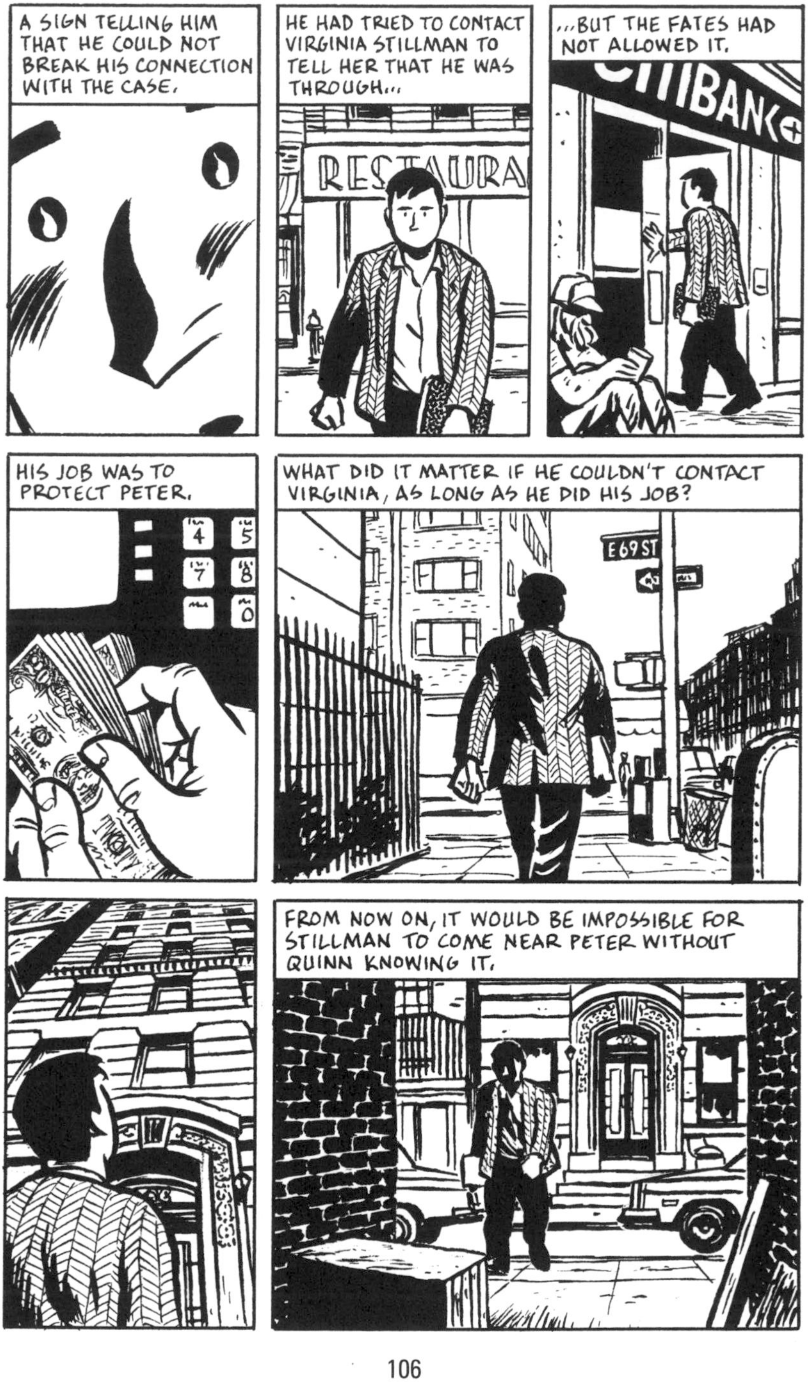
A SIGN TELLING HIM THAT HE COULD NOT BREAK HIS CONNECTION WITH THE CASE.
HE HAD TRIED TO CONTACT VIRGINIA STILLMAN TO TELL HER THAT HE WAS THROUGH...
RESTAURA
...BUT THE FATES HAD NOT ALLOWED IT.
ITIBANK
HIS JOB WAS TO PROTECT PETER.
4
5
7
8
0
WHAT DID IT MATTER IF HE COULDN'T CONTACT VIRGINIA, AS LONG AS HE DID HIS JOB?
E 69 ST
FROM NOW ON, IT WOULD BE IMPOSSIBLE FOR STILLMAN TO COME NEAR PETER WITHOUT QUINN KNOWING IT.

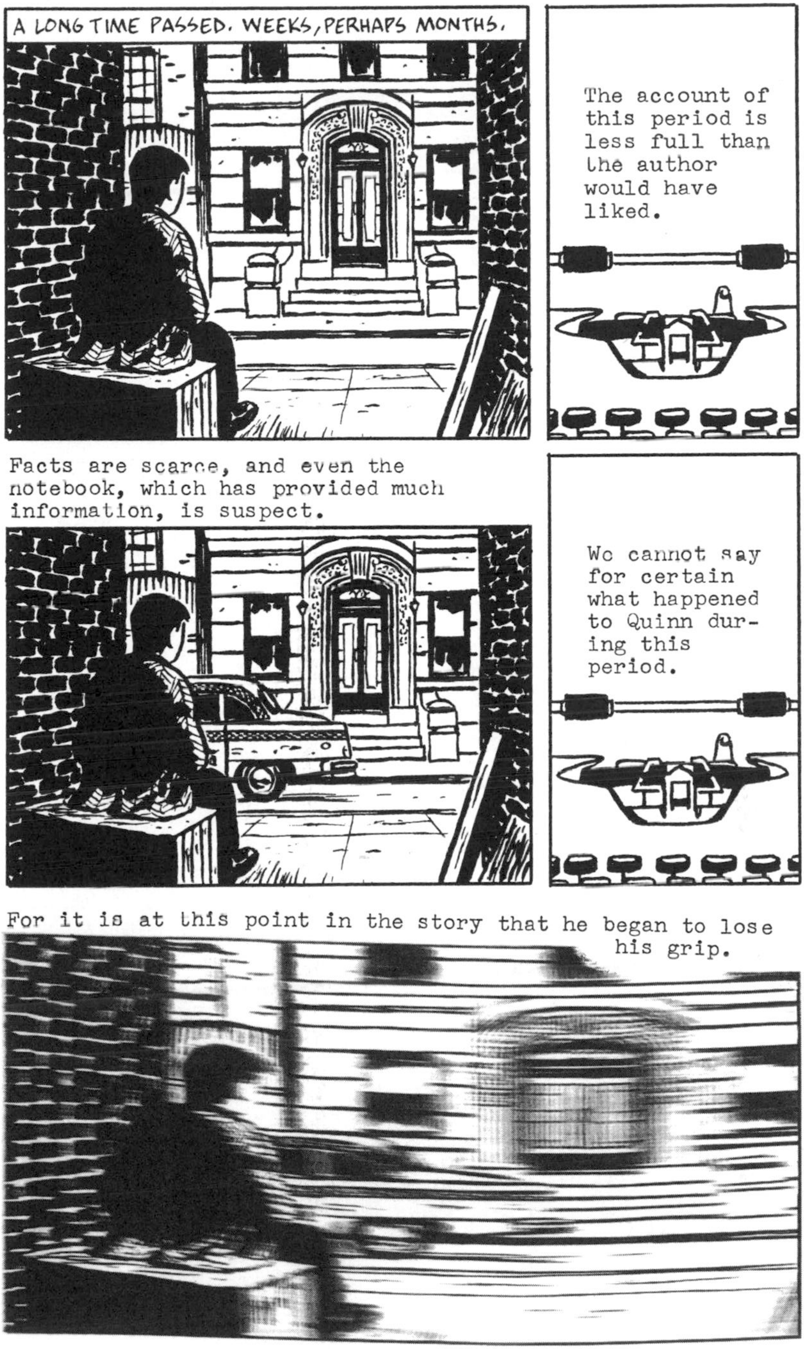
A LONG TIME PASSED. WEEKS, PERHAPS MONTHS.
The account of this period is less full than the author would have liked.
Facts are scarce, and even the notebook, which has provided much information, is suspect.
We cannot say for certain what happened to Quinn during this period.
For it is at this point in the story that he began to lose his grip.

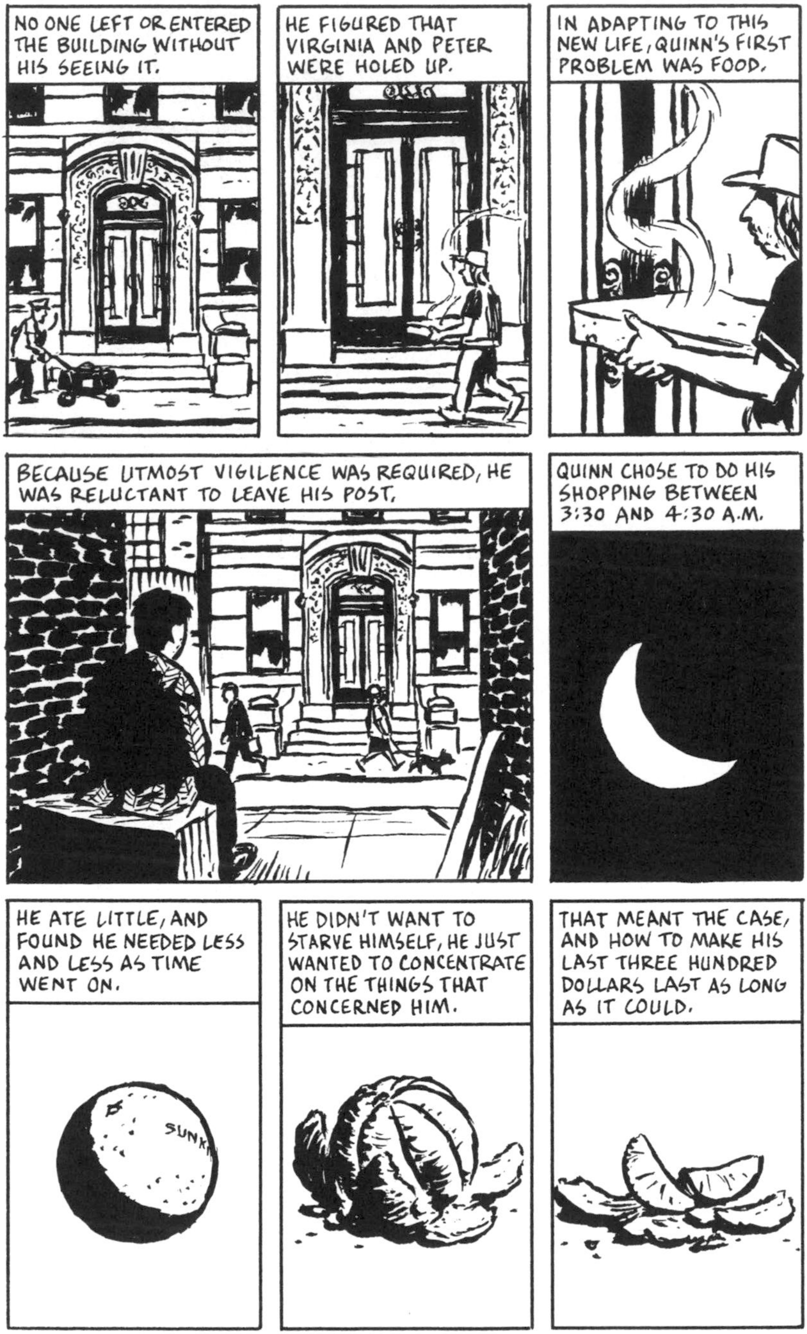
NO ONE LEFT OR ENTERED THE BUILDING WITHOUT HIS SEEING IT.
HE FIGURED THAT VIRGINIA AND PETER WERE HOLED UP.
IN ADAPTING TO THIS NEW LIFE, QUINN'S FIRST PROBLEM WAS FOOD.
BECAUSE UTMOST VIGILENCE WAS REQUIRED, HE WAS RELUCTANT TO LEAVE HIS POST.
QUINN CHOSE TO DO HIS SHOPPING BETWEEN 3:30 AND 4:30 A.M.
HE ATE LITTLE, AND FOUND HE NEEDED LESS AND LESS AS TIME WENT ON.
HE DIDN'T WANT TO STARVE HIMSELF, HE JUST WANTED TO CONCENTRATE ON THE THINGS THAT CONCERNED HIM.
THAT MEANT THE CASE, AND HOW TO MAKE HIS LAST THREE HUNDRED DOLLARS LAST AS LONG AS IT COULD.

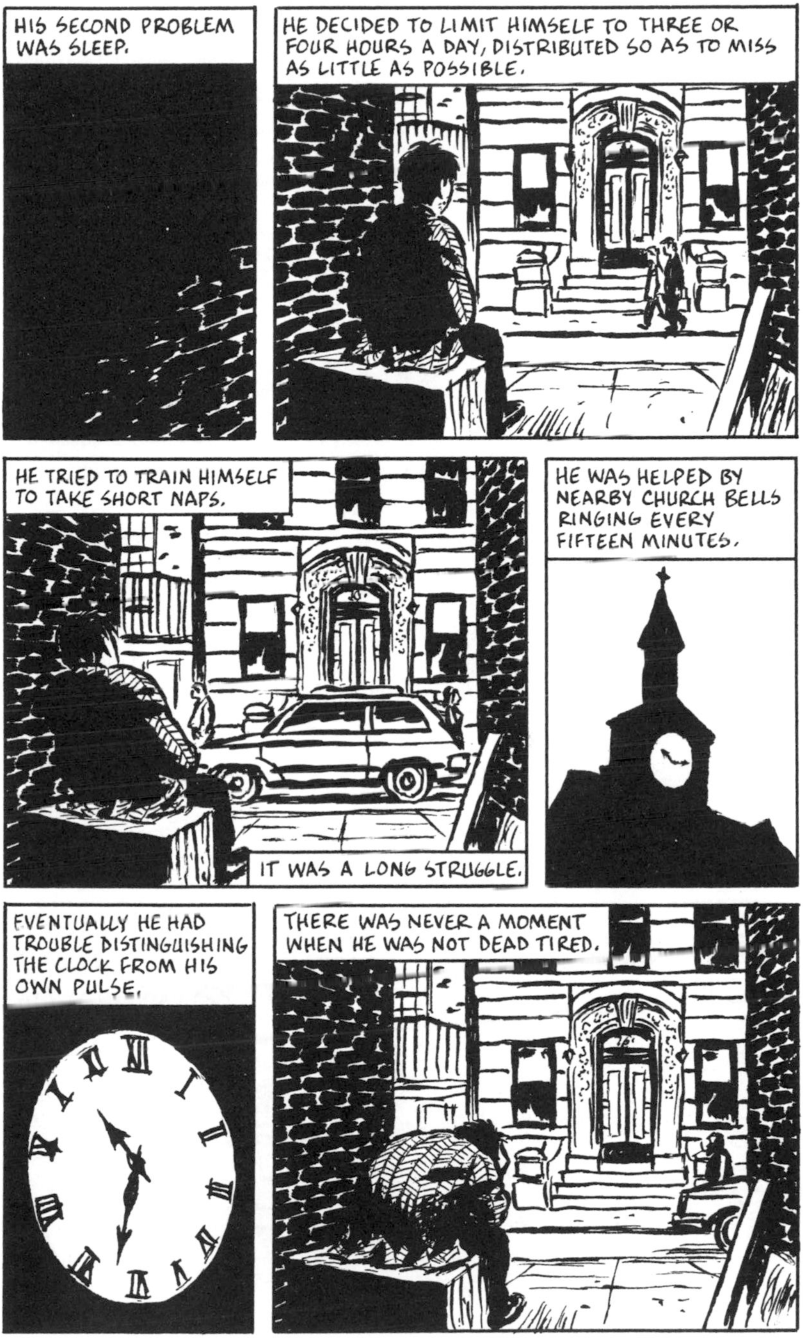
HIS SECOND PROBLEM WAS SLEEP.
HE DECIDED TO LIMIT HIMSELF TO THREE OR FOUR HOURS A DAY, DISTRIBUTED SO AS TO MISS AS LITTLE AS POSSIBLE.
HE TRIED TO TRAIN HIMSELF TO TAKE SHORT NAPS.
IT WAS A LONG STRUGGLE.
HE WAS HELPED BY NEARBY CHURCH BELLS RINGING EVERY FIFTEEN MINUTES.
EVENTUALLY HE HAD TROUBLE DISTINGUISHING THE CLOCK FROM HIS OWN PULSE.
THERE WAS NEVER A MOMENT WHEN HE WAS NOT DEAD TIRED.

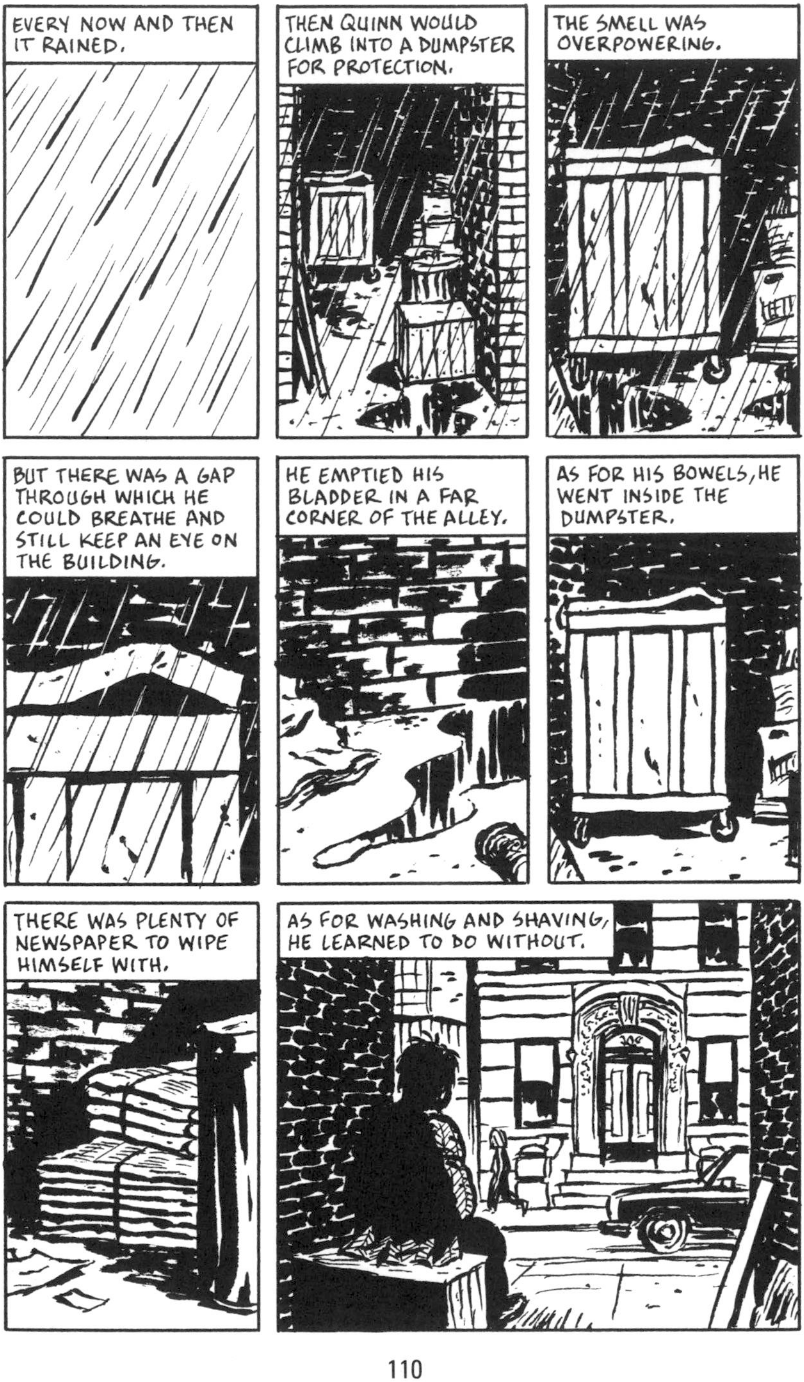

EVERY NOW AND THEN IT RAINED.
THEN QUINN WOULD CLIMB INTO A DUMPSTER FOR PROTECTION.
THE SMELL WAS OVERPOWERING.
BUT THERE WAS A GAP THROUGH WHICH HE COULD BREATHE AND STILL KEEP AN EYE ON THE BUILDING.
HE EMPTIED HIS BLADDER IN A FAR CORNER OF THE ALLEY.
AS FOR HIS BOWELS, HE WENT INSIDE THE DUMPSTER.
THERE WAS PLENTY OF NEWSPAPER TO WIPE HIMSELF WITH.
AS FOR WASHING AND SHAVING, HE LEARNED TO DO WITHOUT.

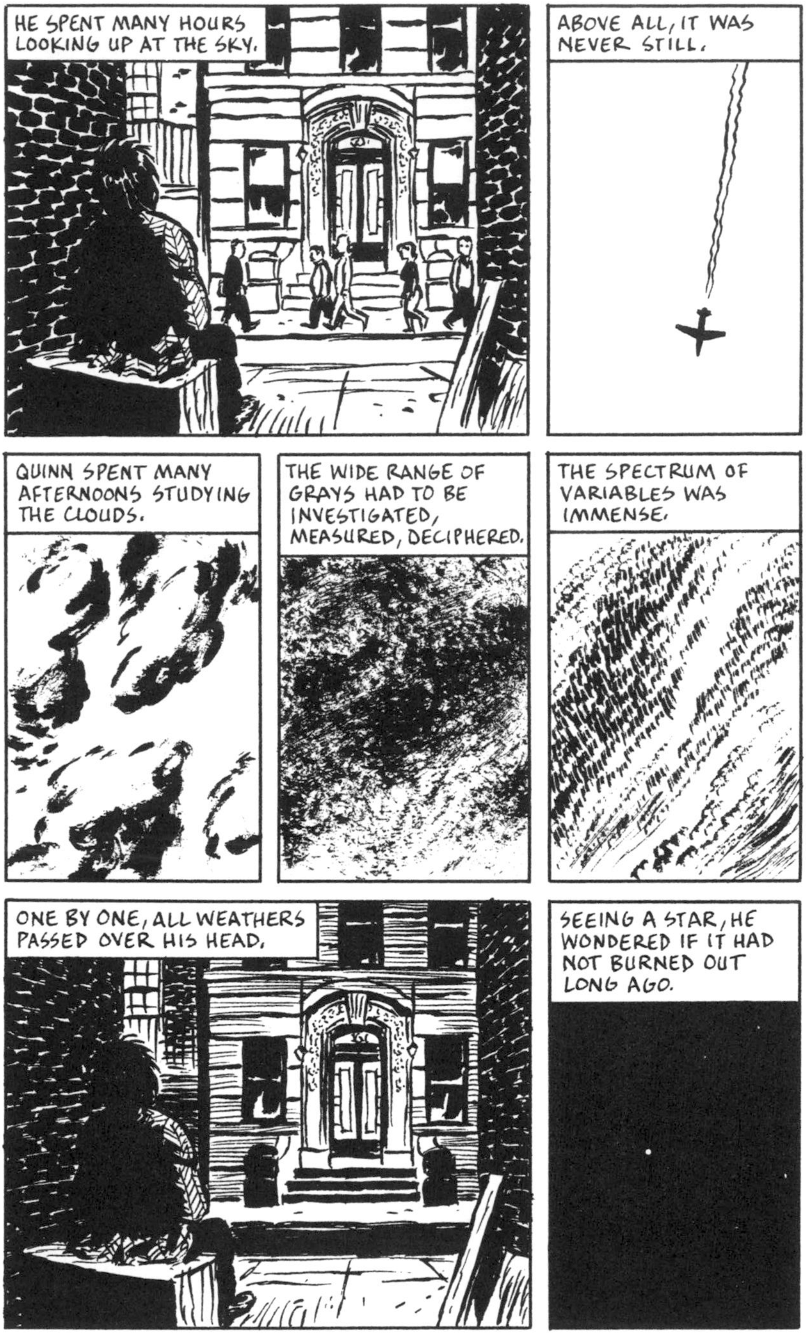

HE SPENT MANY HOURS LOOKING UP AT THE SKY.
ABOVE ALL, IT WAS NEVER STILL.
QUINN SPENT MANY AFTERNOONS STUDYING THE CLOUDS.
THE WIDE RANGE OF GRAYS HAD TO BE INVESTIGATED, MEASURED, DECIPHERED.
THE SPECTRUM OF VARIABLES WAS IMMENSE.
ONE BY ONE, ALL WEATHERS PASSED OVER HIS HEAD.
SEEING A STAR, HE WONDERED IF IT HAD NOT BURNED OUT LONG AGO.

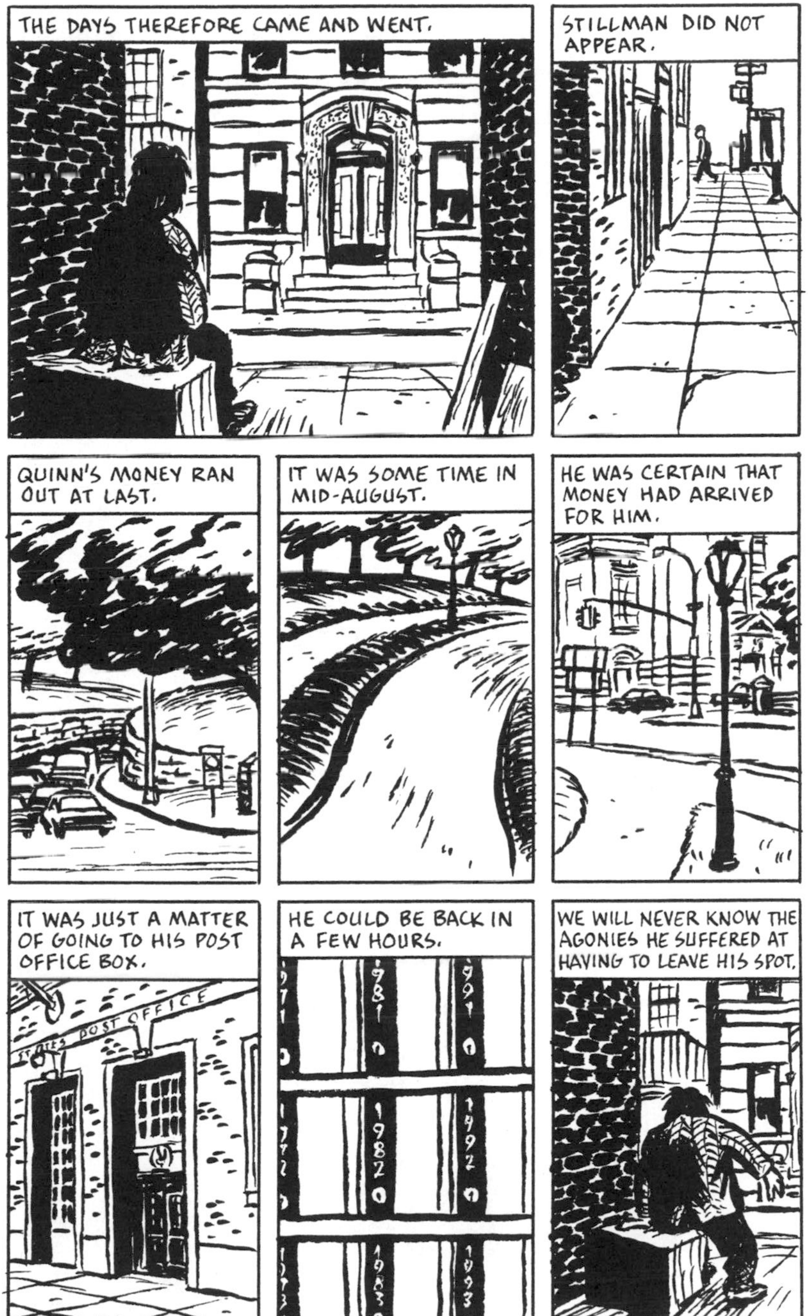
THE DAYS THEREFORE CAME AND WENT.
STILLMAN DID NOT APPEAR.
QUINN'S MONEY RAN OUT AT LAST.
IT WAS SOME TIME IN MID-AUGUST.
HE WAS CERTAIN THAT MONEY HAD ARRIVED FOR HIM.
IT WAS JUST A MATTER OF GOING TO HIS POST OFFICE BOX.
POST OFFICE
HE COULD BE BACK IN A FEW HOURS.
WE WILL NEVER KNOW THE AGONIES HE SUFFERED AT HAVING TO LEAVE HIS SPOT.

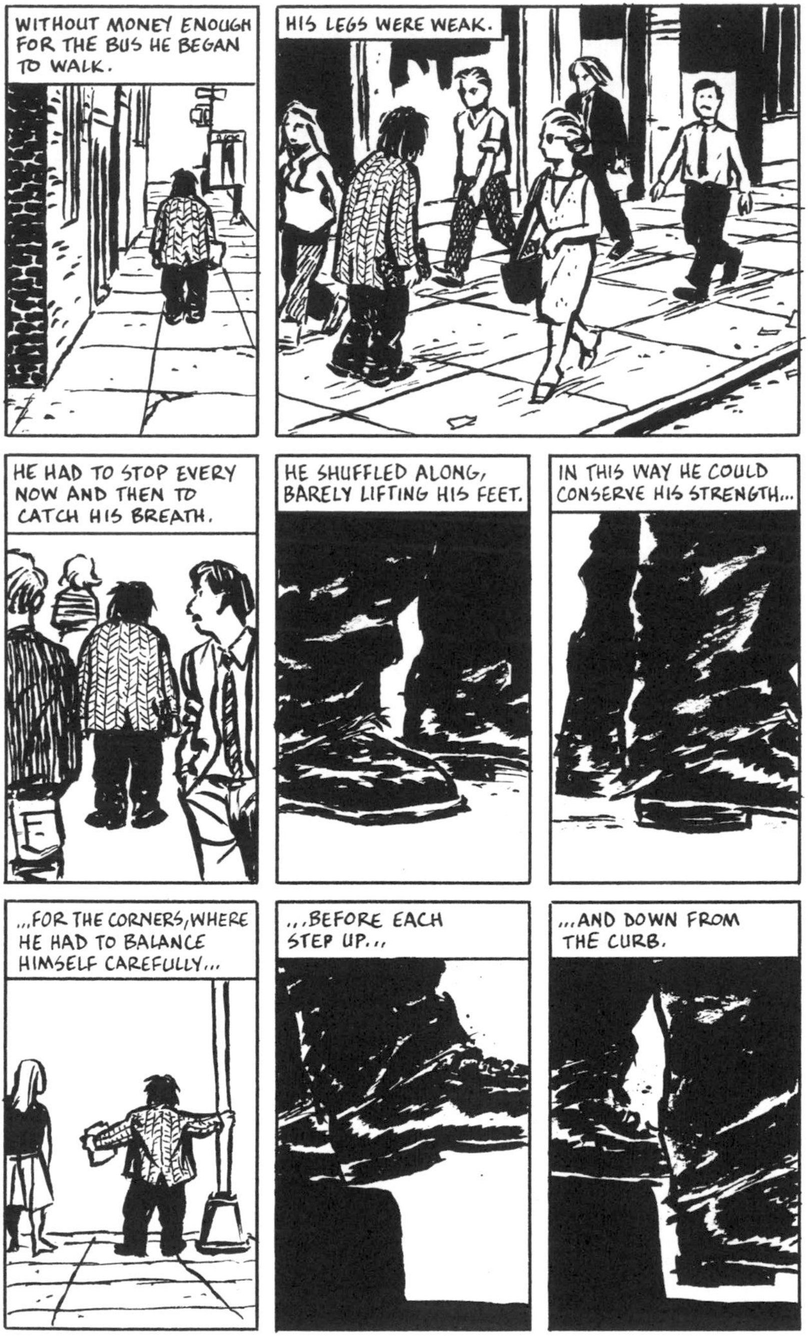
WITHOUT MONEY ENOUGH FOR THE BUS HE BEGAN TO WALK.
HIS LEGS WERE WEAK.
HE HAD TO STOP EVERY NOW AND THEN TO CATCH HIS BREATH.
HE SHUFFLED ALONG, BARELY LIFTING HIS FEET.
IN THIS WAY HE COULD CONSERVE HIS STRENGTH...
...FOR THE CORNERS, WHERE HE HAD TO BALANCE HIMSELF CAREFULLY...
...BEFORE EACH STEP UP...
...AND DOWN FROM THE CURB.

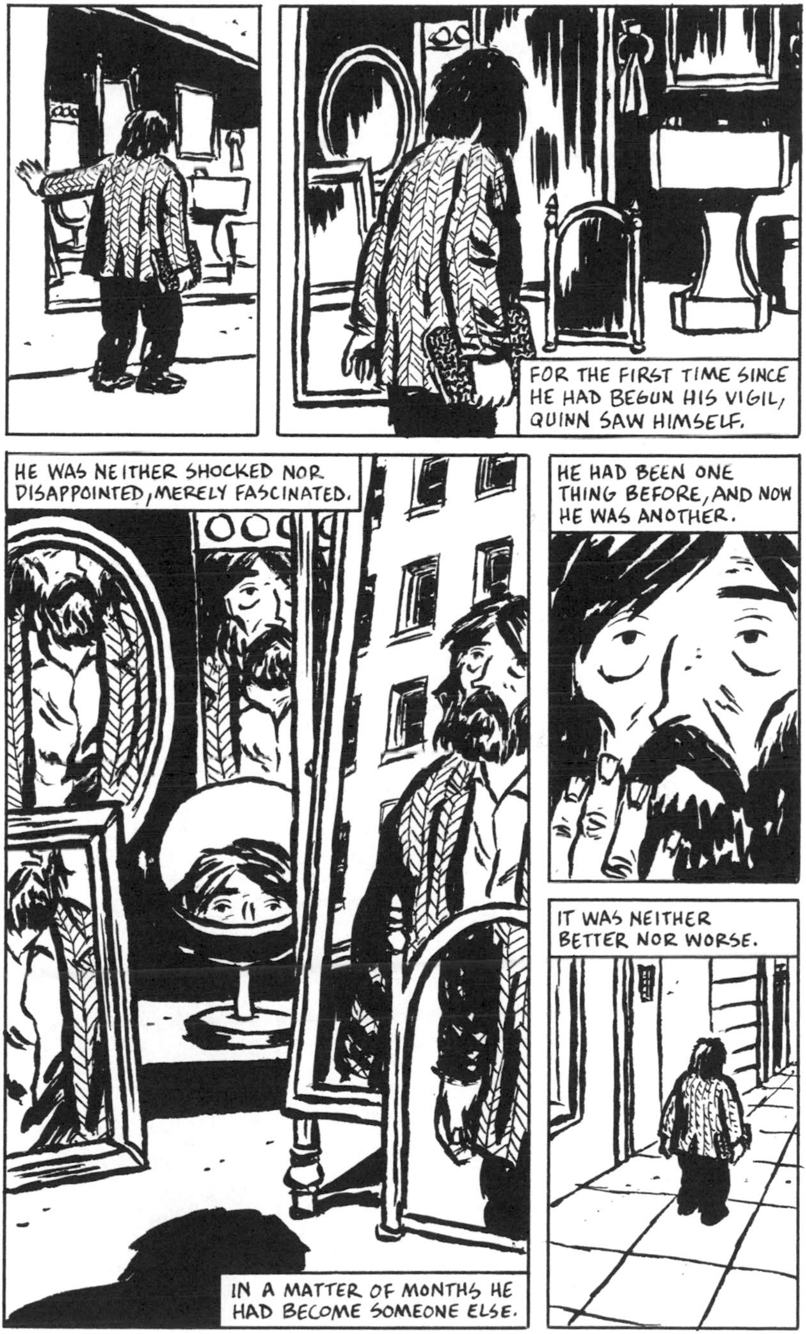
FOR THE FIRST TIME SINCE HE HAD BEGUN HIS VIGIL, QUINN SAW HIMSELF.
HE WAS NEITHER SHOCKED NOR DISAPPOINTED, MERELY FASCINATED.
IN A MATTER OF MONTHS HE HAD BECOME SOMEONE ELSE.
HE HAD BEEN ONE THING BEFORE, AND NOW HE WAS ANOTHER.
IT WAS NEITHER BETTER NOR WORSE.

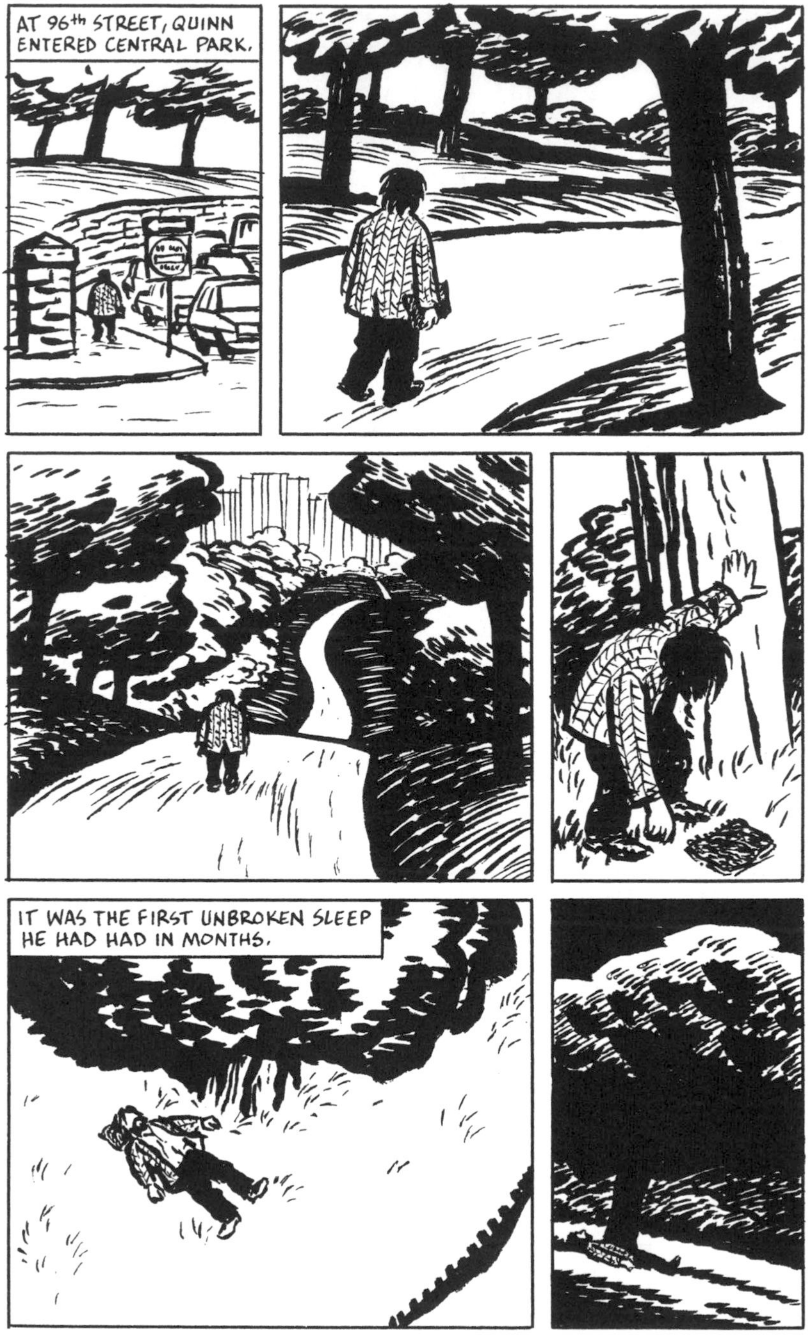
AT 96th STREET, QUINN ENTERED CENTRAL PARK.
IT WAS THE FIRST UNBROKEN SLEEP HE HAD HAD IN MONTHS.

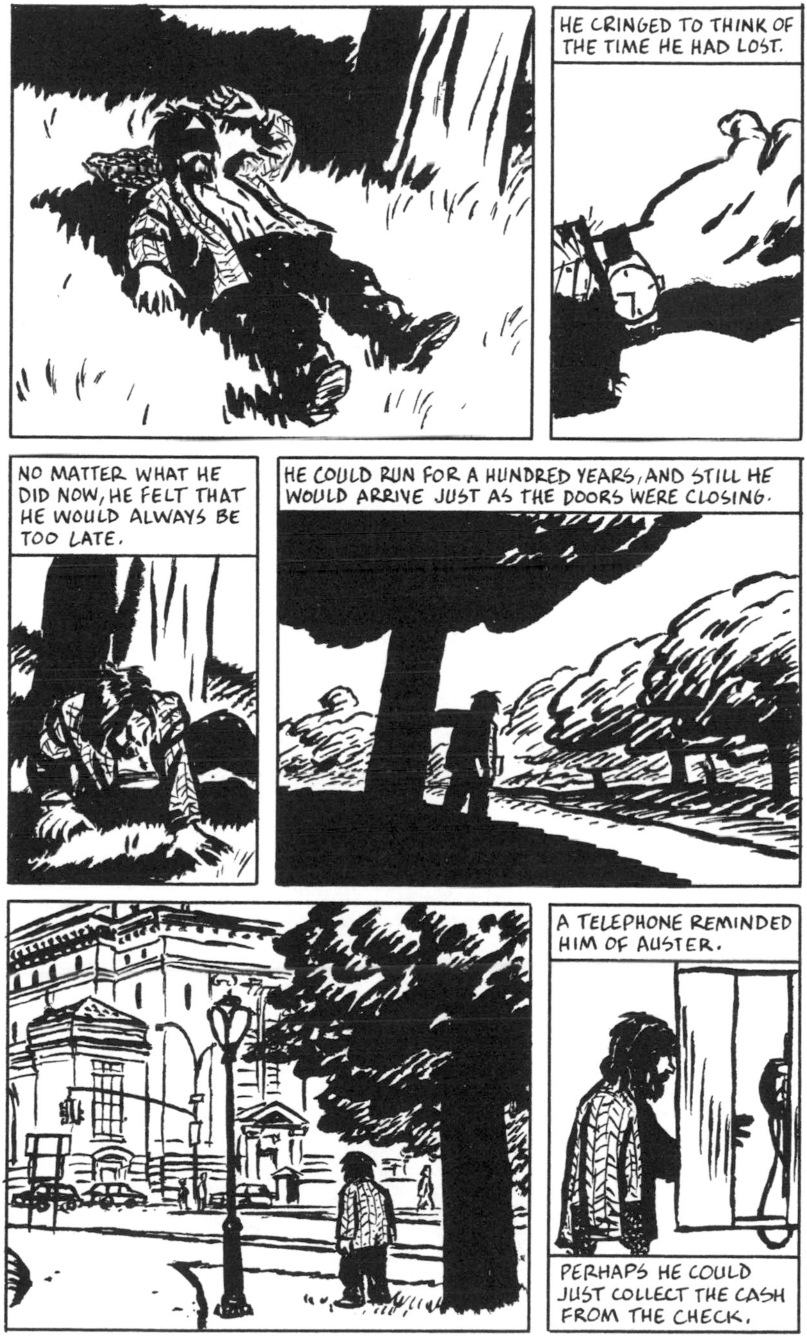
HE CRINGED TO THINK OF THE TIME HE HAD LOST.
NO MATTER WHAT HE DID NOW, HE FELT THAT HE WOULD ALWAYS BE TOO LATE.
HE COULD RUN FOR A HUNDRED YEARS, AND STILL HE WOULD ARRIVE JUST AS THE DOORS WERE CLOSING.
A TELEPHONE REMINDED HIM OF AUSTER.
PERHAPS HE COULD JUST COLLECT THE CASH FROM THE CHECK.

118

119

120

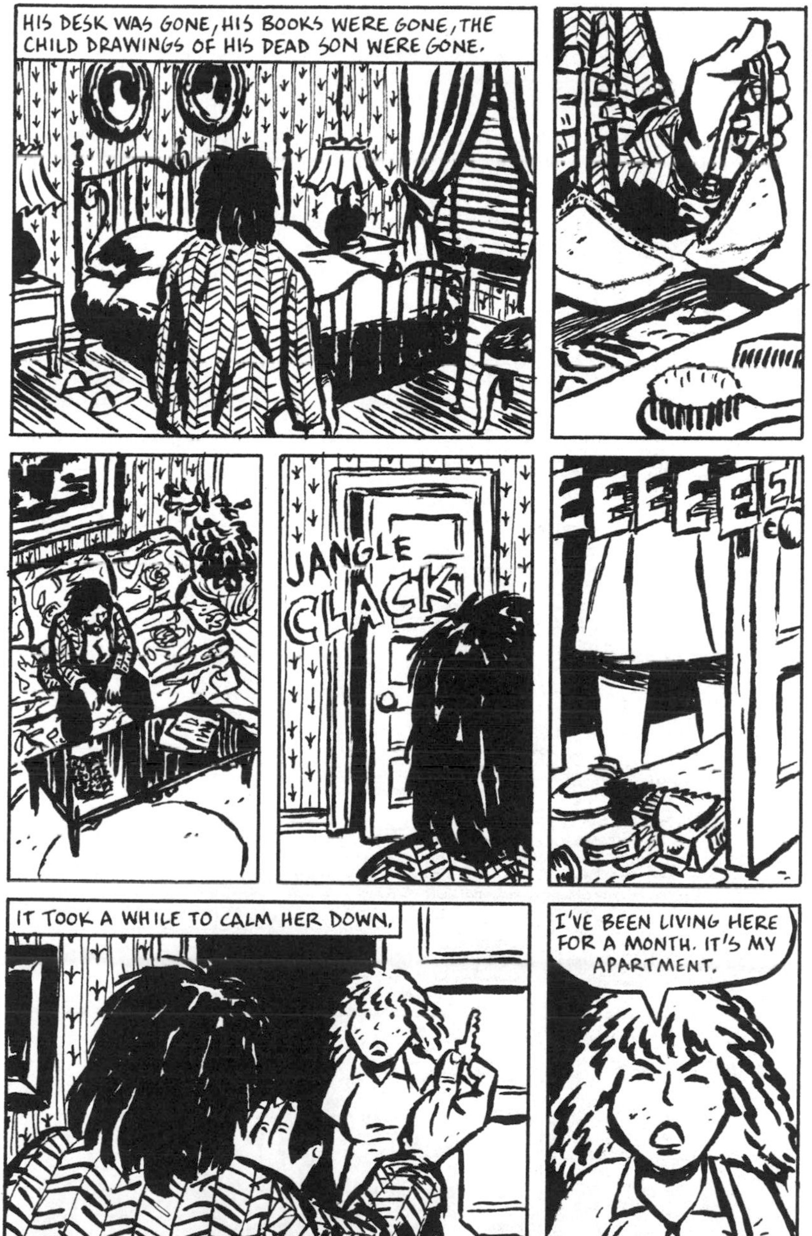
HIS DESK WAS GONE, HIS BOOKS WERE GONE, THE CHILD DRAWINGS OF HIS DEAD SON WERE GONE.
JANGLE
CLACK
EEEEEE
IT TOOK A WHILE TO CALM HER DOWN.
I'VE BEEN LIVING HERE FOR A MONTH. IT'S MY APARTMENT.
BUT I HAVE THE KEY. DOESN'T THAT CONVINCE YOU?

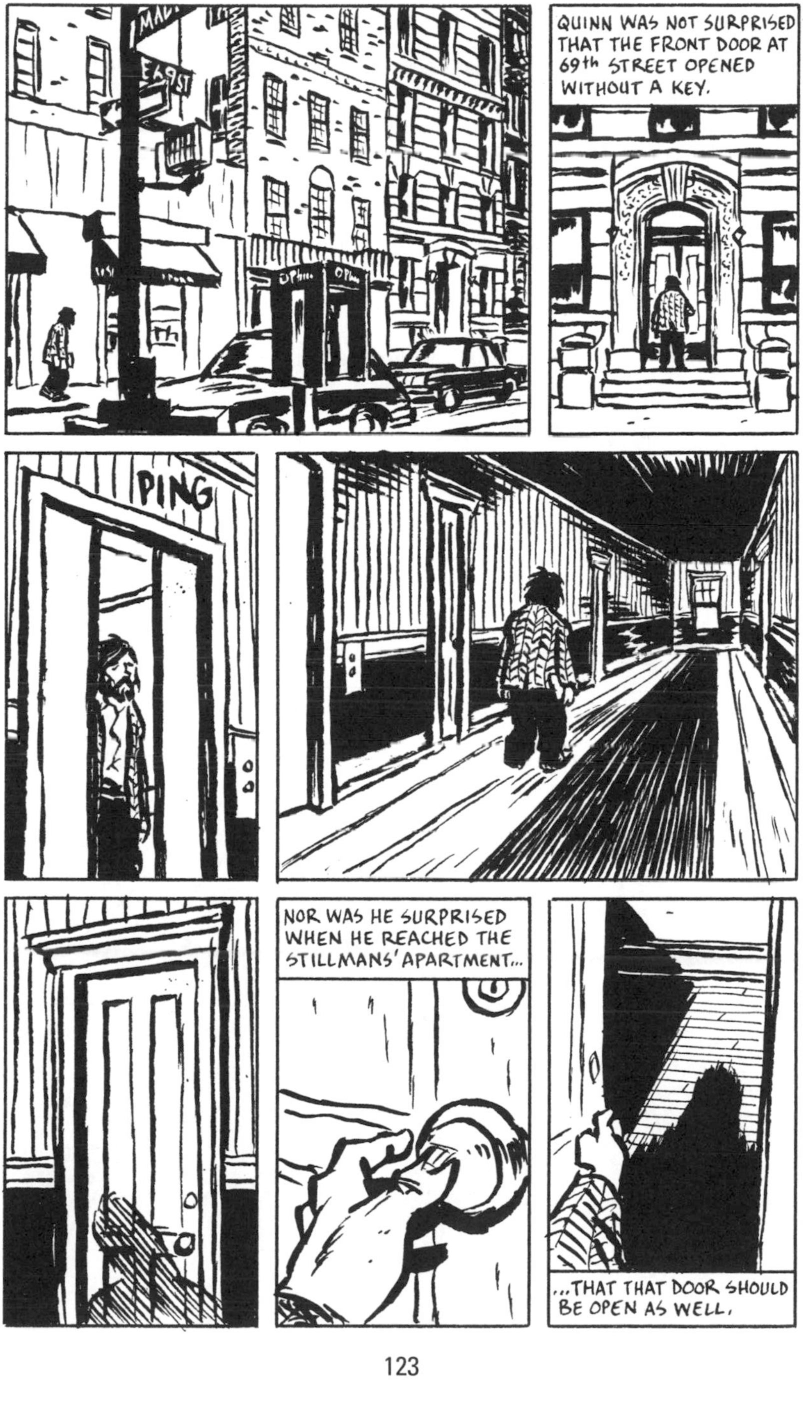
QUINN WAS NOT SURPRISED THAT THE FRONT DOOR AT 69th STREET OPENED WITHOUT A KEY.
PING
NOR WAS HE SURPRISED WHEN HE REACHED THE STILLMANS' APARTMENT...
...THAT THAT DOOR SHOULD BE OPEN AS WELL.

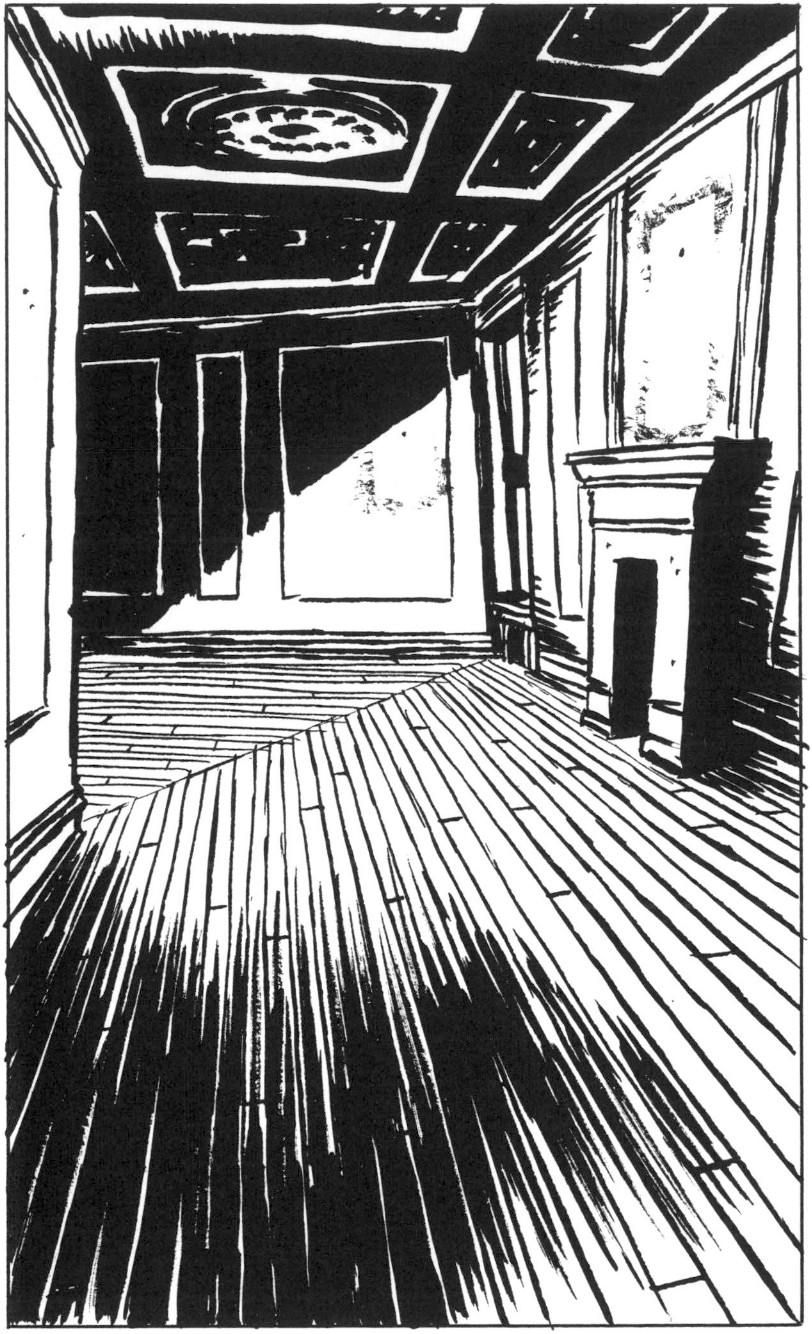

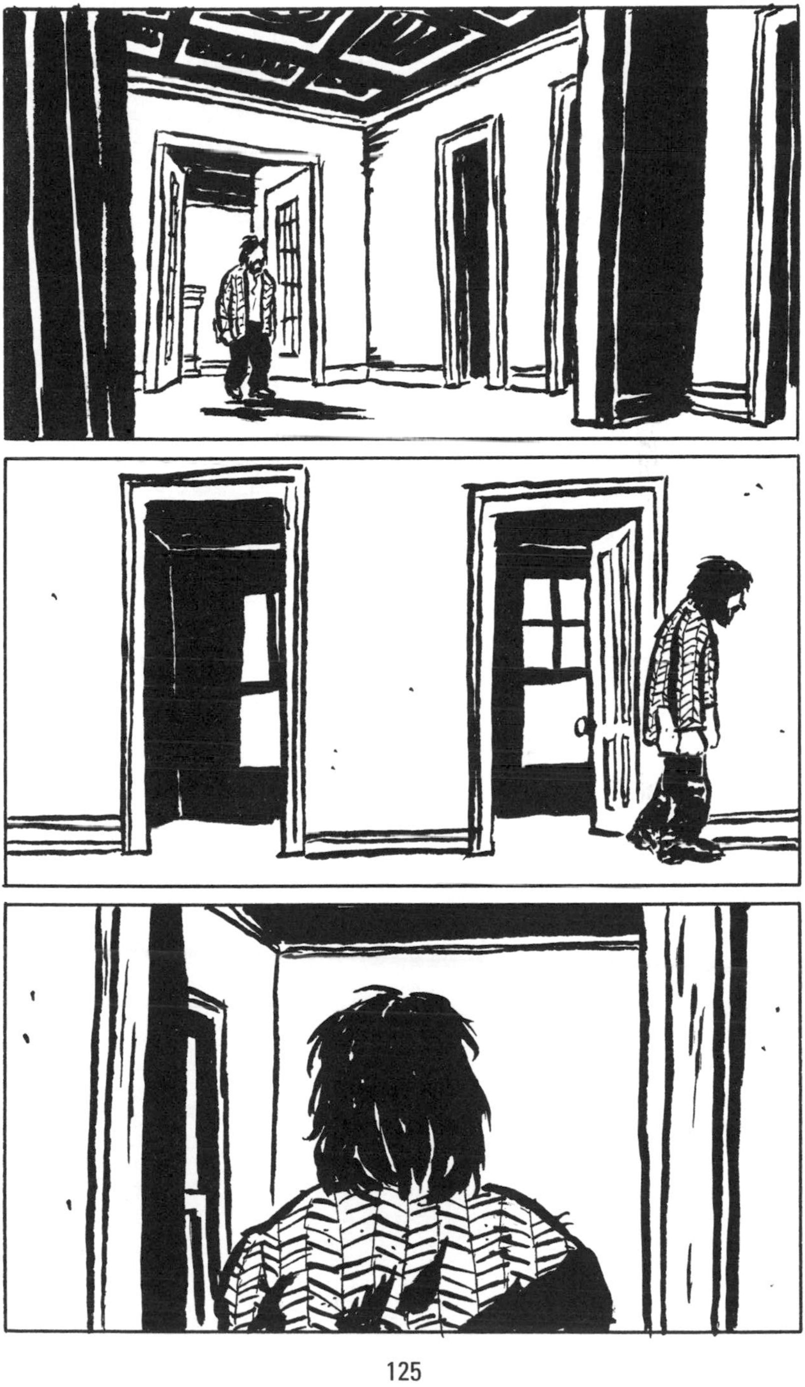

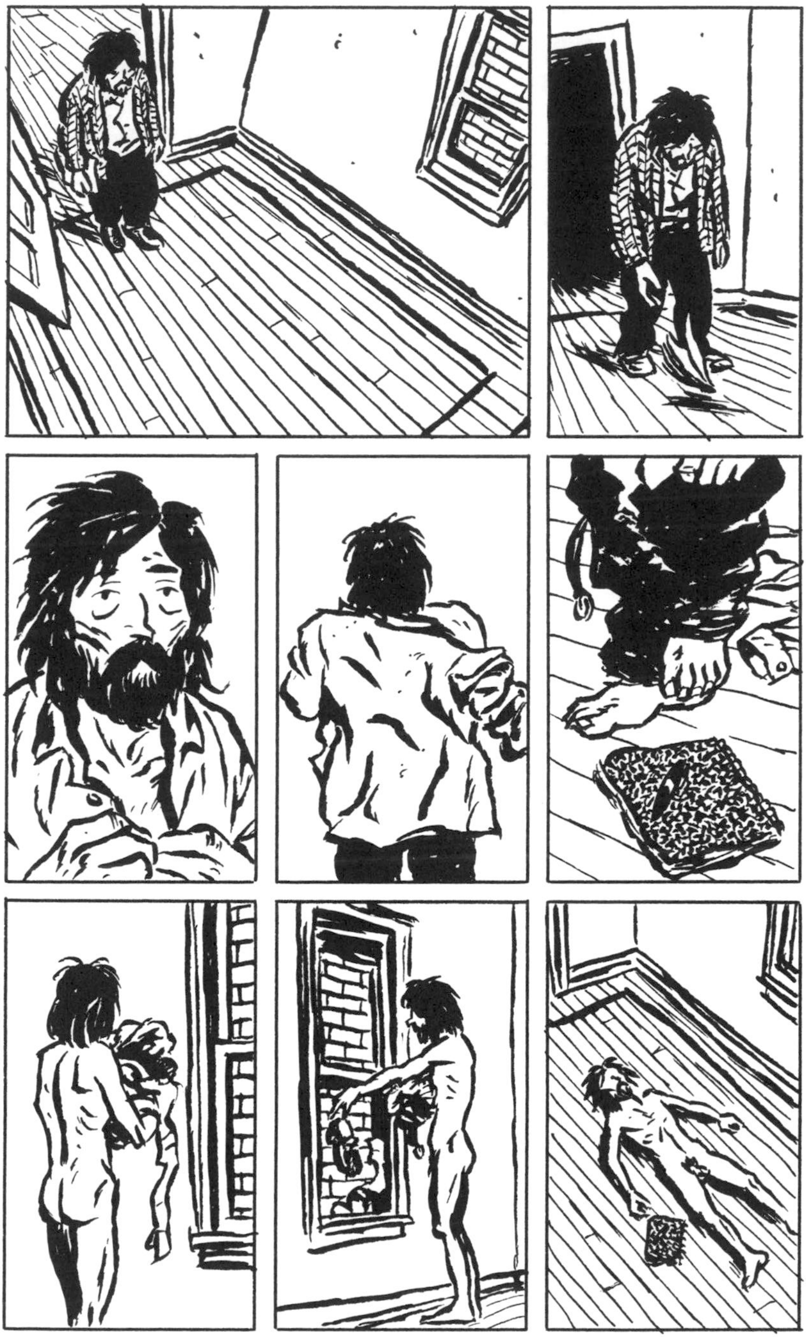

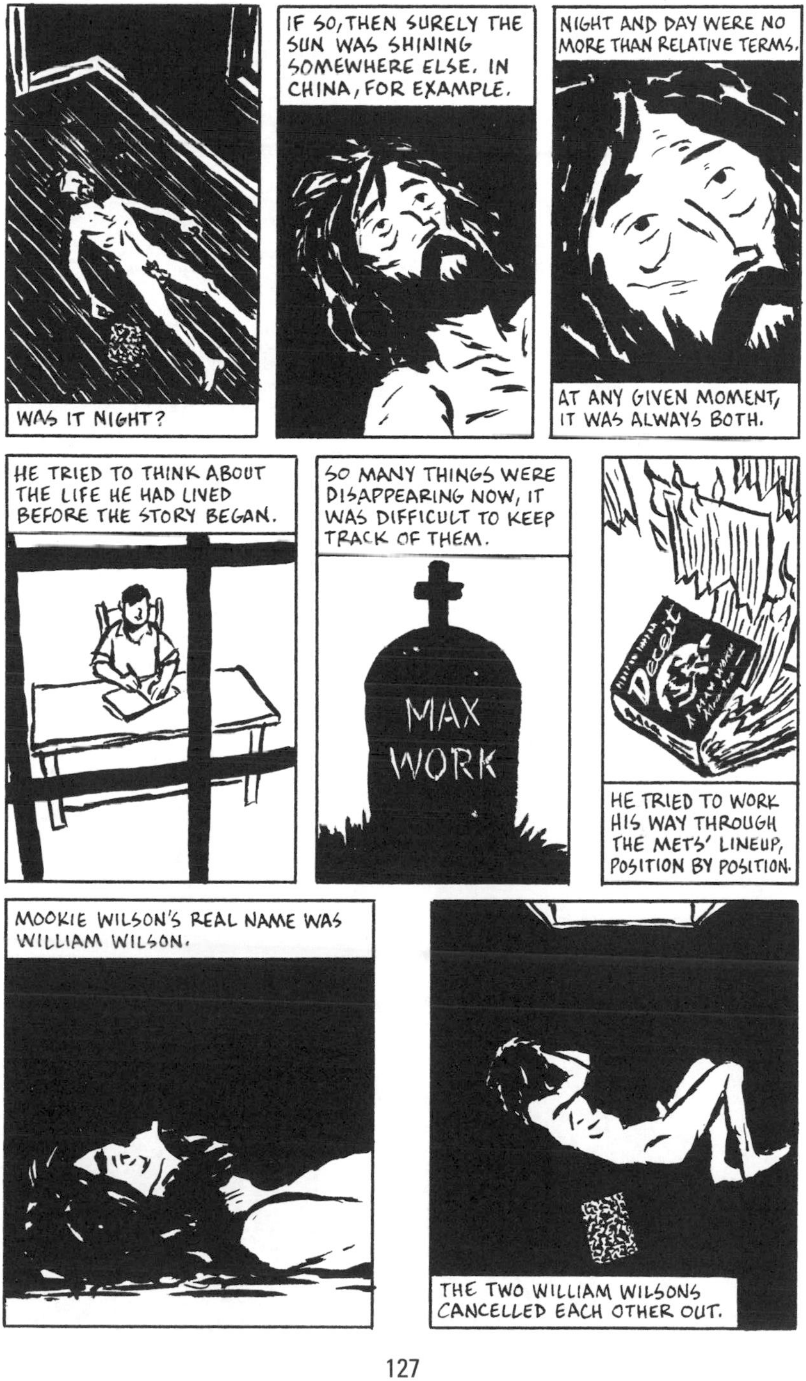
WAS IT NIGHT?
IF SO, THEN SURELY THE SUN WAS SHINING SOMEWHERE ELSE. IN CHINA, FOR EXAMPLE.
NIGHT AND DAY WERE NO MORE THAN RELATIVE TERMS.
AT ANY GIVEN MOMENT, IT WAS ALWAYS BOTH.
HE TRIED TO THINK ABOUT THE LIFE HE HAD LIVED BEFORE THE STORY BEGAN.
SO MANY THINGS WERE DISAPPEARING NOW, IT WAS DIFFICULT TO KEEP TRACK OF THEM.
MAX WORK
Deceit
HE TRIED TO WORK HIS WAY THROUGH THE METS' LINEUP, POSITION BY POSITION.
MOOKIE WILSON'S REAL NAME WAS WILLIAM WILSON.
THE TWO WILLIAM WILSONS CANCELLED EACH OTHER OUT.

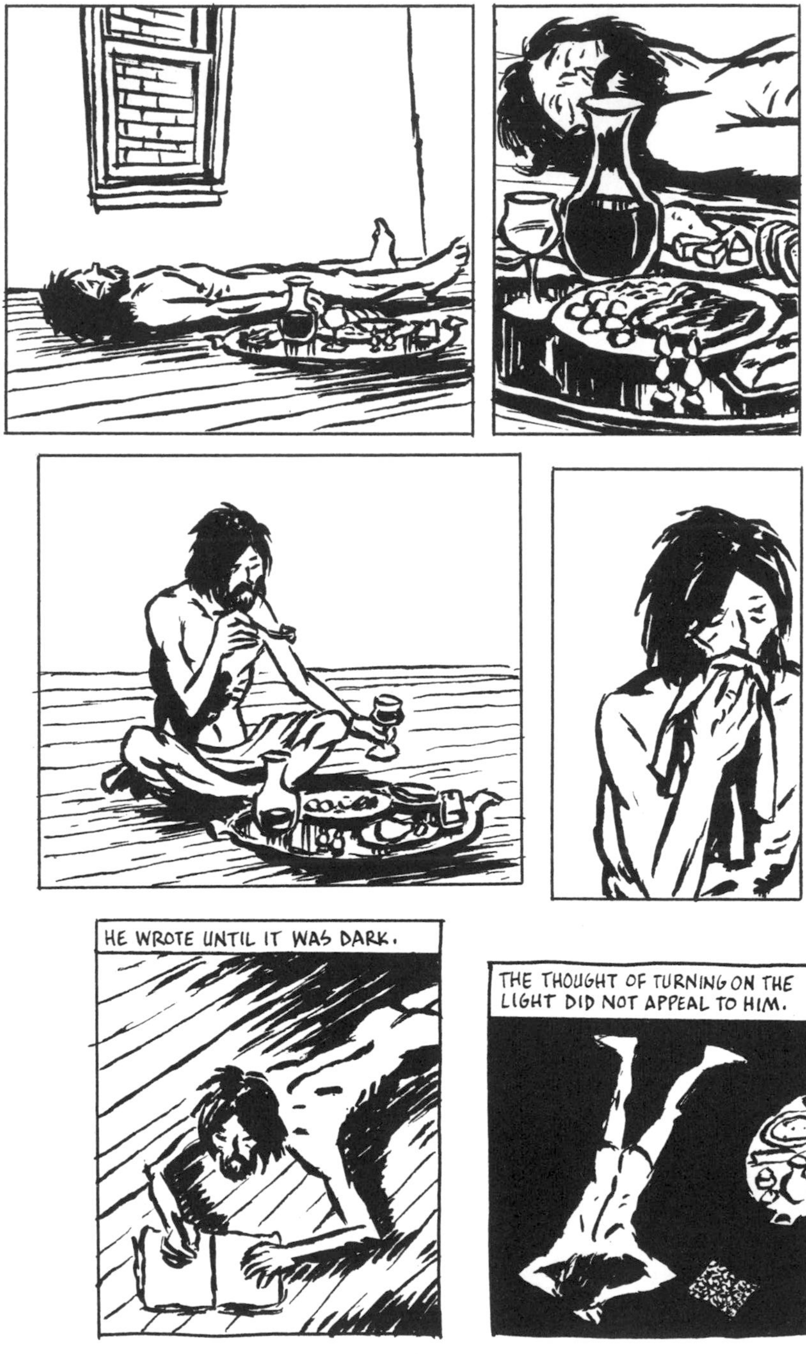
HE WROTE UNTIL IT WAS DARK.
THE THOUGHT OF TURNING ON THE LIGHT DID NOT APPEAL TO HIM.

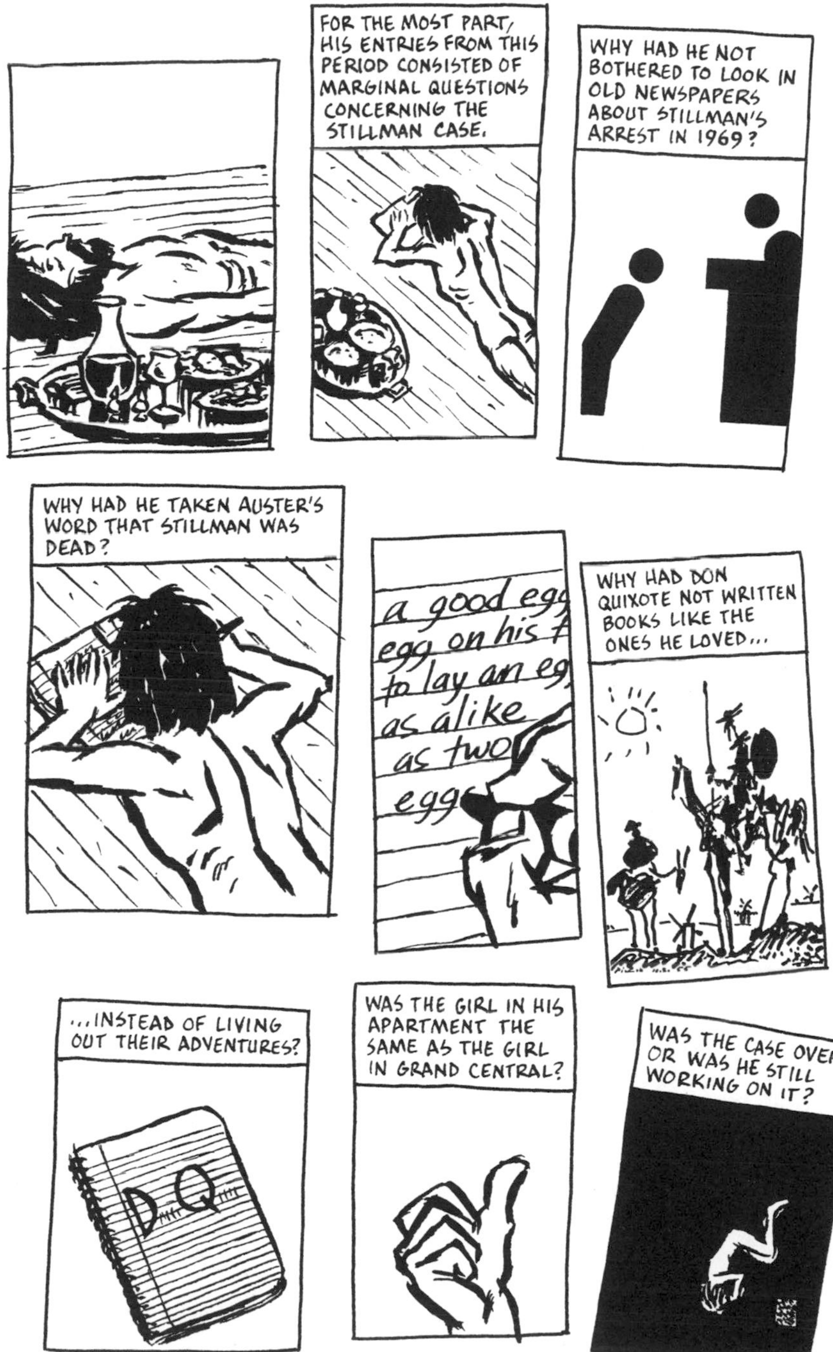
FOR THE MOST PART, HIS ENTRIES FROM THIS PERIOD CONSISTED OF MARGINAL QUESTIONS CONCERNING THE STILLMAN CASE.
WHY HAD HE NOT BOTHERED TO LOOK IN OLD NEWSPAPERS ABOUT STILLMAN'S ARREST IN 1969?
WHY HAD HE TAKEN AUSTER'S WORD THAT STILLMAN WAS DEAD?
a good eg
egg on his
to lay an eg
as alike
as two
egg
WHY HAD DON QUIXOTE NOT WRITTEN BOOKS LIKE THE ONES HE LOVED...
...INSTEAD OF LIVING OUT THEIR ADVENTURES?
DQ
WAS THE GIRL IN HIS APARTMENT THE SAME AS THE GIRL IN GRAND CENTRAL?
WAS THE CASE OVER, OR WAS HE STILL WORKING ON IT?

He wondered if he
had it in him to
write without a
pen, if he could
learn to speak in-
stead, filling the
darkness with his
voice, speaking
the words into the
air, into the walls,
into the city, even
if the light never
came back again.

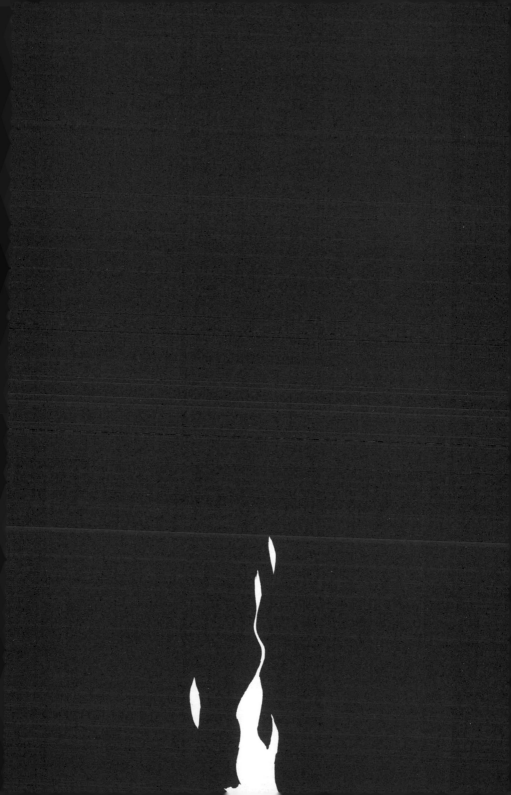

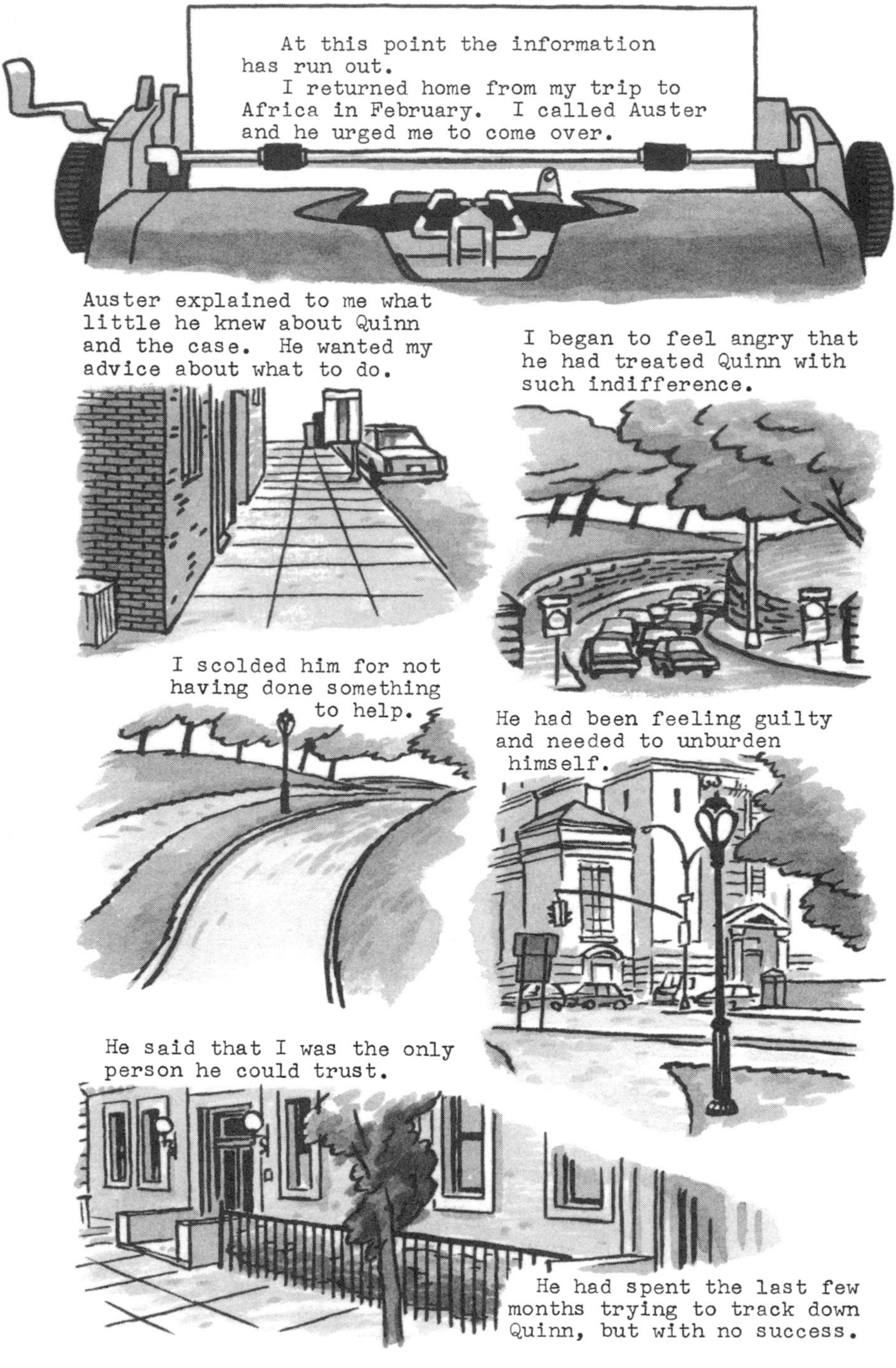
At this point the information has run out.
I returned home from my trip to Africa in February. I called Auster and he urged me to come over.
Auster explained to me what little he knew about Quinn and the case. He wanted my advice about what to do.
I began to feel angry that he had treated Quinn with such indifference.
I scolded him for not having done something to help.
He had been feeling guilty and needed to unburden himself.
He said that I was the only person he could trust.
He had spent the last few months trying to track down Quinn, but with no success.

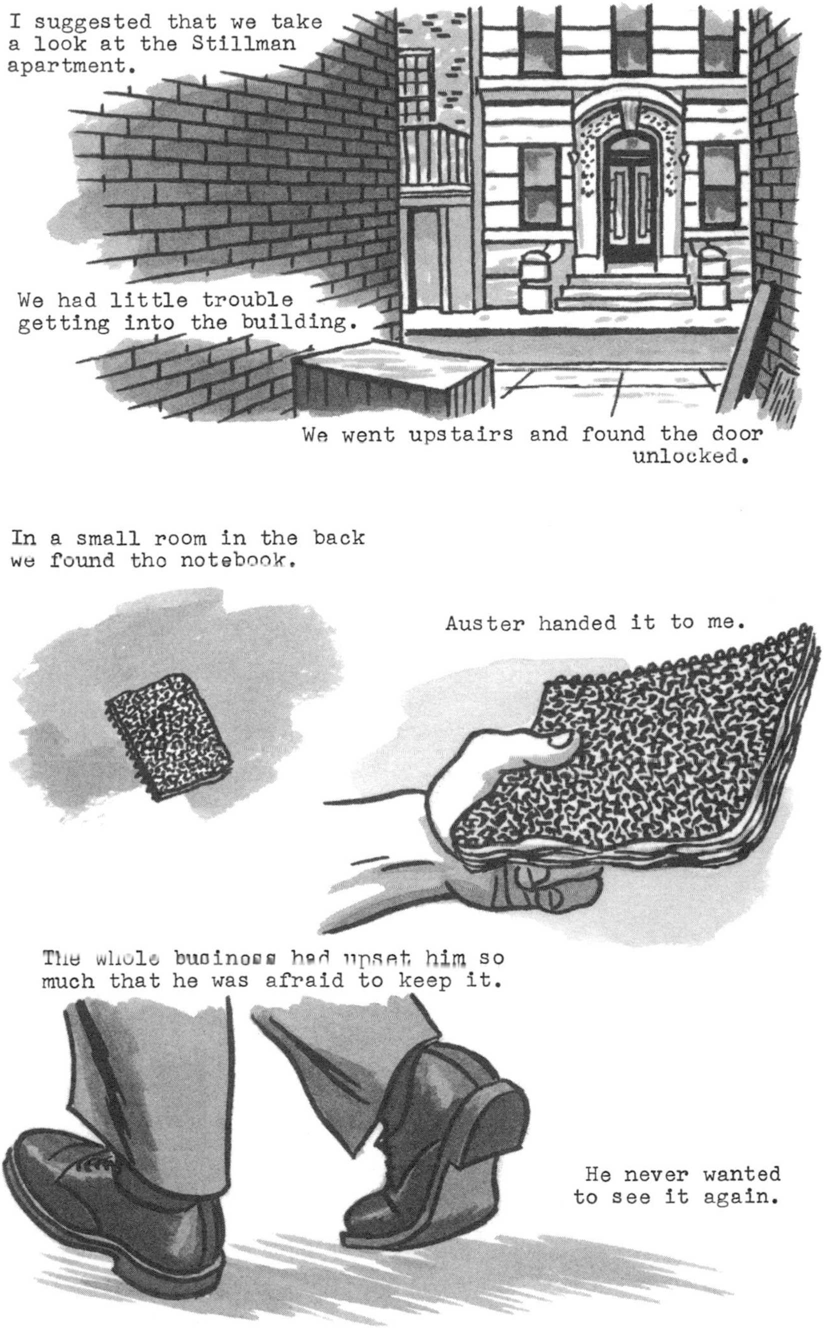
I suggested that we take a look at the Stillman apartment.
We had little trouble getting into the building.
We went upstairs and found the door unlocked.
In a small room in the back we found tho notebook.
Auster handed it to me.
The whole business had upset him so much that he was afraid to keep it.
He never wanted to see it again.

As for Quinn, it is impossible for me to say where he is now. I have followed the notebook as closely as I could, and any inaccuracies should be blamed on me. There were moments when the text was difficult to decipher, but I have done my best. The notebook, of course, is only half the story, as any sensitive reader will understand. As for Auster, I am convinced that he behaved badly throughout. If our friendship has ended, he has only himself to blame. As for me, my thoughts remain with Quinn. He will be with me always.